P301 KEN

COMPARATIVE RHETORIC

COMPARATIVE RHETORIC

An Historical and Cross-Cultural Introduction

GEORGE A. KENNEDY

New York   Oxford

OXFORD UNIVERSITY PRESS

1998

OXFORD UNIVERSITY PRESS

Oxford New York
Athens Auckland Bangkok Bogota Bombay
Buenos Aires Calcutta Cape Town Dar es Salaam Delhi
Florence Hong Kong Istanbul Karachi
Kuala Lumpur Madras Madrid Melbourne
Mexico City Nairobi Paris Singapore
Taipei Tokyo Toronto

and associated companies in
Berlin Ibadan

Published by Oxford University Press, Inc.
198 Madison Avenue, New York, New York 10016

Oxford is a registered trademark of Oxford University Press

Library of Congress Cataloging-in-Publication Data
Kennedy, George Alexander, 1928–
Comparative rhetoric : an historical and cross-cultural
introduction / George A. Kennedy.
p.   cm.
Includes bibliographical references and index.
ISBN 0-19-510932-5 (cloth) — ISBN 0-19-510933-3 (pbk.)
1. Rhetoric, Ancient—History.   I. Title.
P301.K45   1997
808—dc20   96–33010

3 5 7 9 8 6 4 2
Printed in the United States of America
on acid-free paper.

To my Granddaughter,
Emily Ruth Morton

Contents

Acknowledgments

The aboriginal Australian song, "Why do you come here every day to my grave," in chapter 3 is quoted from *The World of the First Australians* by Ronald M. and Catherine H. Berndt with the permission of the publisher, the Australian Institute of Aboriginal and Torres Strait Islander Studies; the other aboriginal myths and songs in chapter 3 are quoted from *Songs of Central Australia* by T. G. H. Strehlow with the permission of Harper Collins Publishers (Australia) Ltd. The Petition of the Eloquent Peasant, Maxims of Ptahhotep, and the Complaint of Khakeperre-Sonb in chapter 5 are quoted from *Ancient Egyptian Literature* by Miriam Lichtheim with the permission of the University of California Press. The *Hymn of Vak* in chapter 7 is quoted from *The Hymns of the Rigveda* translated by R. G. Griffith with the permission of Motilal Banarsidass Publishers.

In writing this book I have been indebted to the National Endowment for the Humanities for a summer stipend in 1992 and a Fellowship for College Teachers in 1994–95; to the Institute of Arts and Humanities of the University of North Carolina at Chapel Hill for a summer fellowship in 1993; to the same university for a Kenan leave in 1994–95; and to the Department of Speech Communication of Colorado State University for providing me with faculty privileges and an opportunity to teach comparative rhetoric in the fall of 1995 on the basis of a draft of this book. Reactions and suggestions by my students were helpful as I made final revisions in the manuscript. In addition, for comments and bibliographical suggestions I wish to thank Don Abbott, Lloyd Bitzer, Carl Burgchardt, Richard Enos, Michael Fox, Mary Garrett, Kurt Raaflaub, and anonymous referees for Oxford University Press. Finally, I am grateful to Robert Miller, Mark Naccarelli, and other members of the staff of the press who have seen the book through to publication.

COMPARATIVE RHETORIC

D

The Comparative Study of Rhetoric

Comparative Rhetoric is the cross-cultural study of rhetorical traditions as they exist or have existed in different societies around the world. It has at least four objectives:

> One is to use comparative methods to identify what is universal and what is distinctive about any one rhetorical tradition in comparison to others. How, for example, have traditional rhetorical practices in China resembled or differed from those in Europe? A comparative approach has often proved to be useful in the natural and human sciences to reveal features of some object of study that may not be immediately evident in its own context.

> A second, drawing on the first, is to try to formulate a General Theory of Rhetoric that will apply in all societies. This would be the innate or "deep" rhetorical faculty that we all share but which takes different forms in different cultures.

> A third is to develop and test structures and terminology that can be used to describe rhetorical practices cross-culturally.

> And a fourth is to apply what has been learned from comparative study to contemporary cross-cultural communication. This fourth objective goes beyond my present undertaking, but I hope greater historical perspective may be useful in understanding how cultures other than our own have come to view conventions of discourse.

This book is divided into two parts. In the first five chapters I give a picture of rhetorical practices in social groups that do not make use of writing. The chapters will differ somewhat in the order of topics discussed, depending on the nature of the evidence. Readers may be surprised to discover that I begin with analogies to human rhetoric in animal communication. Animals, however, use vocal and bodily signs to get what they want or avoid danger, and study of animal communication tells us something about the natural basis of rhetoric. The chapter that follows provides a connecting link between animal communication and rhetoric as practiced in nonliterate societies that survived until modern times by speculating briefly about possible rhetorical factors in the early stages of human speech and language. Part I then continues with consideration of traditional rhetorical practices among the aboriginal inhabitants of Australia, a hunter–gatherer society with little technology that had been isolated from cultural development elsewhere for thousands of years and which thus provides a good introduction to rhetoric as existing in a very different world from our own. Then comes a longer chapter giving a broad and more organized survey of features of rhetoric in a variety of other oral cultures in Africa, the Americas, and the South Pacific, and finally a chapter on the rhetoric of North American Indians, the traditional oral culture to which my readers probably have the easiest access.

In Part II I turn to rhetorical practices in the major ancient cultures that developed systems of writing: Mesopotamia, Egypt, Palestine, China, India, and Greece. Writing had an important impact on composition and on the conceptualization of rhetoric.

No previous book has attempted to study such a wide range of materials. I hope that my readers will view what I have to say as a preliminary attempt to provide an introduction to a vast, and fascinating, subject, an account that will doubtless need revision in the future by others who take up the subject. Neither I nor any one else I know of is competent to give an authoritative account of the rhetorical practices of these many different cultures, primarily because no one has the requisite knowledge of the many languages and societies of the world. I draw on a large body of research by linguists, anthropologists, social biologists, and experts in non-Western societies, most of whom never use the word "rhetoric," though to me that is often what they seem to be discussing. Although I hope that readers in these disciplines, anthropologists in particular, may find some of the discussion interesting, I view my primary audience as the general reader, curious about the world, and teachers of classics, English (both literature and composition), philosophy, and speech communication, who are seriously interested in the phenomenon of rhetoric and welcome a new approach to understanding it.

Two matters important for the objectives of comparative rhetoric, as set out at the beginning of this chapter, need some preliminary consideration here: What do I mean by "rhetoric" in the context of this book? And what terms can be used to describe the structures of General Rhetoric and those of non-Western societies?

Some might argue that "rhetoric" is a peculiarly Western phenomenon, a structured system of teaching public speaking and written composition, developed in classical Greece, taught in Roman, medieval, renaissance, and early modern schools, and, with some revisions, still in use today. Nothing exactly like this has existed in other cultures, though there are some partial parallels in Aztec schools and in literate cultures. This, however, is only one meaning of "rhetoric," a subset of a more general meaning that also goes back to the beginnings of Western rhetorical consciousness. "Rhetoric," and its variations in European languages, is indeed derived from the Greek, from *rhêtorikê*, of which the earliest occurrences are in Plato's dialogue *Gorgias*. It is used there, somewhat pejoratively, of the technique of a public speaker or politician (*rhêtôr*). A common brief definition of "rhetoric" in classical antiquity was "the art of persuasion," or in Aristotle's fuller form (*Rhetoric* 1.2.1) "an ability, in each case, to see the available means of persuasion." Aristotle traced the beginning of the study of rhetoric back a century before Plato's use of the word, and constantly cited examples of rhetorical usages from the Homeric poems, Greek drama, and earlier prose writers. Rhetoric thus existed in Greece before "rhetoric," that is, before it had the name that came to designate it as a specific area of study. "Rhetoric" in this broader sense is a universal phenomenon, one found even among animals, for individuals everywhere seek to persuade others to take or refrain from some action, or to hold or discard some belief. Traditional nonliterate cultures have not, so far as I can discover, developed an abstract term to describe the "art" of persuasion; they usually speak in more specific terms. Almost all cultures have a word for an "orator," someone with special skills at public speaking; most have terms for different speech situations or different kinds of traditional literature. Some have words that correspond to "metaphor," "comparison," or other features of discourse. The conceptualization and discussion of something analogous to what we call "rhetoric" occurred in other early literate cultures besides the Greek: in ancient Egypt and ancient China, for example, where there were even something resembling handbooks of good speaking and good writing, as I shall explain in later chapters.

Although rhetoric in Greece and Rome was primarily taught as an art of persuasive speaking or writing, it was widely recognized that rhetorical techniques were also employed in imaginative compositions not explicitly intended to persuade an audience to some action or belief, though that might be present as a subtext, but aimed at an aesthetic effect, to give enjoyment to an audience or to demonstrate the imaginative and linguistic skills of the speaker or writer. The definition of rhetoric as the "art of persuasion" might thus easily be extended to the "art of effective expression."

I would, however, like to push the definition of rhetoric beyond an abstract concept of an art, skill, or technique of composition to try to identify a place for it in nature. Rhetoric is not, I think, just a convenient concept existing only in the mind of speakers, audiences, writers, critics, and teachers. It has an essence or reality that has not been appreciated. I shall argue in this book that rhetoric, in essence, is a form of mental and emotional energy. This is most clearly seen when an individual, animal or human, is faced with some serious threat or opportunity that may be affected by utterance. An emotional reaction takes place in the mind. The emotion may be fear, anger, lust, hunger, pity, curiosity, love—any of the basic emotions of sentient life. The probable source of such basic emotions, and thus of rhetoric, is the instinct for self-preservation, which in turn derives from nature's impulse to preserve the genetic line. As will emerge in the next chapter, nature has preferred communication to physical force as least costly of energy. Rhetoric is thus a "conservative" faculty.

The emotional reaction in the mind of the individual, consciously or unconsciously, then sparks utterance—speech or gesture—aimed at affecting the situation. Utterance requires physical energy and conveys rhetorical energy; so do gestures. The simplest forms of rhetorical energy are heard in volume, pitch, and repetition; for example, "help! Help! HELP!" In complex human communication, rhetorical energy is conveyed also by logical reasons, ethical and pathetical appeals, metaphors, and figures of speech that give emphasis or encourage audience contact. My understanding of rhetoric has a partial precedent in the concept of "vivacity" as taught by eighteenth-century British rhetoricians and resembles some ideas in Chinese philosophy to be discussed in chapter 7.

A speaker ordinarily has some perceived audience on whom some effect is intended. The audience may be the self, God, some force or object of nature, an animal, or one or more human beings. If the audience is a sentient being, communication can take place and something may be effected. The energy of the message, however, may not be sufficient to accomplish its purpose. The speaker may be too tired or weak to give the message enough energy to make it heard through the noise of the environment or to awaken the interest of a recipient. If the energy is sufficient to reach an audience, a reaction takes place in the mind of the hearer. The cognitive content of the message may be decoded; the energy of the message may spark a reaction, sympathetic or hostile, depending on the self-interest of the hearer. The hearer may be persuaded to do or believe something and may respond with another message.

I argue in this book that rhetoric is a natural phenomenon: the potential for it exists in all life forms that can give signals, it is practiced in limited forms by nonhuman animals, and it contributed to the evolution of human speech and language from animal communication. Within human history, rhetoric has culturally evolved into more complex forms in conjunction with other aspects of cultural evolution. These other aspects of culture include political institutions, such as chiefdoms, councils, and courts of law; religious practices, such as myth-making, rituals, and sorcery; and artistic representations creating symbols. A major stage in cultural evolution was the invention of writing systems, thus the division of this book into two parts. Writing greatly facilitated the possibility of conscious creation, analysis, and criticism of discourse, thus conceptualization, abstract thinking, and complex reasoning. Metarhetoric, or a theory of rhetoric, is a product of writing and is first to be found in early literate societies.

Rhetoric can be distinguished from communication and communication would not take place without a rhetorical impulse to drive it. There is no "zero degree" rhetoric in any utterance because there would be no utterance without a rhetorical impulse. Communication is, I take it, a general term for the transmission of a message and often involves the creation of new thought by the reaction of a receiver of the message to an original statement, which then in turn may impel the sender to revise the statement, making it clearer or more forceful, or meeting some objection. The meaning or effect can thus be negotiated. There are varying degrees of rhetoric in communications. "The window is shut" is a communication. Its rhetorical energy is dependent on how it is said and the context in which it is said. It might, for example, be a mild reasssurance to a recipient concerned about rain blowing into a room, or an exclamation of frustration by a thief who had planned to climb in. "Shut the window," even without knowing its context, seems to carry a higher degree of rhetorical energy. The speaker is expressing an order. The statement carries some claim of authority to make the statement. The recipient's responses are limited to executing the order, failing or refusing to execute the order, thus denying the authority of the speaker, or demanding some equality in negotiating the situation. The recipient might say "Shut it yourself." Or, "Why? It's stuffy in here." The latter statement is an example of what in traditional rhetorical theory is called an "enthymeme" or rhetorical syllogism, for it implies a major premise ("fresh air is desirable in a room") and supports a conclusion with a reason. The first speaker can also create an enthymeme by adding a reason (e.g., "Shut the window because the wind is blowing the papers off the desk"). In so doing, the abruptness of the utterance is reduced: authority is less obvious, appeal to the judgment of the recipient is implied. I would describe the rhetoric of these statements as a matter of their energy level. It is easy to see that they might be expressed in different degrees of shrillness or calmness of voice. Thus they also involve different degrees of expenditure of physical energy in their utterance. Rhetoric, in the most general sense, may thus be identified with the energy inherent in an utterance (or an artistic representation): the mental or emotional energy that impels the speaker to expression, the energy level coded in the message, and the energy received by the recipient who then uses mental energy in decoding and perhaps acting on the message. Rhetorical labor takes place.

A second problem facing any student of comparative rhetoric is what terminology to use to describe rhetorical practices in non-Western cultures. The only fully developed system of rhetorical terminology we have is that derived from Greco-Roman rhetoric. In China and in India a considerable number of rhetorical terms came into use in the last centuries BCE and eventually detailed systems of literary criticism were developed. These terms, however, are unfamiliar to most Western readers and to try to use them as a basis of analysis of discourse in other cultures would be confusing. Comparative rhetoric, it seems to me, offers us a unique opportunity to test the applicability of Western rhetorical concepts outside the West. I have no intention of trying to impose Western assumptions about rhetoric on exotic cultures. Quite the opposite, I hope to encourage the development of a standard cross-cultural rhetorical terminology by modifying Western concepts to describe what is found everywhere. From time to time I shall use some of the more familiar terms in discussing non-Western rhetoric—ethos, epideictic, and metaphor, for example—but often indicating the need for some qualification. Some Western terms are relatively unproblematic: for example, all human societies engage in some form of deliberation and it seems reasonable to speak of "deliberative rhetoric" as a general species.

Some readers may not be familiar with the structure and terminology of classical rhetoric, so I here offer a brief outline of it, raising in each case the question of how valid or useful it may be in describing rhetoric outside the Western tradition. In the Conclusion to the book I shall return to offer tenative answers to these questions.

Traditional Western rhetoric is divided into five parts, sometimes called "canons," which represent the stages of planning, composing, and delivering a speech": invention, arrangement, style, memory, and delivery. How well do these stages describe composition outside of Western schools? In chapters 6 and 7 the reader will learn that there are what have been called "canons" of rhetoric from ancient Egypt and China, and they are rather different.

Traditional Western rhetoric identifies three, and only three, species of discourse: judicial, deliberative, and epideictic. The criterion is the function of the audience. Aristotle argued (*Rhetoric* 1.3) that every audience is either a judge or not a judge. If the audience is a judge of what has happened in the past, the species is judicial (or in older terminology, forensic); if it judges what action to take in the future the species is deliberative. If the audience is not a judge but hearers or readers who are not asked to take any specific action, the species is epideictic. How valid are these categories for a general theory of rhetoric? Are there species of rhetoric not provided for in this classification?

Traditional Western rhetoric makes a distinction between "nonartistic" means of persuasion, such as citation of a law that a speaker "uses," and "artistic" means, which the speaker "invents." There are three, and only three, artistic means of persuasion: ethos, or the credibility of the character of the speaker; logos, or the rational arguments employed; and pathos, or the awakening of the audience's emotions. How valid are these classifications generally?

Logos, or argument, is traditionally divided into inductive and deductive. In Western rhetorical theory inductive argument is the use of "paradigms." A paradigm, or example, supports a proposition by implying a universal conclusion from experience, which need not be expressed. Deductive argument is the use of a rhetorical syllogism, called an "enthymeme." Such an argument is usually probable, not a certainty, and it tends to assume one premise that is unexpressed. Is logical argument in the Western sense a feature of non-Western discourse? Use of examples and analogies will prove to be common. But what about enthymemes? And are there other forms of argument?

A student of traditional Western rhetoric looks for what to say in "topoi," "places." Some of these, called "common topics," are strategies of argument such as definition, division of the question, and argument from cause to effect. Others are "specific topics" appropriate to the subject at hand: things one might say, for example, in favor of war or peace, or things one might say to praise or blame someone. Are topoi a feature of non-Western discourse? And if so, how do they resemble or differ from those used in the West?

Ethos, logos, pathos, and topoi fall under the heading of "invention." "Arrangement" in traditional Western rhetoric concerns the division of a work into identifiable parts that perform specific functions: the "proemium" or introduction should get the attention, interest, and good will of the audience; the "narration" should provide the audience with background and necessary facts to understand the argument; the "proof" should identify the question at issue and the thesis, followed by supporting arguments. It may also refute the arguments of an opponent. The final part is the "epilogue," which should recapitulate the main points made earlier and stir the emotions of the audience to belief or action. How generally does discourse, Western or non-Western, conform to this pattern?

"Style" in traditional Western rhetoric is divided into choice of word and composition of words into sentences. Word choice includes the use of "tropes," such as metaphor, metonymy, and synecdoche, in which one word is regarded as being substituted for another or expresses a concept for which there is no common word; composition includes figures of speech, such as anaphora or alliteration, and figures of thought, such as apostrophe or rhetorical question. Composition also includes construction of sentences, rhythm, and the use of proverbial or gnomic sayings. What are the common devices of style in non-Western discourse? I shall have much to say about metaphor in particular. In addition, the theory of style identifies different kinds, levels, or registers of style appropriate to different occasions or subjects. The most common traditional classification is a grand, a middle, and a plain style. Are different levels of style recognized in other cultures, and if so how are they best classified? This will prove to be an especially important issue.

Western theory of "memory" elaborated a system of mnemonic devices based on visualization of what was to be said. "Delivery" is a matter of the control of voice and use of gestures. These are clearly important features of public address, all the more so in nonliterate cultures. There is, however, less evidence about them in my sources and I can only occasionally comment on them.

After these introductory remarks I can now begin with the use of rhetoric, or something very like it, by nonhuman animals.

PART **I**

RHETORIC IN SOCIETIES WITHOUT WRITING

CHAPTER 1

Rhetoric Among Social Animals

Charles Darwin entitled the third chapter of *The Descent of Man*, published in 1871 with a revised edition in 1874, "Comparison of the Mental Powers of Man and the Lower Animals." Although prudently recognizing the "immense gulf" between the intellect of the most intelligent animals and that of the least civilized human beings—"savages" as he calls them—he sought to show that life is a continuum across the species from simplest to most complex, and he identified, largely on the basis of his own extensive observation and the anecdotal reports of others, the existence in one or more species of animal of emotions and mental powers often regarded, then and now, as distinctive of the human race. He cited instances of fear, suspicion, courage, anger, wonder, curiosity, imitation, attention, memory, imagination, reason, the use of tools, individuality, communication by voice and gesture, sense of beauty, and even a rudimentary form of religion. To this I would add that animals also employ features of what we call rhetoric.

The ability of nonhuman social animals—that is, those who live in groups—to understand, reason, and communicate with each other, primarily with members of their own species, sometimes with other species, has been extensively studied by biologists since Darwin's time, and especially with the emergence of controlled experiments much progress has been made to confirm, or in some cases to revise, Darwin's observations and to provide detailed scientific evidence about all these phenomena of life. Much is known, much can be conjectured with some probability, and much remains speculative. *Animal Language* by

Michael Bright is a readable survey of the subject as understood in 1984 and can be supplemented by more recent studies such as *Animal Minds* by Donald R. Griffin (1992) and *Animal Talk* by Eugene S. Morton and Jake Page (1992). My discussion here revises and expands what I wrote earlier in an article on the subject (Kennedy 1992). Scientific research on animal communication has benefited from the recent reaction against rigid behaviorism in psychology, which reduced not only animal life, but human life to conditioned instincts, and toward a more cognitive or even mentalist approach that allows for the existence of feelings and thoughts on the part of social animals. Social biologists and animal psychologists never, so far as I know, use the term "rhetoric" to describe features of animal communication, but it seems possible to find in their descriptions of behavior features that are analogous to what has been regarded as rhetoric among human beings.

Animal lovers are prone to anthropomorphize their pets and unscientifically attribute to them qualities they are unlikely to have. To some people, at some times, animals can even seem morally superior to human beings, and we can easily fantasize their lives to a simpler, more natural existence that we long for ourselves. Certainly animals are spared much of the worry about the future and guilt about the past that human beings feel, though they can and often do find themselves in highly stressful situations. Some popular books about animals have little scientific value, while others manage to escape sentimentality by focusing on the life of animals in their own terms. Konrad Lorenz's classic works, *King Solomon's Ring* (1952) and *Behind the Mirror* (1977), record experiences of a major scientist living with animals and are in a form that has continued to delight readers, though recent research has shown that many subtleties of animal communication escaped even his sympathetic and inquiring mind. An excellent, recent, and popular book is *The Hidden Life of Dogs* by Elizabeth Marshall Thomas (1993). A modest degree of disciplined anthropomorphism is not a negative factor in studying animals; without it scientists would never have suspected that what seem irrational roars, grunts, or squakings, actually constitute codes with different meanings understood within each species. Our own experience and metaphors from human life are often the only terms we have to describe what we observe among animals (Burghardt 1985:917). Anyone who has lived intimately with animals knows that they use a combination of vocal sounds and body language to express their feelings, influence others, and get what they want from human masters. The rhetorical study of animal communication primarily seeks to identify basic principles and formal aspects of communication that are fundamental to all rhetorical structures and used by both human and nonhuman animals.

The opposite of the sentimental approach to animal life is the radical humanism that draws a sharp line between nonhuman and human animals, sometimes on the basis of religious doctrine of the soul, sometimes on the assumption that animals lack reason because they lack human speech. Among scientific observers, a prominent exponent of this latter view has been Noam Chomsky, who has argued that human language is not a higher stage of evolution of animal communication, but a result of a specific type of mental organization lacking in animals (Chomsky 1972:66–71; see also Pinker 1994). Chomsky does not mention rhetoric, but rhetoric seems to me one thing that animal and human communication, as he describes them, have in common. Animals, whether for physical or mental reasons, do not naturally employ human speech, though some birds can learn to do so in limited ways (Pepperberg 1991; Griffin 1992:169–71) and chimpanzees can learn American Sign Language to some extent (Gardner et al. 1989); conversely, human beings are inept at employing most systems of animal communication. We can, however, by observation learn to understand animal rhetoric and many animals can understand some features of human rhetoric that they share with us, such as gestures or sounds that express anger or friendliness or commands. We share a "deep" natural rhetoric.

Life on earth has evolved from simple to more complex forms. We are closest in most ways to primates, especially to chimpanzees, with whom we share about 98% of our DNA, but we have shared physical characteristics and mental faculties with all creatures that have brains. We are not, of course, descended from any existing species of animal, though it is likely that humans, chimpanzees, and gorillas share a common ancestor perhaps 5 to 7 million years ago (Weiss 1987); each of us has evolved in our own natural environment. But insofar as there are shared characteristics among a variety of species, including human beings, these point to a common source in nature that established basic potentialities, functions, and forms of rhetorical communication. In what follows I shall explore the extent to which some categories of Western rhetoric might apply to communication practices among social animals.

Examples of Rhetoric among Social Animals

A simple example of what I mean by rhetoric in animal communication is provided by the behavior of red deer stages during the rutting season as described by Michael Bright (1984:203–6). Similar behavior exists generally among male deer, elk, musk oxen, and some other quadrupeds; in America it can be observed each fall in Rocky Mountain National Park, where park rangers conduct tours for those interested in watching the elk in the rutting season and hearing their "bugeling." As described by Bright, red deer stags compete for the hinds primarily by staging loud vocal encounters. They are, of course, equipped with dangerous antlers and occasionally—perhaps 30% of the time—the encounters end in a physical fight if both stags stand their ground. More often, one is "persuaded" to retreat, leaving his opponent free to mate with the females. The encounter takes the form of a contest in which each stag tries to out-roar the other; the options offered are "flight or fight," and the one who roars the loudest and longest often wins. If the challenger fails to retreat, this may be followed by parallel strutting at right angles a few meters apart, and only if that is not persuasive by a fight. The performance resembles confrontation between hostile states: a series of ultimata, deployment of weapons, war as a last resort.

The rhetoric of the stags is a display of raw physical and psychological energy conveyed by the simplest possible techniques and thus illustrates my contention that rhetoric, in essence, can be viewed as a form of energy that results from reaction to a situation and is transmitted by a code. Though costly in energy, since it can go on as much as an hour, it is less costly and less dangerous than an actual fight. From this and from similar evidence it seems clear that nature has encouraged the evolution of rhetorical communication as a substitute for physical encounters. The rhetorical energy a stag can exhibit is directly proportional to his physical strength and potential as the best mate for a female. This is tested by debate. The evolutionary function of the display is to determine who is the fittest to survive and transmit his genes to future generations of the species. The social function is to secure authority, territory, and mating rights.

In terms of the traditional Western concept of the five parts of rhetoric, the confrontation of stages seems to contain elements of invention, arrangement, style, memory, and delivery, though these are natural attributes and not conscious "art." The inventional elements, the code by which the stag's energy is transmitted, are of the simplest sort: repetition of the same utterance, with increasing volume, for as long as possible, up to about an hour. Here, as in all animal communication and to a considerable extent in human communication, overstatement and redundancy are the means of overcoming distracting noise in the environment, securing attention, and expressing confidence and resolve to prevail. Morton and Page (1992:113–21) provide evidence suggesting that low-pitched sounds by animals convey the meaning of relatively large size; these sounds are aggressive and tend to frighten others. High-pitched sounds generally indicate smallness and imply either fear or appeasement. Among the stags there is rational argument only in the sense that one opponent usually concludes from the evidence that he is outmatched and should retire. There is, however, a strong element of rhetorical ethos in that the contestants' technique is the exhibition of their determination and personal character. Rhetorical pathos is present in that each stag intensifies the emotional state of the other. Arrangement is by three successive parts: the vocal display, the display of stalking, and, when it occurs, the fight. The stalking might be said to provide "evidence" of a stag's intention to carry through the struggle; the fight is the ultimate "proof." Human beings in the past, and occasionally today, have resorted to threats and duels as a way to settle disputes and prove something, whether it be their manhood or that God is on their side. In terms of style, there are individual variations encoded in most animal calls that enable other members of their species to recognize individuals when out of sight, even if this is generally not evident to human observers. Although Bright does not comment on it, both male and female deer can probably recognize each other as individuals by a combination of sound, smell, sight, and behavior. Memory, in the case of the stags, is presumably an innate pattern of behavior imprinted in the brain of the male of the species. Learning, imitation, and recall of appropriate utterances certainly occur among some mammals and birds; I do not know whether young male deer can be said to learn behavior from imitation of their elders. Delivery is clearly an important rhetorical element in the confrontation of the stags and successful delivery largely determines the outcome.

The vocal repertory of stags is very limited. Other animals, especially primates and birds, are more versatile and their calls can carry distinct semantic elements that are identified by others of their species. Perhaps the most interesting research in this connection was that carried out in observing vervet monkeys in Kenya by Dorothy L. Cheney and Robert M. Seyfarth and published in their book *How Monkeys See the World* (1990). Vervets in the wild, according to Cheney and Seyfarth (98–130), give six acoustically different alarm calls identifying the presence of different predators, each of which evokes a somewhat different evasive defense strategy from the other monkeys in the group, and four acoustically different grunts in social behavior. The alarm calls are said to identify leopards, eagles, snakes, smaller mammals, baboons, and unfamiliar humans, respectively; grunts differ on the basis of whether given to a subordinate or a dominant animal with group interaction, and thus express the social structure of the group; or they indicate that the speaker or another monkey is moving into an open area, perhaps increasing vigilance against predators; or they are directed out from the group as a warning to another group that is approaching.

The alarm calls are rhetorically interesting, a feature not discussed by Cheney and Seyfarth, in that by identifying the nature of a predator and thus the evasive action to take—climb out in the branches of a tree in the case of a leopard, hide in a bush in the case of an eagle—the monkey might be said to provide a reason for alarm. Thus, translated into human language, the call means "Look out, (for) there is a leopard (or eagle, etc.) approaching." Animal calls identify the state of mind of a speaker and convey information; when translated into human language they contain propositions (for some support of this view, see Stelkis 1988), though semioticians consistently ignore the possibility. The complexity of animal calls is proportional to the complexity of social organization of animal species: "The greater a species's social complexity, the more complex the range of sound qualities—that is, the more points along the motivational gradient—that will be expressed. In other words, increasingly complex social life will lead to increasingly subtle expression of an animal's mood" (Morton and Page 1992:121). The history of the evolution of rhetorical invention is the history of the growth of information in communication. In a simple animal cry or a primordial human cry of "Help!" there is great energy but the least information. Human rhetoric, with its conceptualization of rational argument, its ability to give a narrative account of previous or possible future events, and its great creativity can convey a much greater amount of information in an effort to spark mental energy in the recipient in an efficient way (Dewart 1989:233).

Among all social animals there is a hierarchy of authority—a "pecking order"—based on age, sex, and vitality or intelligence. Within groups of social animals, as in human societies, the leadership role is regularly challenged by an ambitious younger animal. There is thus an implicit distinction in nature between office and office holder, explicit in human rhetoric when a speaker draws a distinction between the honor due to an office, such as the presidency of the United States, and the weakness, corruption, or stupidity of the present office holder. In a fascinating article entitled "Chimpanzee Politics," Frans de Waal (1988) has described some of the tactics used by male chimpanzees to gain and keep dominance in their group. Dominance requires support of a majority of the group. Ways of maintaining control, thus order and harmony, that some ambitious chimps have discovered include a systematic policy of supporting "losers" in fights within the group, thus counterbalancing the increased influence of "winners." Or a relatively weak leader may curry the favor of another stronger (but possibly less intelligent) chimp, thus forming a coalition in which the stronger animal acts as chief of police and minister of war while the weaker retains the social perquisites of head of state. These tactics are analogous to those found historically in human society.

Vervet monkeys can identify other individuals, evaluate their authority, and may ignore a call from an unreliable speaker. The calls are interesting linguistically in that they seem to identify classes rather than species of predators. Leopards are the only large, carnivorous quadripeds regularly a threat to the monkeys, eagles similarly the only large birds of which they are much afraid; there thus was no environmental need for the evolution of more specific identifications or for different defensive strategies against other predators. Synecdoche, whether genus for species or species for genus, is apparently a natural rhetorical trope. Some animals can understand metonymy, as when a leash denotes a walk or the appearance of a bowl denotes food to a dog, and some dogs learn to use metonymy by bringing a leash to a master as a suggestion for a walk, but I do not know of any understanding of metaphor—that is, the substitution of something from an analogous but distinct order of signs—among animals. Much of the neurological development needed for distinction between common and proper nouns, or between the general and the specific, seems to have taken place among the ancestors of modern apes. A chimpanzee instinctively understands that "banana" is a common noun, referring to all bananas, and that "Roger" as the name of a trainer refers only to one unique human being.

Lying, Deception, and Veracity

Rhetoric has a long history of association with lying and deception. Some philosophers have tried to claim that only humans lie (e.g., Dewart 1989:104–5). We should not flatter ourselves. Animals engage in deceit all the time, as when they hide under a bush awaiting prey. Some birds give calls that seem to be intended to deceive other birds (Terborgh 1996:44). Cheney and Sefarth devote an interesting chapter (1990:184–203) to the vervets' techniques of deception, which I would label rhetorical strategies, and Savage-Rumbaugh and McDonald (1988) describe even more complex deception on the part of apes. Deceptions by animals usually disguise actions they are about to take: a gorilla, for example, ambling along with a group, sees some food the others do not notice; she sits down and pretends to groom herself until the others pass, then seizes the food for herself. Or an ape may pretend to see or hear something that is not there to mislead others for its own advantage. Chimpanzees who can communicate with trainers by sign language or keyboards play tricks on them to get what they want. The chimp Matata would send a trainer out of the room on an errand, then grab something from another animal and yell and scream as though she were being attacked. When the trainer rushed back she would look at him with a pleading expression and make threatening sounds at the other animals. Chimps who use keyboards to communicate apparently realize that the opinions of others can be influenced not only by what one does, but also by what one says, and that they can attain goals by indirect means. This is also a basic principle of human rhetoric.

Other principles emerge from the conditions that make deception possible. Both human and nonhuman deception only succeeds if an audience has some disposition to believe the speaker. An inveterate liar, or even a well-intentioned individual whose judgment has often proved wrong, soon loses authority in the hierarchical world of social animals, human and nonhuman. The eighteenth-century Scottish philosopher, Thomas Reid, who sought to establish a "common sense" basis of knowledge in response to the skepticism of David Hume, enunciated three grounds of belief that he regarded as instinctive and not learned from experience. They seem as applicable to communication among nonhuman animals as in human society. The first principle is "a propensity to speak the truth, and to use the signs of language, so as to convey our real sentiments. This principle has a powerful operation, even in the greatest liars: for, where they lie once, they speak the truth a hundred times" (Reid 1970:238). Reid called this "the principle of veracity." Second is "the principle of credulity" on the part of a listener: "It is unlimited in children, until they meet with instances of deceit and falsehood: and it retains a very considerable degree of strength through life" (240). Reid then raised the question of why we believe that the future will be like the past and thus are willing to accept statements about what is going to happen in the future, for example, that the sun will rise tomorrow. Hume had denied that knowledge of the future was based on reason and attributed it to the "vivacity" of ideas: Our vivid image of the sun's rising in the past inclines us to project belief of its doing so into the future. For this, Reid substituted "the inductive principle" (246), an instinctive belief in the continuity of nature. Both the principle of credulity and the inductive principle, Reid cautioned, can lead to mistakes: "There must be many accidental conjunctions of things, as well as natural connections; and the former are apt to be mistaken for the latter" (247). By this we infer cause and effect when there is no natural connection between events: post hoc ergo propter hoc. I would take exception, however, to Reid's use of "inductive" to describe the third principle. If, as he claims, the principle is instinctive and not inferred from repeated experience, the process of reasoning would seem to be a deductive one from the assumed major premise of the continuity of nature. I shall return in future chapters to the relation between inductive and deductive reasoning.

Animals, like humans, are naturally disposed to the principle of veracity; both depart from it occasionally when they think they can gain something, think the deceit will escape notice, or are under such stress that a lie is the only apparent option for self-preservation. Animals, like humans, are also naturally disposed to the principle of credulity, to believe communications of others, especially if that other is a figure of some authority; both depart from it occasionally if the speaker has lost their confidence by past calls of "wolf," or if the speaker is young and inexperienced. Although we need not believe that animals conceptualize the inductive—or as I would say the deductive—principle, many of their actions are based on the presumption of natural causes and effects and they are occasionally mistaken in their judgments, wrongly attributing a shadow or a movement in the bush, for example, to the presence of a predator, or failing to note the signs of a predator's real presence. Without the principles of veracity, credulity, and induction, and the possibility of deceit or misinterpretation of cause and effect, there would be little opportunity for prosecution and defense, exhortation and dissuasion, and thus little opening for debate and rhetoric in human affairs. These principles seem equally to apply to animal communication and thus can be regarded as grounds for the general rhetoric of nature. Although they are not learned from experience by each individual, they have doubtless evolved in accordance with natural selection and nature's preference for vocal communication over physical violence. It has been in the survival interest of each species that its members be veracious, credulous, and capable of reasoning from cause to effect, and the genes of those who exhibited these capabilities have had a natural advantage over the genes of those who did not.

Deliberative Rhetoric among Animals

The behavior of stags and vervet monkeys clearly falls within the traditional Western concept of "deliberative" rhetoric. What is at issue is the best action to take for the immediate advantage of the individual participants and the best interest of the species. Recipients judge the message and either act on it or reject it in favor of some other action. One of the best examples of deliberation among animals occurs during the swarming and search for a new hive by honeybees. The waggle dances of honeybees in the hive, by which they provide each other with specific information about the direction and distance of supplies of nectar, are a remarkable phenomenon, of which most of my readers probably have some knowledge. The bees' communication when a queen leaves the hive followed by a swarm of workers is less well known but of greater rhetorical interest. The colony takes up temporary residence in a tree, but unless a hive is provided by a human beekeeper, it needs relatively soon to find an appropriate cavity in a hollow tree, rock, or building in which to build a comb and store food. The cavity should be large enough for the swarm, dry, and have an opening near the bottom. Messenger bees go out searching and report their findings back to the swarm by means of waggle dances that indicate the direction of the cavity; the suitability of the cavity is expressed by the energy exhibited in the dance: The more suitable the place, the more vigorous the bee's performance (Griffin 1992:192–93). What is especially interesting is that bees that have discovered only mediocre cavities sometimes are persuaded by the energetic dance of another bee and become followers of one who has found a better possibility. They fly out to investigate the report firsthand and then return to dance a new, more excited, dance indicating their support of the alternate cavity. Gradually, a consensus develops about what is in the best interest of the swarm and the queen then takes flight to the site chosen by the group. The analogy to features of a human deliberative assembly seem obvious: a series of recommendations are made by speakers; their evidence is investigated and reported or rejected; a consensus emerges; finally, the administrative official accepts the recommendation and implements it.

Judicial Rhetoric among Animals

A second species of Western rhetoric is "judicial," in which a judgment is made about a past action. Judicial rhetoric is relatively undeveloped among animals; as subsequent chapters will reveal, it was also relatively undeveloped in early human societies. Both among animals and early human groups, corporal punishment, including death, or exile from a group occurs as sanctions imposed on offenders against group norms or individuals that are physically or psychologically deviant. From an evolutionary perspective, their genes are not appropriate for the propagation of the species and nature seeks to eliminate them. Judgment against the offender is often made collectively and without any apparent deliberation by the group, though it may be made by the group leader on the basis of his or her own authority. It is not unusual for a female animal to reject a newborn offspring, which is a form of judgment, based presumably on some evidence meaningful to the mother. As in the case of debates between stags, vocal threats may first be used to drive off an offender, who has the choice of answering with submissive behavior, which may sometimes be accepted, with snarls, by fighting, or by accepting the decision and leaving the group.

In domestic situations among social animals there is a kind of gentler judicial rhetoric. An example is described by de Waal (1988). Two chimpanzee mothers are sitting in the shade while their children play. Lying asleep between them is an older female who holds high rank in the group hierarchy. The children begin to fight. One of the mothers gives threatening grunts, the other moves uneasily, but the quarreling goes on and neither mother is willing to intervene in the presence of the other. Finally, one of the mothers wakes up the older female and points to the quarreling children. She gets up, takes a threatening step forward, waves her arms in the air, and barks loudly. The children immediately stop fighting. Here we have an appeal to a higher authority, one with the power to act and not only stop the fight, but prevent dispute between the two mothers, each defending her own child. The situation is perhaps only quasi-judicial. The older female does not so much judge the children's conduct or fix blame as she imposes order on what they may do now. But in human society as well, the general function of adjudication is preservation of law and order. Merlin Donald labels the cognitive culture of nonhuman social animals "episodic": "Their lives are lived entirely in the present, as a series of concrete episodes, and the highest element in their system of memory representation seems to be at the level of event representation" (Donald 1991:149). This allows little opening for judicial rhetoric.

Epideictic Rhetoric among Animals

Epideictic is the most problematic of the traditional Western species of discourse, that in which an audience is not called on to make some specific judgment or take some specific action. In his description of epideictic (*Rhetoric* 1.3 and 9) Aristotle treats it as characterized by praise or blame and concerned with the honorable or dishonorable. He sees its primary manifestations in practices of his own culture, especially funeral eulogies and displays by sophists. In the history of public address, epideictic has usually been associated with any kind of ceremonial oratory such as speeches on public holidays or religious and academic occasions. Famous examples include Lincoln's "Gettysburg Address" and Martin Luther King's "I Have a Dream." Such speeches console or inspire an audience by instilling or renewing values and beliefs and a sense of group identity.

Analogies to epideictic rhetoric in this sense exist among social animals. My first awareness of it happened when I arrived on my college campus early one Saturday morning and discovered that a large number of crows had gathered in several trees. Crows are territorial and spend much of their time in small family groups, though in some areas these groups roost together nightly in large flocks (Gilbert 1992). My initial impression of the morning assembly of crows was that they had come together to debate some issue of general interest: There was a great deal of cawing; most of the crows seemed to be facing the center of the group, though I could not identify the chaircrow; some had turned their backs on the proceedings; a few flew off in apparent disgust. Some research on the habits of the American crow, among the most intelligent and adaptable of birds, revealed that they were not deliberating about any of the subjects of most interest to crows: territory, food, or mating. They had abandoned their usual territories or roosting places, there was no food supply at hand, it was not the mating season. Zoologists have identified what is known as an "assembly call" among crows, which consists of a succession of long raucous cries, distinct from the short caws they use as contact calls in their own territory (Goodwin 1981:84–88). Their assembly, or "flocking," and the vocalization associated with it seem to be a reaffirmation of group identity analogous to human ceremonial speech on public occasions. Crows, like some other birds, get together to renew their "crowness." Gilbert (1992:111) cites a Bengali visitor who compared the flocking of crows to "giving adda" among her people: "When we give adda we talk a great deal, often all at the same time. The attraction is hearing, seeing, being in touch with each other." It is perhaps not a coincidence that the Greeks gave the nickname "Corax," meaning "crow," to the "inventor" of rhetoric.

Ritualization accompanied by epideictic utterance is a feature of animal rhetoric as it is of human life. Although the display and singing of birds in the mating season can be regarded as deliberative rhetoric, bird song outside the mating season is often epideictic in that it reaffirms existing relationships with other birds. One of the most elaborate examples of ritual epideictic among animals is the morning duet of mated pileated gibbons, which follows a distinct rhetorical arrangement. The female gives a soft "hoo-hoo-hoo" as a proemium. The male and female then join in a rhythmic "ooh-a-ooh-a-ooh." "Eventually, the female utters some short 'hoots' that tell the male to be quiet; this is the signal that she wants to sing the long series of whoops of the spectacular 'great call'—a kind of south-east Asian yodel. At the climax, male and female swing around in the tops of the trees, making a considerable commotion—it is a period of intense excitement" (Bright 1985:217). Since the performance is very loud, it is thought to function to defend territory, but it is also important in the cohesion of the pair, who mate for life and achieve increased coordination in the ritual over time. Morning visitors to the San Diego Zoo can see and hear the similar behavior of a mated pair of siamang gibbons, as I did in December 1995, a remarkable experience. In some species of birds the male sings and the female repeats his song. Ritualization, dialogue, and antiphonal singing among animals is perhaps analogous to the early stages of poetry, drama, and literature and may point to some rhetorical functions of these forms, which include territorial interests (strong in the *Iliad*, for example) and family integrity (strong in the *Odyssey*).

Eloquence in Nature

Human cultures that have developed and taught concepts of rhetoric—in Egypt, Palestine, China, India, and Greece—have usually regarded it as an art with aesthetic as well as cognitive value and they have often associated it with the use of beautiful language. Eloquence contributes to persuasion: as the writer of Proverbs 16:24 puts it, "Pleasant words are like a honeycomb, sweetness to the soul and health to the body." The most eloquent form of animal communication is certainly the singing of birds. All birds give simple, sometimes raucous, calls to perform various functions such as establishing territory, making threats, warning others of danger, announcing readiness to mate, maintaining contact with mates and offspring, or signaling an intent to fly (Jellis 1977:81–82; Catchpole and Slater 1995). Some birds, however, also "sing" musical compositions that are intricately structured and capable of variation and amplification to considerable length. Most singing is done by males during the mating season; female birds either do not sing or have less elaborate songs, which are sometimes echoes of the male. The biological functions of singing are to obtain and hold territory and a mate, and singing is often accompanied by visual displays (Jellis 1977:200), though the most elaborate use of visual rhetoric by birds is found in species that do not sing—the peacock, for example. Both singing and visual displays are indications of the health, strength, and fitness for mating of a male bird; they arouse sexual receptivity in females and deter other males from intruding into the territory. In contrast to social calls or displays within a group, the acoustic qualities of singing, including pitch variation and repetition, make it audible at a greater distance through the "noise" of the forest or marsh and allow others who are out of sight of the singer to hear and understand.

Birds learn to sing as they grow up. Some patterning is genetic and innate and is the basis of recognition of the bird's species, a major requirement for successful mating. Fledgling birds, however, imitate older birds in their group, ineptly at first, then more accurately, and gradually learn family motifs. Distinct dialects of calls and songs exist in groups of birds of the same species in different regions. Some birds—mocking birds are the most familiar example—incorporate segments of song of other species into their repertory. The most versatile singers, of which blackbirds and warblers are examples, go beyond this to invent dozens of new motifs, combinations, and variations and can give virtuoso performances, unique to the individual singer, lasting over a minute and containing as many as 300 acoustic units (Jellis 1977:200).

Poets and bird fanciers have long seen in bird song expressions of joy and sadness. Many biologists have been doubtful, but it is clear that the informational content of animal communication includes the animal's state of mind. Birds express panic and anger, and it seems unreasonable to suppose that they do not also sometimes express gentler emotions. The fact that some birds continue to sing and even elaborate their songs after the mating season suggests that they find satisfaction in doing so. As Jellis says (1977:204), "We are presented with some tantalizing possibilities: that in some species at least, these sound signals have evolved beyond the point which is necessary (so far as we can tell) for survival and reproduction; and that the birds may be exercising a rudimentary sense of musical form, very like our own, in the shaping of their songs." Although bird song is basically deliberative in that its natural purpose is to persuade other birds to take some action, in its most amplified form as an artistic performance it takes on epideictic qualities.

Arrangement and Style in Bird Song

The rhetorical interest of bird song relates to arrangement and style, the second and third parts of rhetoric as traditionally understood. The energy in bird songs can be transcribed as sonograms and as musical notation, allowing patterns of arrangement to be observed (examples in Jellis 1977 passim and Bright 1985:66–68). Frequently a short phrase functions as a proemium to attract attention and announce the song; then a theme is stated and varied and may be followed by other themes repeated, interwoven, and varied. Sometimes there is a flourish at the end of a theme or at the end of a whole song that functions as a kind of very brief epilogue, signifying closure but not recapitulating the themes. More often a song seems to trail off gradually or to end abruptly. The emotional high point of a song is likely to be in the middle. Although some form of proemium is often apparent in nature, epilogue or closure is either lacking or a relatively undeveloped potential.

Several features of style can be remarked in bird song, and since these are performances, style includes delivery. Separate species, separate groups within a species, and individual birds within a group have their own styles of composition and delivery (pitch, volume, rhythm, gestures, etc.). Some simple songs are innate, but more complex styles are learned by imitation of authority figures, just as classical and renaissance rhetorical schools taught composition by imitation of canonical models of style. Once facility begins to be acquired, a fledgling bird begins experiments by amplifying topics. Amplification involves repetition, variation, combination, and substitution of themes. Erasmus's famous treatise *On Copia* is the fullest description of how this was traditionally done in the West, using tropes and figures. Bird song exemplifies many figures of speech that are based on sound patterns: anaphora, homoeoteleuton, paronomasia, and the like. It does not employ figures of thought such as rhetorical question, apostrophe, or irony. It uses tropes only in the most literal sense that acoustic patterns or syllables seem sometimes to be substituted for others. Since these units do not appear to have cognitive value, there is no metaphor or metonymy, but the ability to make substitutions is fundamental to any development of troping. I noted earlier that synecdoche (genus for species or species for genus) is present in the communication of vervet monkeys and that some other animals understand metonymy. The ability of birds to combine their themes into different songs is significant because it illustrates in nature the potential to combine sounds into words that is the basis of human speech.

Another feature of bird behavior with some aesthetic implications is nest building. Nests vary with species from almost nothing to complex structures of mud, sticks, leaves, down, or other materials, often carefully woven together; in some species the male builds the nest and the female chooses a mate based on the quality of the housing offered; more often the female builds the nest, either alone or with the help of the male who brings materials for her (Collias and Collias 1984). The English word "text" derives from the Latin *textum*, which means "woven," and nests can be said to be a natural example of textuality. Basic instruction in how to build a nest is genetically transmitted in each species, and birds do not seem to learn nest building by imitation, but in some species there is a process of experimentation and the building of "play nests" by young male birds who eventually produce a quality structure and persuade a female to share it (Collias and Collias 1984:211–24). If the usual materials are not readily available, birds will sometimes adapt substitute materials. A bird has an idea of what is a good nest and seeks to achieve this in the construction; occasionally a partly built nest is abandoned as unsatisfactory in some way. This instinct reflects a natural principle of what is "appropriate," equally stressed as an artistic principle in Greek and Latin rhetoric: The rhetor should seek diction and a style of composition that is appropriate to the subject and the occasion. In Horace's *Art of Poetry* and in renaissance writings on poetics indebted to Horace, what is appropriate, under the term decorum, became a fundamental principle of poetic composition, including attributing to fictional characters thoughts and speeches appropriate to their character and situation. As such, it is a reflection of conventions and restraints of social and economic class and gender rules imposed by hierarchical societies and until the twentieth century more often unconsciously accepted than analyzed. The social life of animals is also hierarchical and also encourages an innate notion of what is appropriate in action and utterance.

Ornamentation in the form of tropes, figures, vivid narrative, ekphrases, and other devices of composition is a traditional feature of rhetoric; although they can have a persuasive function, the rhetoricians regarded them primarily as ways to attract attention and to please an audience so the message will be received. In the Renaissance, tropes and figures were often called the "colors" of rhetoric. There is in nature an attraction to ornamentation that provided the potential for ornamentation in rhetoric and poetry. Insects and hummingbirds are attracted to bright flowers, not for their beauty but because the color is a sign of the presence of nectar. The nectar is itself sweet, and "honeyed words" is another phrase that has been used to describe eloquence, as in the passage from Proverbs quoted earlier or the description of the speech of Nestor in *Iliad* 1.249. Since the activity of insects and birds is essential to disseminating pollen and thus to the survival of the plants' species, by coloration and sweetness even plants can be said to practice a rudimentary form of rhetoric. Some birds and mammals are attracted to brightly colored objects that have no food value and engage in play with them. Lorenz (1952:53) describes an instance: His father was sleeping in the garden when a tame cockatoo bit off all his buttons and then arranged them in a neat pattern where he had been lying.

Intentionality

Lorenz regarded the cockatoo as playing a joke on his father. If so, the bird was acting intentionally and was anticipating a reaction on the part of the old gentleman. Intentionality, both in animal and human actions, is a complex and elusive subject, much discussed by philosophers (e.g., Sorabji 1993:84–85). It is an important issue in rhetoric also, where the intent of a speaker to persuade an audience of some thesis is often regarded as basic to a speech act. But in daily life, many human speech acts are not consciously intentional; they are automatic reactions to situations, culturally (rather than genetically) imprinted in the brain or rising from the speaker's subconscious. They may have effects rather different from what the speaker might consciously want, or they may employ "Freudian slips." Even in the more controlled situation of public address, the real intent of the speaker may be open to question; prejudice, insecurity, or hostility may unwittingly be conveyed, and a rhetorical tactic may have a different or the opposite effect from what is intended. In nature there seems to be a wide range of degrees of intentionality. What Dennett (1987:246) calls "zero order" intentionality occurs when an organism gives off a sign, such as a protective change in coloration or shape, in response to a stimulus without making a conscious decision. Very simple organisms can do no more than this in their own defense; higher orders of animals have not only such reflex actions, but other capacities as well. "First order" intentionality occurs in animals capable of choosing whether or not to react to a stimulus: A response, for example, might attract the attention of a predator or conversely attract help from another of its species. "Second order" intentionality involves a conception on the part of an animal of its own and another animal's beliefs. As discussed earlier, deception as practiced by animals seems to imply some belief about others' beliefs. Although the existence of second order intentionality among nonhuman animals remains controversial, there is evidence that primates have beliefs they wish others to believe—e.g., that a leopard is nearby—or, in the case of chimpanzees, understand, to some extent, each others' goals and motives (Cheney and Seyfarth 1990:143, 254).

At what stage in the evolution of intentionality does rhetoric first exist? I am inclined to say that its potential is already present in the ability of an organism to give a sign, even without intent or belief. The potential is activated in first-order intentionality when vocal signs are employed, which express varying degrees of intensity, reflecting the animal's emotions, and more fully in second-order intentionality, where various rhetorical techniques are exploited. Nature as a whole is purposive: That is, evolution occurs because certain random mutations prove useful in improving the ability of the descendants of an organism to survive in the environment. Among the phenomena of life that have evolved are those of communication, with a natural advantage over physical acts in conserving the energy of forms of life. I do not myself think that nature is consciously purpose*ful*, working out a grand design with some ultimate meaning and end, though many others so believe, or would like to. The evolution of rhetoric, however, has made it possible for human beings to act and speak in a purposeful way, to defend themselves, secure what seems in their best interest, and give meaning to their lives.

Conclusion

Analogies between features of nonhuman animal behavior and traditional concepts of rhetoric among human beings suggest that rhetoric has its basis in natural instincts and supports the hypothesis that it is a form of energy. Rhetoric is biologically prior to speech and to conscious intentionality. The most fundamental of the instincts that created rhetoric is the instinct for self-preservation and for preservation of the genetic line. Among social animals this has been broadened to include the preservation and well-being of the family, the social group, and other members of the species. In this sense it is conservative and defensive. It is often an instrument of change, but this results from the efforts of individuals or groups to improve their lot or gain advantages denied them by others: It develops from a defensive instinct. When rhetorical techniques are used offensively by animals the functions are to secure territory, to acquire access to food, or to gain a mate. These functions lie behind much of human rhetoric in the form of the acquisitions of power and possessions.

Among different species of animals rhetorical potentialities have evolved differently in response to their physical and environmental needs. Genetic evolution has produced the possibilities of "cultural evolution" among animals. I here adopt Bonner's definition of "cultural evolution" as "the transfer of information by behavioural means, most particularly by the process of teaching and learning" (Bonner 1980:10). Human beings have genetically inherited a rhetorical instinct, but human rhetoric has culturally evolved beyond that evident in animals to serve human needs in different environments.

Persuasion can be achieved in several ways, but nature has favored the use of signs because it is less expensive of energy than is the use of force. Rhetoric may be regarded as a form of mental energy, sparked by an emotional reaction to a situation in which an individual feels threatened or perceives the opportunity to gain some advantage. The emotion felt is then transferred into action, either bodily action or utterance (a speech act). Utterance conveys energy by volume, pitch, duration, and repetition. Some animal utterances carry semantic values in that they are the equivalent of propositions and identify to others the reason for the emotion or intended action. Some animal utterances, bird songs in particular, have a complex arrangement suggestive of a proemium, the statement and amplification of themes, and less often, an epilogue.

Social animals live in highly structured, hierarchical groups, determined by age, sex, and physical and emotional stamina. Individuals can recognize each other by behavior and utterance. The rhetoric of a high-ranking animal carries greater weight than that of others. Since higher ranking animals usually produce more offspring, their genes are more often reproduced. This was probably the mechanism by which rhetorical ability evolved: Some genetic mutation enhanced the ability of some animals to gain advantage by utterance, and this advantage was handed on to their descendants and further developed. Authority has remained a major means of persuasion in human society.

Human language and rhetoric are far more complex than anything found in the animal kingdom. Among other things, human beings can reflect on the past, speculate about the future, tell stories, create literature, philosophize about politics and ethics, and speak about speech. These capabilities evolved with the evolution of the human brain and of human society. In the next chapter I offer some thoughts about rhetorical factors in the evolution of language beyond the limited form it seems to have taken in our primate ancestors.

References

Bonner, John Tyler (1980). *The Evolution of Culture in Animals*. Princeton: Princeton University Press.

Bright, Michael (1984). *Animal Language*. Ithaca: Cornell University Press.

Burghardt, Gordon M. (1985). "Animal Awareness: Current Perceptions and Historical Perspective," *American Psychologist* 40:905–19.

Catchpole, Clive K., and Peter J. B. Slater (1995). *Bird Song: Biological Themes and Variations*. Cambridge: Cambridge University Press.

Cheney, Dorothy L., and Robert M. Seyfarth (1990). *How Monkeys See the World*. Chicago: University of Chicago Press.

Chomsky, Norm (1972). *Language and Mind*. New York: Harcourt Brace Jovanovich.

Collias, Nicholas E., and Elsie C. Collias (1984). *Nest Building and Bird Behavior*. Princeton: Princeton University Press.

Darwin, Charles (1874). *The Descent of Man and Selection in Relation to Sex*. 2nd ed., New York: D. Appleton & Co., 1897.

Dennett, Daniel C. (1987). *The Intentional Stance*. Cambridge, MA: MIT/Bradford Press.

Dewart, Leslie (1989). *Evolution and Consciousness: The Role of Speech in the Origin and Development of Human Nature*. Toronto: University of Toronto Press.

Donald, Merlin (1991). *Origins of the Modern Mind: Three Stages in the Evolution of Culture and Cognition*. Cambridge, MA: Harvard University Press.

Gardner, R. Allen, Beatrix T. Gardner, and Thomas E. Van Cantfort, eds. (1989). *Teaching Sign Language to Chimpanzees*. Albany: State University of New York Press.

Gilbert, Bil [sic] (1992). "Commuter Crows: Why They Come Home to Roost," *Smithsonian Magazine* 23:101–11.

Goodwin, Derek (1981). *Crows of the World*. London: British Museum.

Griffin, Donald R. (1992). *Animal Minds*. Chicago: University of Chicago Press.

Jellis, Rosemary (1977). *Bird Sounds and Their Meaning*. London: British Broadcasting Corporation.

Kennedy, George A. (1992). "A Hoot in the Dark: The Evolution of General Rhetoric," *Philosophy and Rhetoric* 25:1–21.

Lorenz, Konrad Z. (1952). *King Solomon's Ring*, trans. by Marjorie Kerr Wilson. London: Methuen; reprinted, Chicago: Time-Life Books, 1980.

———(1977). *Behind the Mirror: A Search for a Natural History of Human Knowledge*, trans. by Ronald Taylor. New York: Harcourt Brace Jovanovich.

Morton, Eugene S., and Jake Page (1992). *Animal Talk: Science and the Voices of Nature*. New York: Random House.

Pepperberg, Irene M. (1991). "Referential Communication with an African Gray Parrot," *Harvard Graduate Society Newsletter*, spring, 1–4.

Pinker, Steven (1994). *The Language Instinct: How the Mind Creates Language*. New York: William Morrow & Co.

Reid, Thomas (1970). *Inquiry into the Human Mind*, ed. with an introduction by Timothy Duggan. Chicago: University of Chicago Press.

Savage-Rambaugh, Sue, and Kelly McDonald (1988). "Deception and Social Manipulation in Symbol-Using Apes," in *Machiavellian Intelligence: Social Expertise and the Evolution of Intellect in Monkeys, Apes, and Humans*, ed. Richard Byrne and Andrew Whiten, pp. 224–37. Oxford: Clarendon Press.

Sorabji, Richard (1993). *Animal Minds and Human Morals: The Origins of the Western Debate*. London: Duckworth.

Stelkis, Horst D. (1988). "Primate Communication: Comparative Neurology and the Origin of Language Re-Examined," in *The Genesis of Language: A Different Judgement of Evidence*, ed. by Marge E. Landsberg, pp. 37–63. Amsterdam: Mouton de Gruyter.

Terborgh, John (1996). "Cracking the Bird Code," *New York Review of Books* 43,1:40–44.

Thomas, Elizabeth Marshall (1993). *The Hidden Life of Dogs*. Boston: Houghton Mifflin.

Waal, Frans de (1988). "Chimpanzee Politics," in *Machiavellian Intelligence: Social Expertise and the Evolution of Intellect in Monkeys, Apes, and Humans*, ed. by Richard Byrne and Andrew Whiten, pp. 122–31. Oxford: Clarendon Press.

Weiss, Mark L. (1987). "Nucleic Acid Evidence Bearing on Hominid Relationships," *Yearbook of Physical Anthropology* 30:40–74.

Bibliography

Animal Communication: Techniques of Study and Results of Research, ed. by Thomas A. Sebeock. Ithaca: Cornell University Press, 1968.

The Oxford Companion to Animal Behaviour, ed. by David McFarland. Oxford and New York: Oxford University Press, 1987.

CHAPTER   2
_____

Rhetorical Factors in the Early Development of Human Language

Animal calls are physical actions that require the expenditure of energy, take a particular acoustic form that can carry meaning, and can transmit a simple message to a potential hearer. Human speech differs from animal calls phonetically in an ability to make a much greater differentiation of sounds by manipulation of the lips, teeth, and tongue and much greater control of the vocal cords, thus producing a large variety of words, and morphologically in an ability to combine and inflect sound segments to produce a variety of meanings. The primary reason that apes cannot learn to speak is not that they have nothing to say, nor that they cannot combine simple ideas, nor that their brains lack the requisite neurological structure for uses of language at the level of two-year-old human children; the primary impediment is the structure of their mouths and throats, which do not permit them to voice many of the sounds, especially consonants, of human languages. A good discussion of the physiological and neurological evolution of the capacity for speech is to be found in Philip Lieberman's book, *The Biology and Evolution of Language* (1984). Although some human beings have continued until modern times to live in hunter–gatherer societies with very limited technological support, no human society failed to develop language into a subtle and complex social tool. We cannot directly study the early stages of human language. These have to be extrapolated from information about animal communication, acquisition of language in childhood, reconstruction of earlier stages of existing languages, and more or less probable hypotheses about conditions in the distant past, of which there have been many.

Theories of the Origin of Human Language

Speculation about the origin of human languages and speech can be found in the writings of Western philosophers and theologians over the last twenty-five hundred years with major periods of interest in the fourth century BCE, when the subject was discussed in the schools of Plato and Epicurus, and in the eighteenth and early nineteenth centuries of our era among enlightenment philosophers (summaries in Borst 1957–61; Stam 1976; Fano 1992:117–83). Although the mythologies of the world tell of name-givers or offer some explanation of the origin of speech, non-Western thinkers of historical times seem not to have much concerned themselves with the subject. It is characteristic of Western logocentric thought to want to find origins, and preferably a single originative principle, to which everything can be traced. Jacques Derrida (1976:167) has warned against this: "The concept of origin or nature is nothing but the myth of addition, of supplementarity annulled by being purely additive." Any hypothesis of the origin of speech is a rhetorical act that inscribes the hypothesis within some totality of meaning to which the author is already committed. In my case, I suppose this includes the belief in the material basis of life, in human evolution from primate ancestors, and in the importance of rhetoric in human society. Postclassical theories were for long strongly colored by the biblical account. In chapter one of Genesis, God creates by speech (in what language was for long a vexing question, perhaps Hebrew); in chapter two God orders Adam to give names to all living creatures; in chapter eleven then comes the account of the building of the Tower of Babel, God's anger, and his decision to "confuse" human languages so that mortals will no longer join in concerted action against his will. Seventeenth- and eighteenth-century accounts were also influenced by contemporary assumptions about the nature of mankind, the soul, the human spirit, or other idealistic or metaphysical theories, all of which were abstract and lacked scientific evidence. Among the most famous of the early moderns to speculate on the subject were J. G. Herder in his *Treatise on the Origin of Language*, which won a prize for an essay on the subject from the Berlin Academy in 1771 and illustrates much of the inherent vagueness of German idealism, and Jean-Jacques Rousseau in his *Discourse on the Origin of Inequality among Men* (1753) and in *Essay on the Origin of Language*, the latter left unfinished at the time of his death in 1778.

Rousseau's views (well summarized by Stam 1976:80–93) are the starting point of Derrida's objections, but, as one might expect, they were rationally much in advance of those of his contemporaries. He envisioned a long development from the condition of an unsociable, mute beast to the life of a linguistically empowered "noble savage," and he associated this development with the invention of artifacts, tools, and weapons and the evolution of family life in a patriarchal system; the first speaking, Rousseau speculated, probably grew out of the passions and was thus figurative and poetic. But he confessed to a basic dilemma:

He could not imagine the opportunity or necessity for language to develop in the earlier, brutish stage, nor the development of the later "noble" stage unless speech already existed. Rousseau's dilemma may be said to have been resolved by modern realization that some social development, use of simple tools, and forms of communication already existed among prehuman primates and that when, a million years or more ago, our ancestors, already living in family groups, came down out of the trees, learned to walk on their hind legs, and engaged in cooperative hunting and gathering, the physiological, sociological, and psychological conditions for development of speech were in place.

Darwin offered some thoughts on the origin of language in the third chapter of *The Descent of Man*, to which reference was made at the beginning of the last chapter, and in *The Expression of Emotions in Man and Animals*. "I cannot doubt," he wrote (1874:87), "that language owes its origin to the imitation and modification of various natural sounds, the voices of other animals, and man's own instinctive cries, aided by signs and gestures. When we treat of sexual selection we shall see that primeval man, or rather some progenitor of man, probably first used his voice in producing true musical cadences, that is in singing, as do some of the gibbon-apes at the present day; and we may conclude from a widely-spread analogy, that this power would have been especially exerted during the courtship of the sexes—would have expressed various emotions, such as love, jealousy, triumph—and would have served as a challenge to rivals."

How a specific meaning could become attached to a specific utterance is one of the important questions in the evolution of speech. In the previous chapter I noted that some animal calls already carry specific meanings understood by others of the species. Presumably this resulted from the habitual use of the same call by some animal and the gradual awareness of others that the call was followed by some event, such as the appearance of a predator; then other animals imitated the call in similar circumstances. We can safely assume that the earliest hominids, before the emergence of homo sapiens, were already making grunts and cries that conveyed something to each other.

A second basic question is how human beings discovered that distinct groups of sounds—the equivalent of phonemes and syllables—could be combined in different ways to specify or modify meaning, opening up the possibility of numberless combinations that create the power and flexibility of modern languages. Primates do not do this in their natural environment, but as noted in the previous chapter, some birds combine acoustic segments in a variety of ways. Although these do not carry semantic differences, they show that there can exist in nature an inclination to acoustic experimentation and recombination that could provide a potentiality for human language in creatures with greater mental development.

Although the new possibilities for research provided by Darwinian theory were taken up by biologists and social philosophers in the second half of the nineteenth century, linguists largely abandoned direct speculation on the origin of speech as unprofitable. What took its place was an attempt to reconstruct earlier versions of existing languages, to find relationships among language groups, and perhaps ultimately to reconstruct the original language of the earliest human beings. This scholarly effort has continued over the last century from the hypothetical reconstruction of proto–Indo-European to the even more hypothetical reconstruction of a common ancestor of several language groups, called "Nostratic," and beyond that to "proto-World" (Danesi 1993:20–21). Shevoroshkin and Ramer (1991) provide a survey of how such reconstruction proceeds (see also Kelley 1992:155–206; Ruhlen 1994). In such studies there is an underlying hope of showing that all known languages derive from a single source.

Genetic evidence has recently been published pointing to the conclusion that all human beings are ultimately descended from one woman (Brown 1990:23–29) and one man (Hammer 1995) who lived in Africa between 100,000 and 200,000 years ago, whether from the copulation of these two individuals or from that by two of their descendants. If the genetic origin of the human race in two individuals is accepted as fact, the theory of a single origin for human languages would be strengthened but not proved. The sounds made by these particular individuals and learned by their offspring would be a significant factor in molding a language that would continue to be used by their descendants, but proto-languages, developed from sounds made by primate ancestors, certainly already existed in hominid societes and would have been a force toward diversity. Moreover, the research to be mentioned below suggests there may be a natural link between the configuration of the mouth in uttering phonemes and the semantic value originally carried by the resulting utterance, which might suggest the natural emergence of vocabularies with similar roots among diverse groups of individuals as they spread over the world, leading to languages that seem to have some similarities but were historically unrelated to each other. Even if some of the earliest words go back to prehuman grunts and cries, as they probably do, and even if some originated in imitation of natural sounds or were physically linked to meanings, the grunts and cries of different groups may have differed, different natural sounds are encountered in different environments, and how human beings make these imitations differs somewhat. The development of additional vocabulary using arbitrary sounds and the development of syntax, marking a transition from primitive speech to distinctively human language, is likely to have been specific to a particular group. The beginnings of speech and a common potential for language had certainly evolved in our remote ancestors, but that does not mean that its actualization might not have taken many different forms.

Glossogenetics

Scientific research on the origin of speech has reemerged in the last quarter of the twentieth century under the term "glossogenetics" or "glottogenetics" (the two spellings go back to two forms of the Greek word for "tongue"), utilizing new evidence from anthropology, biology, child development studies, linguistics, physiology, and psychology. Controversy still abounds and there are schools of thought emphasizing physiological, behaviorist, and cognitive approaches, but it seems to me that a majority view exists about some major factors involved and some of the steps in the beginnings of human speech. In particular, the ability of apes to reason and communicate has strengthened the view that a potentiality for speech evolved naturally over millions of years and that changes in the human brain, mouth, and throat, the latter two partly resulting from walking upright, together with the recognition of the utility of cooperation and communication, facilitated the development of more complex forms of oral communication perhaps a hundred thousand years ago. It is sometimes claimed that speech was at some point "invented" by early human beings, as were tools and the use of fire, that it is specifically a phenomenon of living in human society. I do not entirely agree with this: Human speech, the use of tools, and human social organization seem to me developments out of already existing primate practices, while the use of fire was a distinctively human invention. Although the equipment and potentiality for speech exists at birth among humans, children acquire language by imitation; a German child adopted at birth by Americans will learn to speak English, not German. Apparently speech has to be learned at an early stage of life: In the best documented instances of children reared without hearing speech no normal facility to use language subsequently developed (Danesi 1993:6).

I do not intend here to offer still another theory of the origin of human speech and the development of human language. Rather, I would like to try to identify some rhetorical factors, which, so far as I can see, have gone unnoticed or unstressed in recent discussions. But since my readers may not be familiar with theories of the origin of speech it may be helpful first to summarize some of the major theories briefly, drawing on a variety of sources, all of which disagree about many details. Beginning in the midnineteenth century humorous, sometimes belittling, names were given to theories of language origin and have become traditional in glossogenetics (Jespersen 1922; Stam 1976:243; Danesi 1993:6–7).

What is called the "bow-wow" theory attributes the first creation of words to the imitation of natural sounds; this usage survives in onomatopoetic words in modern languages. As an explanation of the origin of language the theory is often much ridiculed, since the number of onomatopoetic words in any language is small. It explains only the origin of the words for some natural sounds—in English, for example, "bang, smash, tinkle"—or for the names of some animals based on their calls, but these words differ somewhat in different languages. Still, it seems reasonable that early humans, like their modern descendants, may have signified some actions or animals by imitation of natural sounds, thus enlarging their inherited vocabulary. There are usually assumed to be parallels between the first emergence of speech among human beings and the stages of language learning among children: "Ontogeny recapitulates phylology" (sometimes). The fact that onomatopoetic coinages are easily understood and used by small children is some support for the possibility that they played at least a small role in early human language development.

The "pooh-pooh" theory is the name given by the midnineteenth-century linguist Max Müller to the claim that words originated in instinctive cries made in response to painful or pleasurable experiences—in modern English words like "ouch! wow! hey!" This might account for the development of interjections, which have become conventionalized in different forms in different modern languages.

The "ding-dong" theory is more subtle. It finds the origin of the first words in the configuration of the mouth in response to some stimulation. The usual example is "mama," representing the movement of the lips as an infant approaches the breast. Or the smacking of lips at a pleasurable taste might produce a word like "yummy." Some such words may have been added to early vocabularies.

The "yo-he-ho" theory attributes the earliest words to grunts or chants made during communal efforts, such as an effort to move some heavy object. This might not have created many specific words but could have contributed to the development of a sense of rhythm and encouraged the use of utterance in other contexts.

The "la-la" theory suggests that language began with sounds made during love-making, play, or other social activities with emotional content. Both the "yo-he-ho" and the "la-la" theory can be associated with the view of Rousseau and Darwin that the use of speech in practical situations was preceded by "poetry" of a sort: primitive rhythmical utterances expressive of emotion. The morning duet of the pileated gibbons mentioned in the previous chapter illustrates the existence of this among primates, and bird song is a commonly cited analogy.

No one of these theories in themselves seems adequate to explain the origin of speech; it is not impossible, however, that each of the processes occurred among some early human groups and that each contributed something. If any words were created as described in the "bow-wow" or "ding-dong" theory, this would constitute some evidence for linkage between words and natural objects or actions, between signs and signified, in the earliest stage of language. Modern languages, with the minor exception of onomatopoetic words, are, as Saussure (1959) argued, arbitrary systems: Words are not defined by their resemblance to their signified but by other words in the dictionary in an endless circle. This apparent fact is the basis of deconstruction as practiced by Jacques Derrida and other poststructuralist philosophers, who conclude that there is no ultimate foundation for language, reason, or truth. It seems possible, however, that the history of language is dominated by entropy: that at least some of the earliest words had linkages or resemblances to natural realities and were not totally random or conventional signs. Once the use of words became common, selective variation occurred both by chance and by simplification of utterance, language became stylized and conventionalized, and new words were invented arbitrarily (Englefield 1977:38–45). I shall return to the question of by whom and how later in this chapter. The history of writing in both the East and West provides a parallel: first picture writing, then simplification, stylization, and the creation of conventional symbols; eventually, alphabets and the creation of new, largely arbitrary symbols to signify sounds. I say "largely" arbitrary since there are a few letters in our alphabet that preserve some natural link to the shape of the mouth in utterance; the best example is O.

A more subtle version of the onomatopoetic theory of language origin was advanced in Plato's dialogue *Cratulus*, where Socrates plays with ideas without finally endorsing any of them. This theory provides a natural link between sign and signified by attributing categories of meaning to the sound of letters of the Greek alphabet. Thus, it is suggested, "liquid" sounds—l, m, n, and r—are characteristically found in words referring to motion and flux; the letter i denotes thin, subtle things; d and t represent binding and rest, hard g a gliding motion, and so forth. Whether the coinage of early human words was conditioned by such feelings cannot be said; certainly poets since antiquity have exploited the use of sounds that seem, whether naturally or conventionally, to suit the sense of the verse:

> Soft is the strain when zephyr gently blows,
> And the smooth stream in smoother numbers flows;
> But when loud surges lash the sounding shore,
> The hoarse, rough verse should like the tempest roar.

> (ALEXANDER POPE, *AN ESSAY ON CRITICISM*)

A similar phenomenon occurs in music, developed especially in romantic tone poems as composed by Debussy, Strauss, and others, in which the composer gives the audience an idea in the title, such as "Afternoon of a Faun" or "A Hero's Life," and the sounds and rhythms of the music then evoke a possible narrative and changes in mood and setting. This is a development of a natural principle: In the previous chapter I noted that in animal calls pitch reflects relative size, with the result that low pitch seems naturally to denote aggression, high pitch fear or appeasement.

Some support for a version of the theory of Plato's *Cratulus* has been offered in recent times by Morris Swadish (1971) from his research on sound symbolism in a wide variety of language groups. He noted that many languages use i or short e vowels in words denoting nearness (e.g., English "this") and a and u vowels in words expressing distance (e.g., English "that"), leading to the conclusion that the nearness or openness of the lips unconsciously represents relative distance (Danesi 1993:9). Mary Foster (1983:457–61; see also Koch 1990:149) has proposed that the shape of the lips in forming p sounds created proto-words that referred to projection or extension outward, whereas t sounds suggested intromission, penetration, and contact, and w sounds suggested surrounding or encircling.

Gesture and Language

The most common explanation of how arbitrary cries could have become linked to specific meaning is that they were accompanied by gestures—in rhetorical terminology, "delivery"—just as the meaning of animal calls is often accompanied by physical display and body movement. This was the view of the ancient Epicureans. They were materialists and naturalists and their cultural theory is evolutionary. The Epicurean poet Lucretius, in the fifth book of his Latin epic *On the Nature of Things*, denies that there was any original name-giver, he closely connects the origin of human speech to a development of the sounds made by animals, and he suggests that sounds acquired specific meanings through the use of gestures that accompanied them. One can easily imagine a variety of scenarios in early human life, frequently repeated, in which a particular sound was accompanied by a particular gesture and came to be associated with it. From the analogy with animal communication, where calls are usually associated with establishing territory, alerting others to predators, keeping off competitors, mating, gathering food, and care of young, one can imagine situations in domestic life and in hunting, food-gathering, and defense. Many such gestures would probably have been ostensive: that is, indicating "this, that," "you, me," "over there," "go, come," or specific objects pointed to; others might be mimicked: drinking, creeping, hiding, stabbing, and so forth.

Many modern scholars have incorporated the gesture theory into their explanations of language origin (e.g., Hewes 1976; Englefield 1977; Gans 1981; Armstrong, Stokoe, and Wilcox 1995). Englefield's book, though largely ignored by scholars of glossogenetics, gives a thoughtful account of the whole subject of language origins and a powerful refutation of the doctrine, still strong in some academic circles, that thought is totally controlled by language. The book is, however, eccentric in one respect: His suggestion that the first spoken languages may have been secret forms of communication among a small group of individuals. Gans's book is also eccentric in that it is strongly influenced by ideas of René Girard about the origin of religious sacrifice. In *Violence and the Sacred* (1972) Girard argued that sacrificial religion originated in an act of violence: A band of human beings experienced some crisis in their ways of life, perhaps from an act of nature. They suddenly and collectively turned their anger and fear on one person, killed the offender, and immediately felt better. This violence, Girard claimed, was "the birth of symbolic thought" and, almost in passing (235–36), he added that it was also the origin of language through "the mechanism of the surrogate victim." The idea is slightly developed in a later book (Girard 1978:103–4) where he says, "It seems possible, during the ritual around the victim, that cries at first inarticulate should fall into a rhythm and become ordered like steps in a dance...." The bizarre conclusion seems to be that the first human word was "kill!" Girard's theory of the origin of sacrificial religion deserves respect, but as a theory of the origin of language it ignores other basic contexts of life analogous to those in which animal communication occurs: establishing a territory, providing for food, securing a mate (as Darwin suggested), and raising young. Among early humans, as among animals, utterance was surely more frequently defensive than offensive—"help! look out! stay away!" Ritualization, which Gans (1981:30), like some others, regards as the source of language, among animals is largely a part of courtship or the preservation of bonds with others, and it seems unnecessarily cynical to imagine that it was totally different among early humans.

Opposition to the gestural theory is occasionally expressed. Bickerton, who also stresses the "gulf between language and animal communication" (1990:10–16), objects to it on three grounds (142): It does not explain how elements acquired reference or how syntax developed and would seem to predict that infants would use gestures prior to vocalizations. It seems to me that the strength of the gestural theory is that it does provide the best explanation of how arbitrary sounds can be linked to referents. The second objection is unfair in that the gestural theory applies specifically to the creation of vocabulary and short phrases, which is a necessary preliminary to the development of syntax by the juxtaposition of words. The third objection, based on the assumption that ontogeny should recapitulate phylogeny, confuses the issue. What is relevant is not the gestures infants make but the gestures adults make in teaching the meaning of words to infants, especially the objects they point out and the actions they perform while saying words.

The importance of syntax in the earliest development of languages, whether through the inflection or order of words or the use of grammatical subordination, is easily exaggerated. The enlargement of vocabulary was far more important for everyday communication. Englefield (1977:98–101) illustrates how much can be conveyed by a succession of words without grammatical connection if a listener shares experience and ideas in common with the speaker and understands the immediate context. The language of archaic Australian songs relies heavily on simple juxtaposition of words with little in the way of grammatical syntax. Syntax is perhaps a rhetorical technique to obtain greater clarity and precision in conveying complex thoughts, characteristic of cultures where some individuals enjoy the luxury of reflection and find a need to make distinctions of tense, mood, and case to express themselves. The most complex systems of syntax, involving the use of subordinate clauses and periodic sentence structure, are a feature of written languages.

Language and Song

Since theories of the origin of human language in ritual, song, and poetry have had powerful advocates from Rousseau to Darwin to Jespersen to Girard and Gans, I would like to make a few observations on the issues involved. First, most meaningful calls of most animals are made in the context of their daily life while gathering food and defending themselves, not in ritual. Some animals engage in ritual cries while mating and some birds and primates have developed complex songs or duets of a ritual nature. Something analogous to these is found among human beings all over the world and is probably very ancient. The need for efficient communication in daily life was, however, surely predominant in enriching vocabulary. Play, love-making, recreational singing, and lamentations of grief provided practice in the formation of sounds and innovative combinations of sound segments expressive of emotions, and these faculties could then be applied to enrich everyday language, giving it greater emotional power and enhancing its aesthetic potentials. Ritual and song were thus important in developing rhetorical features of language beyond such rudimentary techniques as volume, pitch, and repetition of the message. In particular, ritual and song are likely to have been the contexts in which figures of speech originated.

Much early language is likely to have been harsh, depending heavily on shrill sounds and long vowels, as do the languages of primates, probably interspersed with sound segments that expressed the speaker's state of mind but carried no specific cognitive meaning, and highly repetitive. Human beings are still reduced to emotional sounds at times and a great deal of human speech is somewhat sing-song, repetitive, ungrammatical, and illogical. Important historical factors that have disciplined speech in the direction of greater clarity and logic are public address as it emerged with new political forms, such as councils, and the use of writing in urban centers of early historical times. In the case of ritualized singing, whether private or public, a disciplining factor may have been a desire to tell a story and thus to create narrative. Noncognitive song, like instrumental music, can have a dynamics that suggests narrative structure without carrying specific narrative meaning. The introduction of cognitive vocabulary from everyday life could gradually mold this into a narrative of the actions of gods, animals, and human beings. Prose and poetry derive from two different sources, one the practical needs of everyday life, the other the emotional needs of the human psyche. Both, however, reflect the basic need to survive. The two traditions come together most closely in the rhetorical genre of epideictic and in those poetic genres that traditionally perform public functions: epic, drama, and satire. These, however, until modern times have marked themselves off from ordinary language by the use of "formal" language, rhythmical, often highly metaphorical, often archaic. Similarly, religious rituals all over the world proclaim their sacred qualities by otherness from ordinary language, commonly in the form of archaism. The rhetorical effect is twofold: Archaism seems to validate the account of events of the mythical past by conveying them in the language first used to describe them (usually an illusion, since orally transmitted songs change over time); and it increases the authority of the singer, priest, or bard, since he or she, with a special knowledge unavailable to others, seems to have direct access to the truth, which can then be interpreted to the vulgar as the singer wills. Sometimes, as in early Israel and early Greece, the bard claims, and doubtless often believed, direct inspiration from a god or the muses, further authenticating the song.

In subsequent chapters it will emerge that the use of different forms of language for different contexts is a feature of many otherwise different cultures all over the world. It seems possible that the ultimate origin of these linguistic distinctions, to be described more fully in chapter 4, is the very early differentiation of song from everyday speech, which led not only to the modern distinction between poetry and prose, but the differentiation of intermediate levels of style, some poetic, metaphorical, and formulaic, some relatively prosaic, depending on the degree to which the speech situation was or was not perceived as formal and ritualistic.

Some Rhetorical Considerations

The concept of the "rhetorical situation," familiar to students of speech communication, should be the starting point for an approach to the early stages of human language as rhetoric. This concept was first advanced by Lloyd Bitzer (1968:6) in the following terms: "Rhetorical situation may be defined as a complex of persons, events, objects, and relations presenting an actual or potential exigence which can be completely or partially removed if discourse, introduced into the situation, can so constrain human decision or action as to bring about the significant modification of the exigence." With minor modifications, the definition applies to animal communcation as well and in the form given describes the situation in which early humans used language. A situation occurs to which an agent feels an emotional reaction and which impels utterance. I have suggested earlier that the instinct for self-preservation is the fundamental factor, extended in social situations to include the perceived best interest not only of the agent, but of the family, the social group, and their progeny—in biological terms the survival of their genes. The "situation" is the context of a reaction on the part of an individual and of the creation of mental energy that is then transmitted by a rhetorical code.

Bitzer continues with discussion of audience and constraints. Audience, however, need not be limited to the situation of public address as Bitzer might be thought to imply. It may be a small group, it may be one person, it may be an animal, it may be the agent addressing the self or some aspect of the self. "O breath of my life, beset by difficult troubles, rise up ..." exclaimed the early Greek poet Archilochus. The audience may also be a natural phenomenon or physical object such as a storm, a river, a rock, or a tree. Anthropological studies show that personification of the forces and objects of nature, surviving in modern discourse as a rhetorical trope, reflects a literal belief found in societies all over the world that these forces and objects are alive and can be appeased and persuaded to act in some way. Magic, too, is one of the oldest human arts, and magical utterances and incantations surely made up one of the first rhetorical genres to emerge.

The "constraints" encountered by early humans in rhetorical situations were numerous. Most probably still had only a limited control of their vocal apparatus and thus of the variety, pitch, and volume of sound. They had only limited vocabulary, though this could be aided by gesture. They had only a limited range of rhetorical techniques to accomplish persuasion. They could assume only a limited range of ideas on the part of an audience. Finally, traditional societies as known today are highly conservative and resistant toward anything that seems innovative or not part of their experience. Probably we should assume that early societies were equally conservative and resistant to innovation.

An important means of persuasion available to early humans, and the rhetorical factor consistently overlooked in all discussions I have read of the origins of speech, is the authority acquired by individuals. Among social animals, as described in the last chapter, certain animals have high rank and authority. Often there is a hierarchy both among the males and the females, each with authority in certain areas, though the highest ranking male can often ultimately have his own way. Authority is achieved and expressed by physical strength and appearance, power of utterance reflecting that strength, success in mating, hunting, gathering and preparing food, defense of the group, and by self-confidence. These qualities can be inherited as the result of selective mating among the most fit, but there is a more or less constant contest among younger animals, especially males, for higher rank. Some form of social hierarchy is found universally among human groups today and can be assumed to have existed among early humans, certainly within the family circle and probably also within a group of related families cooperating in hunting and food gathering. An ability at self-expression and at persuading others would be an important aspect of leadership, favored by natural selection in the emergence of leaders and their offspring since, as described in the last chapter, nature has favored the development of communication as conservative of energy in contrast to violence. Conversely, the particular form of utterance employed by the natural leader would take on authority within the group and be imitated by others.

The authority of some individuals is likely to have been an important factor in the fixing of the meaning of words and the extension of vocabulary beyond that inherited from prehuman animals and that created by imitation of natural sounds. Every individual, animal or human, to some extent makes habitual sounds that are unique to the individual and can be distinguished by others. Arbitrary sounds invented by leaders and habitually used would carry authority for others and become accepted words within the group. Probably we should imagine at least two major contexts, one dominated by the senior female in the household and productive of vocabulary relating to domestic life, one dominated by the senior male in the field and productive of words useful in hunting and interaction with other groups. Although this process of the development of language doubtless began without conscious consideration on the part of leaders, an intelligent leader eventually is likely to have come to some understanding of his or her role in language creation and certification. One can imagine others turning to the leader to ask what something should be called and the leader giving an answer, whether at random or by adaptation of some existing word or words. The authority of a leader results in part from experience and leadership in turn enlarges experience. Experience, reflected on, leads to wisdom. The classical philosophers who proposed that a primeval wise man gave names to things and led humanity from brutishness to civilization may not have been entirely wrong.

What, beyond the authority of a speaker or the potential use of force or favors, would have been persuasive in early human society? What might be the earliest forms of argument? In chapter 2 I noted that some animal cries inherently carry reasons in that they can express alarm and the reason for the alarm. Vervet monkeys do not state universal propositions such as "all eagles are dangerous; this bird is an eagle; therefore this bird is dangerous." Instead, they communicate the conclusion—"Danger!"—and the minor premise—"Big bird!" The major premise is assumed and instinctively shared. In rhetorical terms, communication takes the form of an enthymeme. It seems likely that early human reasoning took a similar form. A body of experiential wisdom existed but was not conceptualized. Among examples that can be imagined are "Dead! Head crushed"; "Sleep, tired"; "Look out! Hot." Utterances are simply juxtaposed without inferential particles, with logic but without syntax. These examples also suggest that one of the earliest and perhaps most basic of rhetorical topoi may be "cause and effect." Such statements could be accompanied by gestures.

At some point in human history individuals began to formulate and state universal propositions. Some of the evidence to be discussed in the next two chapters suggests that this may be a relatively late development, since it has not fully taken place in some still existing societies. Wisdom in traditional societies still often takes the form of specific stories without generalization of the moral. The application of the story is left to the hearer. Some societies have few or no proverbs, which is one form of generalized wisdom. Generalized statements are persuasive to the degree that they are spoken with authority, but the rhetorical effect can be increased by citing one or more specific examples of something analogous. Formulation of general propositions may be a function of leadership roles, analogous to the creation of arbitrary words as described earlier. Appeal might be made to a father or elder for advice, for example, about how to deal with a marauding animal or hostile stranger, and the response might then be given in general terms that could apply to a variety of situations. The addition of a specific example in support of a general proposition would seem to suggest that the proposition was not immediately clear or that differing views existed, thus that the argument occurred in a deliberative situation. Systematic inductive logic in which evidence is collected and some generalization formulated to account for it is clearly a very late development in human intellectual life, not much cultivated until the scientific revolution of the seventeenth century in Europe.

Beyond authority and enthymematic reasoning, the most common rhetorical device of prehistoric society was doubtless repetition, as it is in animal communication and indeed as it remains in human communication: repetition with increased emphasis, or repetition with some variation, as in bird song. Archaic songs, as found, for example, among the Australian aboriginals, and magical incantations all over the world are characterized by repetition and variation.

From Authority to Ethos

In chapters 1 and 2 I have repeatedly remarked on the role of the hierarchical authority of certain individuals as an important means of persuasion among social animals and early human beings. In the Prologue, however, no mention was made of authority as having any place in traditional rhetorical theory. What we find there is ethos, the moral character of the speaker projected into a speech (or text) to secure credibility or sympathy with audience or reader. Authority from a position in a hierarchy is a powerful means of persuasion that is brought to bear on a rhetorical situation, sometimes without any specific reference to it in the words that are spoken or written. The presence of the speaker or the name of the author is sufficient. It has continued to be important throughout history as a basis of power by rulers, prophets, priests, teachers, military and civilian officials, employers, and parents. Often persons in these positions have no need to supply reasons for their pronouncements to be effective. A General Theory of Rhetoric needs to provide a place for authority within its structures. Probably the best solution is to regard authority as a "nonartistic" counterpart to ethos, analogous to the text of a law or the words of a contract, which are counterparts to logical argument. Like laws and contracts, authority is something external, used but not invented for the occasion.

To be a means of persuasion, ethos, or moral character, requires an understanding of moral values on the part of members of a society. In chapter 1 I argued that social animals have what Thomas Reid called an understanding of "veracity, credulity, and induction." In animal communication the veracity and credulity of a message may be established by the listener's prior knowledge of the animal. In that case, authority and not ethos operates. But if the sender of the message is unknown to the recipient, volume, pitch, and insistent repetition constitute a *claim* to authority in the message, and as such can be regarded as an incipient use of rhetorical ethos.

The ability to distinguish truth from falsehood is probably fundamental to the development of a sense of right and wrong, which resulted over time among early humans from experience of what was in the best interest of the society and was then imposed and reinforced by hierarchical leaders in the interest of order, discipline, and power. We cannot trace the development of artistic ethos in early human rhetoric. It can be recognized in texts when the author directly or indirectly seeks to establish credibility or sympathy. In egalitarian societies to be discussed in chapters 4 and 5, a speaker may lack authority and have need to create ethos. The emphasis on ethos and the neglect of authority in classical rhetoric derives from the egalitarian assumptions of Greek democracy.

Conclusion

Research on animal communication, comparative physiology, child development, and linguistics has begun to provide a scientific basis for theories of language origin. Much still remains speculative. Researchers have neglected to consider the rhetorical situation in which language developed, which was primarily the needs of daily life. Gestures certainly played a role in identifying sounds with meanings. Rhetorical "delivery" was thus an important factor from the beginning. Equally important was the authority of the speaker in the situation, an authority determined by age, sex, strength, and ability at leadership. Human languages developed from animal communication. The rhetorical techniques of early human speech included the authority of the speaker and logical argument in the form of juxtaposed utterances giving a reason for a statement. Ethos, or the artistic creation of credibility and sympathy by a speaker, probably developed slowly over time with the growth of moral values.

References

Armstrong, David F., William C. Stokoe, and Sherman E. Wilcox (1995). *Gesture and the Nature of Language*. Cambridge: Cambridge University Press.

Bickerton, Derek (1990). *Language and Species*. Chicago: University of Chicago Press.

Bitzer, Lloyd (1968). "The Rhetorical Situation," *Philosophy and Rhetoric* 1:1–14; reprinted in supplementary issue, 1992:1–14.

Borst, Arno (1957–61). *Der Turmbau von Babel: Geschichte der Meinungen über Ursprung und Vielfalt der Sprachen und Völker*. 3 vols. in 5. Stuttgart: A Hiersemann.

Brown, Michael H. (1990). *The Search for Eve*. New York: Harper & Row.

Danesi, Marcel (1993). *Vico, Metaphor, and the Origin of Language*. Bloomington: Indiana University Press.

Darwin, Charles (1874). *The Descent of Man and Selection in Relation to Sex*. 2nd edition, New York: D. Appleton & Co., 1897.

Derrida, Jacques (1976). *Of Grammatology*, trans. by Gayatri Chakrovorty Spivak. Baltimore: Johns Hopkins University Press.

Englefield, F. R. H. (1977). *Language: Its Origin and Its Relation to Thought*. New York: Charles Scribner's Sons.

Fano, Giogio (1992). *The Origins and Nature of Language*, trans. by Susan Petrili. Bloomington: Indiana University Press.

Foster, Mary (1983). "Solving the Insoluble: Language Genetics Today," in *Glossogenetics: The Origin and Evolution of Language*, pp. 455–80, ed. by Eric de Grolier. Chur, Switzerland: Harwood Academic Publishers.

Gans, Eric (1981). *The Origin of Language*. Berkeley: University of California Press.

Girard, René (1972). *Violence and the Sacred*, trans. by Patrick Gregory. Baltimore: Johns Hopkins University Press.

———(1978). *Things Hidden Since the Foundation of the World*, trans. by Stephen Bann and Michael Metteer. Stanford: Stanford University Press.

Hammer, Michael F. (1995). "A Recent Common Ancestor for Human Y Chromosomes," *Nature* 378 (23 November), pp. 376–78.

Hewes, G. W. (1976). "The Current Status of the Gestural Theory of Language Origin," in *Origins and Evolution of Language and Speech*, pp. 482–504, ed. by S. R. Harnard, H. D. Steklis, and J. Lancaster. New York: New York Academy of Sciences.

Jespersen, Otto (1922). *Language: Its Nature, Development, and Origin*. London: Allen and Unwin.

Kelley, E. Morgan (1992). *The Metaphorical Basis of Language: A Study in Cross-Cultural Linguistics*. Lewiston, NY: Edwin Mellen.

Koch, Walter A., ed. *The Genesis of Language*. Bochum: Universitätsverlag Brockmeyer.

Lieberman, Philip (1984). *The Biology and Evolution of Language*. Cambridge, MA: Harvard University Press.

Ruhlem, Merritt (1994). *The Origin of Language: Tracing the Evolution of the Mother Tongue*. New York: John Wiley and Sons.

Saussure, Ferdinand de (1959). *Course in General Linguistics*, edited by Charles Bally and Albert Reidlinger, translated by Wade Baskin. New York: Philosophical Library.

Shevoroshkin, Vitaly, and Alexis M. Ramer (1991). "Some Recent Work on the Remote Relations of Languages," in *Sprung from Some Common Source: Investigations into the Prehistory of Languages*, pp.178–99, edited by Sydney M. Lamb and E. Douglas Mitchell. Stanford: Stanford University Press.

Stam, James H. (1976). *Inquiries into the Origin of Language: The Fate of a Question*. New York: Harper & Row.

Swadish, Morris (1971). *The Origin and Diversification of Language*. Chicago: Aldine-Atherton.

Bibliography

Burkert, Walter (1996). *Creation of the Sacred; Tracks of Biology in Early Religions*. Cambridge: Harvard University Press.

Grolier, Eric de, ed. (1981). *Glossogenetics; The Origin and Evolution of Language*. Chur, Switzerland: Harwood Academic Publishers.

Landsberg, Marge E., ed. (1988). *The Genesis of Language: A Different Judgement of Evidence.* Berlin: Mouton de Gruyter.

Wind, Jan (1992). *Language Origin: A Multidisciplinary Approach.* Dordeckt, Netherlands: Kiuwer Academic Publishers.

———, et al., eds. (1989). *Studies in Language Origins*, I. Amsterdam: John Benjamins.

CHAPTER 3

Rhetoric in Aboriginal
Australian Culture

Beginning with the voyages of discovery in the fifteenth and sixteenth centuries, and on a larger scale during colonization in the seventeenth and eighteenth centuries, western Europeans encountered strange new societies in Africa, Asia, the Americas, and islands of the Indian and Pacific oceans. For long, the usual European reaction to this wider world was to view the natives as savages, a lower form of human life, and to exploit or enslave them, while seeking to convert them to Christianity. A few travelers, among them some Jesuit and Franciscan missionaries, took an interest in "outlandish" cultures, especially the more highly developed societies of China, Mexico, and Peru, and compiled accounts that were read with interest in Europe; a few natives were brought across the seas for the edification or amusement of Europeans. By the end of the eighteenth century the world had been mapped and its inhabitants known to a considerable extent except for central South America, central Africa, and Australia. Knowledge of these areas began to be acquired in the nineteenth century. The aboriginal culture of Australia is a particularly interesting one in many ways; discussion of its rhetorical features can provide an introduction to a wider survey of the Third World in the next chapter.

Although early explorers, including Captain Cook, recorded some impressions of the Australian natives, they were little known until after British settlement at the end of the eighteenth century and even then long ignored, perhaps because they were not warlike and either retreated to central regions unappealing to whites or fell into menial roles in white society. In the course of the nineteenth century a number of Anglican missionaries wrote descriptions of the native culture. Then, between 1899 and 1927 Baldwin Spencer and F. J. Gillen compiled comprehensive accounts that are still valuable since they describe features of the culture that no longer exist. Spencer and Gillen (1899) saw what seemed to be a surviving stone-age people who had been isolated from the rest of the world for tens of thousands of years, preserving something like the hunter–gatherer conditions under which prehistoric human beings may have lived. The best overall modern account is that by Ronald M. and Catherine H. Berndt, *The World of the First Australians*, originally published in 1964 and now in a fifth, revised edition (1988). Much of the following discussion is based on this book.

Every society, however "primitive" it may seem to Westerners, is the result of a long history of development within its own environment. Changes, including in some cases decay from a higher to a lower level of culture, can be assumed, and most existing nonliterate societies provide no evidence for prehistoric rhetoric. But most societies also have had some ongoing contact, whether friendly or hostile, with neighbors different from themselves, have been influenced by them in some ways, and have influenced them in turn. Very slowly, technology, ways of life, and ideas have spread over the landmass of Africa, Asia, Europe, and the Americas. The Australians' claim to special consideration is the absence of outside influences for a very long time. Some features of discourse observed among them resemble rhetorical practices of early human beings suggested in the previous chapter, whether these are survivals from ancient times or the result of living in conditions more analogous to ancient times than found elsewhere in the world. It is perhaps relevant that the animals of Australia—for example, the platypus and the echidna—include survivals from earlier stages of evolution.

The aboriginal inhabitants of Australia are thought to be descendants of groups who reached the island continent from East Asia 30,000 or more years ago and who subsequently had no contact with other human groups until the voyages of discovery, except perhaps on the northeast coast where, on rare occasions, a few canoes from the East Indies may occasionally have put ashore. Australian myth contains no memories of migration to the continent and instead describes the origin of the people in Australia in the remote past. When first encountered by whites, the aboriginals lived in small, often isolated groups as hunter–gatherers. They had no technological inventions except the boomerang, the spear-thrower, and the use of fire: no pottery, no weaving, no clothes (though they adorned their bodies in various ways), no chiefs, no formal tribal councils, no fixed homes, no domestic animals. They did not sow and harvest crops, but lived by hunting, fishing, and gathering the produce of nature. They did not even engage in organized warfare, that otherwise most human of institutions, though they had quarrels and occasionally killed each other and sometimes ate the victims. They did not engage in human or animal sacrifice, though they had developed a complex religion, ritual, mythology, and a rich body of stories and songs.

Rhetorical Features of an Aboriginal Prose Myth

Aboriginal Australian culture, unlike many other nonliterate societies, had no provision for councils, assemblies, or formal debate, and unlike cultures to be discussed in the next chapter there were no individuals regarded as civic orators. Doubtless a good deal of informal exchange of opinion occurred about what a family or group of families should do or where they should go, and individuals certainly exercised leadership on the basis of age, success in hunting, or a reputation for knowledge. Information about traditional aboriginal rhetoric has to be derived from transcriptions of orally transmitted myths and songs. Overall, these can be said to fall under the category of epideictic, broadly understood, but some of them describe deliberation between individuals.

Among the best known of the aboriginal Australians are the Arunta (or Aranda), who lived in the geographical center of the content, an arid land similar to parts of the American West. Among their myths is a story about killing a euro (a small, hairy species of kangaroo) by two brothers, Ntjitkantja and Kwaneraka, who are mythical members of the euro totem and were regarded as inventors of the spear and the spear-thrower. Strehlow (1947:22–23) gives the following version:

> They see a large euro nodding in its sleep. And Ntjitkantja tells Kwaneraka to move in a half-circle to the rear of the animal so that he may sneak up to it more closely. When Kwaneraka is at the rear of the euro, Ntjitkantja signals to him, "Come further forward and throw your spear." But Kwaneraka, who can only see the ears of the euro, is misled into thinking that the animal is facing him, and so he signals back, "Not I; come forward yourself!" Again Ntjitkantja calls to him, "No, you should come towards me; the euro is looking at me." And Kwaneraka in reply repeats, "No, it is up to you; I am being watched." They now go around the animal in a wide circle and meet together and take counsel: "What is to be done?" Then Ntjitkantja has a happy thought. He says to Kwaneraka, "Wait here for a moment; I shall go back to our camp."
>
> He went to get a tjurunga; and having taken the tjurunga into his hands, he returned to his younger brother. He held it behind his back. And then Ntjitkantja demonstrated its proper use: the tjurunga flew through the air, it gashed the head and body of the euro. And after the gash had been made, the brothers received the power of scent; their noses had been opened by the smell of the blood. Both men and euros ever since have been able to smell; for before that time their noses had been shut fast.

The story seems to describe a primeval scene, whether 100 or 100,000 years ago. One thing to note is the use of gesture in the first part of the story, something that seems to have been crucial in the earliest stages of speech. The Australians have highly developed sign language systems (Kendon 1988) and sometimes prefer to use gestures even when speech is feasible. Ntjitkantja is the older brother; thus he gives the orders and takes the lead throughout the story, whereas his younger brother is "misled" by what he thinks he sees. At first, Ntjitkantja simply repeats his order, relying on his status as the elder, but when resisted he adds a reason: "You should come towards me; the euro is looking at me." To oppose this order Kwaneraka then needs to support refusal with a reason; thus his reply, "No, you should come towards me; the euro is looking at me." By simple juxtaposition of statements both brothers create enthymemes. Juxtaposition of words or statements, without inferential or subordinating connectives (the equivalent of "for" or "because"), is characteristic of traditional Australian texts, which are almost without syntax, although connectives are used in the colloquial language. Nor does the traditional language have a system of grammatical tenses. There is little differentiation of time: It is an assumption of the culture that everything that ever existed still exists and will always exist. Strehlow does not here provide a literal version of the text, but probably Ntjitkantja says "I go to camp," not "I shall go back to camp."

The enthymeme implies a major premise: that an animal can best be attacked from behind. Both brothers know this and there is no reason to state it. The wisdom of traditional Australian texts is seen through description of specific incidents, without formulating general propositions. The culture did not even have proverbs, which are characteristic of most historical cultures and often used as a basis of argument. All this seems consistent with what was proposed about prehistoric speech in the last chapter.

There are some other features of the story with rhetorical interest. The two mythical brothers kill a euro, but they are themselves original members of the euro totem. They are in fact "euros." Every aboriginal identified with his totem, which was both his mythical ancestor and himself. Ordinarily, one should not kill one's totem, except in dire necessity or by mistake, but this does not apply to heroic figures in mythology. Indeed, one attraction of divine or legendary figures to audiences in many cultures is their ability to break taboos. Something of this survives in modern fiction where the reader can vicariously enter into actions that he or she would fear to do. The rhetorical significance here is that the totem is a synecdoche and not a metaphor: "euro" is a category containing animal, mythical, and human instances. The aboriginal knew perfectly well that there are things a euro can do and that he cannot, and that he can do and the euro cannot. But differentiation of sign and referent has not yet occurred. The individual is both fully and literally a euro and in some hazy way not quite a euro. Compare what Phiney (1934:iv) has said about the Nez Percé Indians in North America: "The Indian does not visualize the characters of a tale as being animal or human. No clear picture is offered or needed. If such tangible features were introduced a tale would lose its overtones of fantasy, its charm." It is this haziness, the possibility that some resemblances overlap and others do not, that creates the potential for metaphor when categories are more systematically perceived.

Something similar is true of the tjurunga that appears in the story. Physically, a tjurunga is a flat stone with some painted markings on it. These were the most

sacred objects in Australian religion and almost the only articles of private property. A tjurunga is identical with the totem but all tjurungas are more or less
alike. Their neutral appearance makes them capable of taking on any meaning.
They are the ultimate synecdoche.

The story has a beginning, a middle, and an end (the successful killing of the
euro). Human communication through story telling acquired the need to satisfy
with some kind of closure, and thus to have rhetorical structure. Archaic Australian songs also regularly show a rhetorical structure of beginning, middle, and
end. They generally consist of three parts: an introduction, which evokes the
mythical ancestors, then descriptions of a series of actions, which are represented
both in words and in dance, and a conclusion, which describes the falling asleep
of the mythical figures. The simplest and most basic story closures, still in common use everywhere, seem to be sleep and death.

The story of the two brothers and the euro has a supplement, not a generalized moral about hunting or the wisdom of older brothers, but a concrete explanation of the origin of the sense of smell. This supplement converts the story
into an aetiological myth, a common feature of story telling all over the world.
It also converts the story from an example of deliberative rhetoric to epideictic.
Although one might guess that the story was invented to explain the origin of
smell, its seems more likely that the story originally existed by itself. The supplement seems to adapt the story to a secondary purpose as part of a pattern of
explanations of causes in myths. This is a simple rhetorical device of giving new
meaning and added significance to the story for the audience.

Traditional stories in all cultures can be revised to fit existing conditions. For
example, when the origin myth of the Gonja people in Ghana was first recorded
in the early twentieth century it told of the seven sons of the mythical founder;
from these were descended the seven parts of the kingdom. When the myth was
transcribed again sixty years later only five divisions existed and the myth had
reduced the seven sons to five (Finnegan 1988:20). Specific incidents of note
such as disasters or unusual human achievements can be, as it were, poured into
traditional form and take on a legendary tone. There is, however, always also a
process of erosion as well as renewal of myth and tradition, resulting partly from
forgetfulness and lack of skill by some transmitters, partly from a desire to please
an audience. Variants naturally occur among different segments of the same population, and some of these variants may be adopted by others in place of their
own versions, though it is a common feature of oral literature that the singer or
bard insists that his version is the true one.

The most important means of persuasion in aboriginal texts is the authority of
the speaker. In the previous chapter I sought to distinguish authority as a nonartistic means of persuasion from ethos, the artistic creation of veracity, credibility, and
sympathy. Ethos substitutes for authority when the speaker lacks prestige. I have
not found examples of ethos in aboriginal texts, though there is some potential for
it in secular songs in which the singer lacks authority. Aboriginal society, and all
other premodern societies, were extremely hierarchical. The mechanism that pre-

serves and implements hierarchical structure consists of, first, religion and myth, and second, the kinship system with its generational gradations. Highest in authority among the aboriginals were their totemic ancestors who created the world and whose deeds, institutions, and instructions were preserved in myth. But these myths required regular presentation to retain their power, and that lay with the authority of older men who knew the religion and explained and taught it. No questions were permitted to them in their expositions of myth. They also had authority in the practical and secular world. The ancestors ranked above the older men, the older men above the younger men, men in general above women, and adult women above children. Wisdom based on age, experience, and knowledge of religion was a powerful influence in aboriginal society.

The traditional cultures of the world are exceedingly conservative; they resist change. Fear of change is an important source of rhetorical energy. Just as the basic impulse for rhetoric in the individual derives from the instinct for self-preservation, so the most common function of rhetoric in traditional societies is preservation of their accustomed beliefs and way of life. Among the ways this is done is by attributing the institution of customs to divine or semidivine authority figures, by stressing the antiquity, continuity, and consistency of the customs, and by seeking to authenticate them by the use of archaic language. Social control is secured by those in the contemporary society who have been initiated into the language and the mysteries of the tradition and can both present it in its allegedly authentic form and interpret it to the public. Opportunity for manipulation for personal gain exists, but probably only becomes a factor when special situations or crises arise. Deliberation of a sort always occurs on the problems of the group, but even in a traditional society with a more developed polity than that of the Australians, decisions are usually taken by consensus. As Malinowski (1922:62) wrote of the Trobrianders, "there is hardly ever much room for doubt or deliberation, as natives communally, as well as individually, never act except on traditional and conventional lines."

Australian oral literature includes both prose myths, like that quoted above, and songs. The prose myths give coherent narrative accounts in language comprehensible to all of legends about totemic ancestors: their birth, their wanderings, the ceremonies they instituted, and their final falling asleep. These stories may be recounted by almost any adult, man or woman, though some individuals acquire a reputation as good story tellers. Some of the stories are told specifically for children. Although the contents are traditional, the actual tellings differ somewhat in language, length, and the elaboration of incidents.

Sacred Songs

Aboriginal songs can be roughly divided into those that are part of religious rites, such as initiations, and those that are more secular in nature, though the latter borrow elements from the former. The religious songs are especially interesting rhetorically since they are in very archaic language and they are regarded as having been composed by the mythical ancestors, not by human authors. Since they are often part of large cycles and tell of great events in the past, they have some similarities to oral epic in other cultures, but they differ from oral epic as usually understood in that they are not "recompositions in performance" based on formulae and themes; they have been memorized and transmitted, allegedly word for word, from generation to generation, memorization being facilitated by meter and sound patterns. The sacred songs do, of course, differ somewhat from performance to performance: The singers do not always remember all the verses and they do not always arrange them in quite the same sequence. There were no professional bards, but some individuals acquired a reputation as "songmen." In the most solemn and sacred initiation ceremonies the songs were performed by older men who had acquired authority for their religious wisdom.

Strehlow extensively studied aboriginal sacred songs and gave a valuable discussion of their poetics, including versification, vocabulary, grammar, structure, and rhetorical devices, with some comparisons to Greek, Anglo-Saxon, and Hebrew poetry (Strehlow 1971:109–236). The songs are part of ritual performances that integrate music, words, and dance. Dance, with pantomime movements and gestures, is important in helping convey something of the narrative to an audience that does not understand the words. The verses consist of couplets in which the second line either repeats the first, sometimes in the same words, sometimes in slightly different words, or introduces a new thought that completes or complements the first line. This "parallelism" is a common feature of oral poetry; the best known examples are the Hebrew Psalms but the technique occurs all over the world (see, e.g., Fox 1974) and will be discussed further in later chapters. Most verses in aboriginal songs consist of only two words, subject and predicate. Two-word sentences, without subordination, are a feature of the language of human infants at around the age of two and are within the capabilities of apes using sign language (Bickerton 1990:110–15); thus, the language of the songs may preserve a very early stage of human linguistic evolution. Another primitive feature is the highly concrete nature of the language, which is dependent on the visualization of perceptible objects or actions; terms for complex mental states are lacking, though such attitudes can be implied by a sequence of actions or by rhetorical questions such as "What is to be done?" As in animal communication, there is a great amount of repetition, and the repetitive effect is increased by the fact that the Australian languages are highly reduplicative in word formation. But there is also variation in the substitution of synonyms and epithets. Anaphora and rhyme tie couplets together. Here is part of a song describing the mythical ancestor in a ritual as transcribed and translated by Strehlow (1971:195):

> /:Nómabaué / rérlanopaí:/
> /:Nómajatín/ tjélanopaí:/

/:Nómabaué / rérlanopai:/
/:Nómaalbé / tínjopaí:/ etc.

I am red like a burning fire;
I am covered with glowing red down.

I am red like a burning fire,
I am gleaming red, glistening with ochre.

I am red like a burning fire;
Red is the hollow in which I am lying.

I am red like the heart of a fire;
Red is the hollow in which I am lying.

A tjurunga is standing on my head;
Red is the hollow in which I am lying.

From this passage one might conclude that simile is a regular feature of aboriginal song. In fact, the similes were introduced by the translator for the English reader. Strehlow (1971:171) notes that "similes in our sense of the term are not found in these aboriginal songs." As in the case of the juxtaposition of propositions that may be read as enthymemes, the original text juxtaposes but does not articulate the nature of the relationship between words. Thus the first line above might more literally be translated "I burn, a red fire." Although red is a favorite color among the aboriginals, there is apparently no general term "red"; its various shades are signified by nouns like "red fire, red clay" (Dixon 1980:274). This is certainly not yet simile, nor is it metaphor, since the meaning is that my redness is literally the redness of red fire. However, by substitution in the second line more than one visual quality can be predicated of an object. For example, of a totem pole (Strehlow 1971:111):

A whirlwind, it is towering upwards;
A pillar of sand, it is towering upwards.

In such combinations one begins to feel that some degree of differentiation between the literal and figurative is implicit. At one moment the pole not only seems but is a whirlwind, at another a pillar of sand, but since it is both it is not quite either. Another form of troping results from the ability of the language to form compound nouns and adjectives, which then are used as epithets to substitute for a proper word: a kangaroo can be referred to as "the-one-with-upright-ears" or "the-one-with-striped-forehead." The songs show the potentiality to develop stock epithets like those found in the Homeric poems and other oral epic but do not actually use them.

For comparison with the descriptive passage given above, here is a narrative passage from a song (Strehlow 1971:164 with minor revision):

> On the following morning he resumes his journey;
> He keeps travelling east of the river, he takes no rest.
> In the morning he rises and goes uphill;
> He proceeds to climb over low ridges.
> He descends on the other side;
> And then ascends a range.
> From here he catches sight of something: the yam men are singing at
>   their ceremonies at Iwopataka;
> They are singing and singing, while he is looking down at them
>   from this hill.

The action is carried forward in a series of jerks. In the original, sentences are tied together by the repetition of words rather than by connecting particles, or words are replaced by synonyms or paraphrases. Each line consists of only two or three words, and the translation thus considerably expands each verse.

The aboriginals had descriptive names for different kinds of songs or parts of songs, and the term *manigaicmir* refers to any creature "mentioned in song," but they do not seem to have developed any poetic or rhetorical terminology to describe the process of song, nor so far as I can discover is song a subject for song, as it is sometimes in Homeric and other epic. This is apparently a later, more reflective stage in the development of discourse. Also, in contrast with stories as instanced earlier and secular songs to be mentioned below, sacred songs make little or no use of direct speech; they are primarily descriptive of settings, characters, and actions. They are thus not easily objects of analysis by theories of narrative voice developed for written literature by Bakhtin and others and recently applied to ethnographic material (Lucy 1993). This may again be an archaic feature, the use of dialogue in Australian prose narrative and in other cultures being a subsequent development.

Since the archaic language of the sacred songs cannot be immediately understood by those not instructed in them, in initiation ceremonies the songs are interpreted by an elder who paraphrases them in contemporary language (Strehlow 1974:4). There are several distinct genres of sacred song, including charms, songs sung at totemic increase ceremonies, songs commemorating the deeds of totemic ancestors, initiation songs, women's songs, and others. The origins of literary genres are in social function, not in formal qualities (meter, language, structure). Where formal qualities differ in early literary forms (e.g., use of archaic language), this is usually a direct result of social function (e.g., the archaic language provides a guarantee of authenticity of sacred song). Even early Greek literary genres are primarily distinguished by social function. Over time, the formal qualities come to dominate the definition of genre. "Diglossia" (or "polyglossia"), the existence of two (or more) registers of language within a culture, is common, and the use of archaic language or of an earlier language (e.g., Latin) in religious cerremony has persisted until modern times in many cultures.

Aboriginal sacred verse is never the ostensible vehicle for a poet's own sentiments: According to native belief sacred songs had no human authors. Although highly functional in defining the world of the aboriginals, in explaining the origin of nature, customs, and ritual institutions, they are often filled with a love of beauty, including much vivid description, and afforded an outlet for the emotions. Their rhetorical functions include producing the emotions in the audience needed for acceptance of the tradition and ritual actions. An extreme case is that of the songs accompanying the ritual circumcision of boys. As practiced by the aboriginals, circumcision was a particularly bloody, cruel, and painful rite. Both boys and girls were schooled in bearing pain from an early age, and in circumcision shortly after puberty boys' ability to tolerate fear and pain was deliberately taxed to the upmost. It is this experience that was thought to make them men. Circumcision and other rites, including subincision and scarification, are processes in which a society permanently marks those it admits to full membership in the group. Among the Aranda, the rite was regarded as having been introduced by culture heroes identified with hawks who delighted in anger and brutality. The myth communicates fury toward all boys who are not circumcised and describes the joy derived by the circumcisers from their action. The Aranda men who sang the song in historical times seem to have used it to nerve themselves to the point where they could carry out the operation on their own youths in the traditional brutal way as well as heightening the fear of the boys. It is thus an unusually grim species of rhetoric. The beginning of the song describes the arrival of the hawk-men, who stand on the ceremonial ground awaiting the victims. It continues with the following passage in which "ringneck parrot's tail" is an epithet for a long, thin stone knife:

> Our stone knives are painted with many stripes;
> Our stone knives are decorated with fresh bands.
>
> Ringneck parrot's tail! Sever it!
> The skin-covered penis! Sever it!
>
> The flayed stump! Let it gleam white!
> The flayed stump! Let it be stripped of its skin!
>
> At the very neck! Cut it through!
> In furious anger! Cut it through!
>
> Up in the sky! Sever it completely! [the boy is lifted up]
> Filled with angry glee! Cut it through!

Up in the sky! Sever it completely!
At the very neck! Cut it through!

The ringneck parrot's tail seves it;
It severs the skin-covered penis.

The flayed stump is stripped of its skin;
The flayed stump is gleaming white.

The hands are dripping with blood; they are dripping with blood.
His knife slashes and slices.

The stone knife has slipped on the ground
He looks down with unflinching eyes.

(STREHLOW 1971:401–2)

Secular Songs

Secular songs, though often including religious elements as in western poetry, are individual compositions within certain established traditions. In aboriginal communities, the evenings have often been times for singing and dancing. At funerals and yam festivals individuals were expected to come forward to sing. The Berndts (1988:377–78) quote a moving song by a woman grieving for her dead husband. It takes the form of a dialogue of voices:

"Why do you come here every day to my grave?" [asks the dead husband]
"Because your posts are painted and ready. [she replies]
Come on, get up from that grave!
I saw you there dancing just now,
Shaking yourself in the dance."
"Why not come to me here?" [he asks]
"I'm not old, I'm too young!" [she responds]
"Well [he says], I'm here, I am waiting for you...
I'm glad my wife's coming near me.
You'll be thirsty, I can't give you water,
I'm taking you to a dry and waterless country."

The woman expresses her sense of loss and anger at her husband for dying, but she reminds herself that she is unwilling to join him in the grave. Both she and the dead husband give logical reasons for their actions and statements. The song makes no use of metaphor. Another popular type are "gossip songs," which deal with contemporary events, often erotic relationships. Names are not mentioned and part of the pleasure for the audience is recognizing the referents. One convention is for the singer to claim the information came in a dream. This is true also of more formal singing and dancing:

> A man, occasionally a woman, claims to have had a set of songs and dance-steps shown to him in a dream; and as "boss" of that series he can expect to receive compensation for passing on this revelation to others. It may be a re-arrangement of an existing song-and-dance combination, or it may introduce new features based on his own observation or experience—new tunes or rhythms, or body decorations, or objects, or new content. Native doctors or "clever" men, or women with a background of participation in love-magic rituals, are especially likely to report dreams of this kind. (Berndt and Berndt 1988:384)

The primary function of such songs, dance, and story-telling is pleasure, but they can be used for a variety of rhetorical purposes: admonition, instruction, moralizing, or imparting information. In song, dance, and story-telling the speaker can teach a lesson and can also satirize and ridicule taboos or human relationships: portraying characters doing things not ordinarily permitted. This is a useful safety valve for inhibited feelings and, like carnival in Western society, apparently produces a catharsis. Since the aboriginals had no administrative structures or anything like police, ridicule and ostracism were important means of social control.

Magic as Rhetoric

Another form of social control was sorcery when used against deviant individuals. The aboriginals practiced a variety of forms of magic, some in public in the interests of the group, some in private in the interests of individuals. Only certain persons, specially inspired and initiated and with a knowledge of the necessary actions and words, could perform magical rites. The distinction between a medicine man, who could perform healing, and a sorcerer, who could inflict harm and suffering, is made in some aboriginal languages but the two often overlap. Sorcery in particular served as social control in that knowledge of the spell often reached victims, on whom it could have a powerful psychological effect because of their own belief in magic (Elkin 1945; Berndt and Berndt 1988:304–35). Magical incantations are clearly a form of rhetoric in that words are being used in an attempt to control or influence natural forces, persons, or objects, and magical rites are often forms of public address (Covino 1994:16–24). I shall return to magic as a rhetorical phenomenon in later chapters.

Aboriginal Judicial Process

Speeches of accusation and defense do not seem to have existed among the aboriginals. Some methods of adjudication, however, did exist (Berndt and Berndt

1988:334–66). Serious violations of sacred law were judged by ritual leaders who decided on the appropriate punishment, which could even be death. Violations against persons could lead to revenge by the injured party's relatives. If the identity of a murderer was uncertain, a kind of inquest was sometimes held by the native doctor who, through divination or other means, sought to find the guilty party. Although witnesses might be interrogated, evidence often took the form of "signs" by which the corpse was thought to point to the murderer. For example, a corpse might be carried on a bier while those surrounding it called out the names of possible aggressors; if those carrying the bier felt movement of the corpse toward one of those who called out, the person named was judged the murderer. Similar procedures were used to identify sorcerers.

Dreaming

"The Dreamtime" has come into common use in English as the term for the mythical world of the aboriginals. Actually, only some of the Australian languages use a word that specifically denotes dreaming. Although ultimately derived from a common source and sharing some grammatical features, the languages differ greatly among themselves in vocabulary. The many different aboriginal groups, however, did share a common belief in a creative period in the distant past. According to this belief, the beings then active, as described in myth, and all that is associated with them continue to exist today and will for the indefinite future, although they may be asleep (Berndt and Berndt 1988:229). Access to this spiritual and sacred world is primarily through transmission of myth and song, but individuals sometimes also have access to it through dreams. All mythologies offer a dream-like world into which individuals can escape from their ordinary lives and problems whether sleeping or awake. Many cultures have a belief that in dreams the spirit departs from the body, sees things otherwise unknown to humans, performs actions, and returns with some new knowledge. Modern psychology reformulates this into a belief that dreams can offer direct access to the unconscious mind, or in the theory of Carl Jung, to archetypes of human experience. The interpretation of dreams has played an important role in many cultures, including those of the Near East and Greece, as offering direct communication from gods to men, but the possible role of dreaming in the beginnings of language and cultural institutions has not been much stressed in the scholarship I have read. A special characteristic of dreams is the way the dreamer's unconscious mind combines images in novel ways. It seems reasonable to suppose that primitive dreaming involved animals and natural objects to a greater extent than do our dreams in the developed nations today, since these bulked large in collective experience. Totemism may thus owe its origin in part to dreaming, or at least to have seemed supported by experiential evidence in dreaming. It may be the case that dreams of individuals in traditional societies, where there is limited variety of experience and great consensus of values and beliefs, are more expressive of the culture, less of unique personality, than is the case in our modern society.

It seems also possible that dreaming contributed something to the development of language when some sounds in a dream had been coupled with some visual experience and were remembered. Certainly, dreaming has contributed to poetry and to troping, since it is the essence of dreams to substitute like for like in a metaphorical way or to link one image to something in a kind of metonymy. Dreaming is thus a possible factor in the development of rhetorical language; it is not likely a source for rational and persuasive features of discourse, which result from experience in the real world. Dreams are not rational and lack artistic design, though some structure may be easily imposed on a remembered dream; however, the contents of dreams in the Near East and early Greece, as reported, for example, by Herodotus, provided materials from which a speaker could construct an argument. When a dreamer in a traditional society reports a dream for rhetorical purposes, in most cases we should assume sincerity: This is what the dreamer remembers; whatever structuring and interpretation has taken place is largely if not entirely unconscious. Even in sophisticated, literate societies reports of dreams may be sincere. Saint Jerome may well have dreamed his famous dream of being judged as a Ciceronian rather than a Christian. Because of the private nature of a dream it is never possible to refute it. This opens the possibility, of course, of deliberately inventing a dream as a rhetorical device apt to be persuasive to an audience that believes dreams provide access to truth or to the will of the gods. I suspect that this has often been done, primarily in societies where the conceptualization of ideas or sophistry is developing, but I can offer no certain example. In modern political discourse in the West dreaming is chiefly referred to as a personal, rational vision of the future and does not imply an origin in sleep. It is thus a figure of speech, as for example, Martin Luther King's "I have a dream...."

The history of the Australian aboriginals since European settlement on the continent is a sorry one of exploitation and degredation. In a number of ways it resembles the experience of American Indians, including the effects of diseases against which the natives had no immunity and of alcoholism, though Australia was spared a counterpart of the Indian wars of North America. In both countries the native cultures have come to attract curious tourists, and in both cultures the natives have begun to work through the political system to demand rights, achieve greater self-determination, and preserve some vestiges of their traditional culture. Rhetoric, of course, plays a role in these developments, combining some native traditions in their discourse among themselves with features of western discourse in their address to the majority population. This subject is beyond the scope of my book; an interesting discussion of it as practiced in Australia can be found in a monograph by Erich Kolig, *Dreamtime Politics* (1989).

Conclusion

Many of the concepts of western rhetorical theory have little application to oral discourse among the aboriginal inhabitants of Australia, primarily because their societies lacked contexts in which civic rhetoric flourishes: formal councils, assemblies, courts of law, public ceremonies at which original speeches are delivered, or schools. Although individuals and small groups certainly engaged in deliberation about what to do, giving reasons for their views, and some description of this is preserved in transcriptions of their oral literature, no "orators" are in evidence, as they are in tribal cultures to be discussed in the next chapter. Our evidence for traditional aboriginal rhetoric comes from an extensive body of prose myths and religious and secular song, which can be classified as epideictic in that its primary function was the transmission and reaffirmation of the beliefs and values of the community. Although this oral literature does not celebrate eloquence, its aesthetic qualities were clearly appreciated.

Religious song utilized a formal, highly archaic style, and was understood only by initiates. Both sacred song and prose myths were thought to have no human author; secular songs, however, were often the creations of individuals and were sometimes attributed to dreams. Pathos was a feature of some songs, such as that used in the circumcision ritual. Both myths and songs exhibit a basic arrangement of beginning, middle, and end.

The primary means of persuasion among the aboriginals was the authority of the speaker. Highest in authority were the totemic ancestors, next the older men. Wisdom, based on age, experience, and knowledge of religion was a powerful influence, but this wisdom was not expressed in general terms; it was implied by specific instances. Logical argument also took the form of the juxtaposition of a conclusion with a statement giving the cause or reason, without inferential particles.

At the linguistic level, archaic aboriginal rhetoric seems to illustrate a stage of what might be called "proto-metaphor." By juxtaposing words, a series of overlapping images, perceptions, or emotions can be projected without differentiating their fields of reference. The absence of explicit simile is evidence of the lack of such differentiation. Most modern theories of metaphor seem to me too intellectual and cognitive to describe this process. Its source lies largely if not entirely in animistic personification: the literal belief in the identification of species of animals with human beings and the animate reality of natural objects, including mountains, lakes, and rocks. All of these merge in kaleidoscopic visualization in the ancient "Dreamtime," to which traditional Australians have continued to have access in their own dreaming. These images supply potential sources for a feeling for metaphor or other tropes and these have been somewhat developed in realistic versions of stories and in the Australian languages as spoken in modern times. Catachresis, synecdoche, and metonymy played leading roles in the early development of language. That is to say, when need occurred for a specific term for something, the initial impulse was not to invent a new term, but to find something in the existing vocabulary to "abuse"—the literal meaning of catachresis—in its place. The chief options then became either the use of genus for species or species for genus (synecdoche), if either existed in the language, or the use of some term that is physically contiguous and might be taken as characteristic of the idea needing expression (metonymy). We have seen that synecdoche can be found already in some animal communication and it may be the most primitive trope. Among the most easily adaptable tropes are those from domestic relationships and activities and from parts of the body. Australian examples of the latter include "shoulder" for "waterfall," "upper arm" for "creek," and "rump" for "butt of a tree" (Dixon 1980:109–11). Many such usages remain in modern languages: the "father" of his country; the "foot" of a mountain (facilitated by personification of nature).

References

Berndt, Ronald M., and Catherine H. Berndt (1988). *The World of the First Australians*, 5th edition. Canberra: Aboriginal Studies Press.

Bickerton, Derek (1990). *Language and Species*. Chicago: University of Chicago Press.

Covino, William A. (1994). *Magic, Rhetoric, and Literacy: An Eccentric History of the Composing Imagination*. Albany: State University of New York Press.

Dixon, Robert M. W. (1980). *The Languages of Australia*. Cambridge: Cambridge University Press.

Elkin, Adolphus P. (1945). *Aboriginal Men of High Degree*. Sydney: Australian Publishing Co.

Fox, James J. (1974). " 'Our Ancestors Spoke in Pairs': Rotinese Views of Language, Dialect, and Code," in *Explorations in the Ethnography of Speaking*, ed. by Richard Bauman and Joel Sherzer, pp. 65–85. Cambridge: Cambridge University Press.

Kendon, Adam (1988). *Sign Languages of Aboriginal Australia: Cultural, Semiotic, and Communicative Perspectives*. Cambridge: Cambridge University Press.

Kolig, Erich (1989). *Dreamtime Politics: Religion, World View, and Utopian Thought in Australian Aboriginal Society*. Berlin: Dietrich Reimer Verlag.

Lucy, John A., ed. (1993). *Reflexive Language: Reported Speech and Metapragmatics*. Cambridge: Cambridge University Press.

Malinowski, Bronislaw (1922). *Argonauts of the Western Pacific*. London: Routledge and Kegan Paul; reprinted, New York: E. P. Dutton, 1961.

Phiney, Archie, ed. (1934). *Nez Percé Texts*. Columbia University Contributions in Anthropology 25; reprinted, New York: American Museum of Natural History, 1969.

Spencer, Baldwin, and Francis J. Gillen (1899). *The Native Tribes of Central Australia*. London: Macmillan.

Strehlow, T. G. H. (1947). *Aranda Traditions*. Melbourne: Melbourne University Press.

———(1971). *Songs of Central Australia*. Sydney: Angus and Robertson.

CHAPTER 4

Formal Speech in Some Nonliterate Cultures

Anthropology, as a scientific subject, developed in the late nineteenth and early twentieth centuries at a time when the ancient discipline of rhetoric was in decline. Although ethnographers—that is, anthropologists who write descriptions of native cultures—analyzed the political structure of the people studied, they rarely utilized rhetorical concepts or terminology. Among the few exceptions was Bronislaw Malinowski, who studied the Trobriand Islanders between 1914 and 1920; his classic work, *Argonauts of the Western Pacific* (1922), is primarily concerned with the unusual gift-exchange system of the islanders, but it also discusses oral communication, forms of persuasion, the rhetorical structure of myths, and the rhetoric of magic. Gift-exchange systems are in themselves a kind of rhetoric in which the givers make symbolic statements about their status and imply what is owed to them, to which the receiver is expected to reply by an even more valuable gift but may counter in various ways (Gewertz 1984). In the 1970s, a time when a rhetorical approach was gaining ground in the humanities, some ethnographers began to take an interest in oratory and rhetoric in native cultures. J. J. Gumperz and Dell Hymes were among the first (1972), followed by Richard Bauman and Joel Sherzer (1974), and Maurice Bloch (1975). Since then, a growing number of books, volumes of collected studies, and articles have addressed aspects of the subject. Some forms and functions of speech common to disparate or widely separated societies in Africa, the Americas, Southeast Asia, and the islands of the Indian and Pacific oceans have emerged.

Orators in Traditional Societies

Some traditionally oral societies are much more given to talk and argument than others, but in most cultures with a political organization beyond what is found in Australia there are individuals who are respected for their ability at public speaking, and the languages of these cultures generally have a native word to designate an orator or membership in the group of respected speakers. This may be an official appointment, as among the Borana Galla in Kenya, or an informal recognition by others in the society, as among the Mursi in Ethiopia (Turton 1975:174). Most native orators are men, and sometimes women are not permitted to be present at important meetings, but the role of women varies greatly from society to society; in some places it is not uncommon for women to speak in informal meetings, and in Samoa there are even women recognized as orators (Duranti 1984:226–27). Oratorical skills derive in part from natural ability, but as Greek and Roman rhetoricians stressed, also require learning rhetorical conventions by observing older speakers, imitating them, and finding opportunities for practice. The opportunities for an individual to achieve recognition as an orator certainly differ with the political structure of the society. In one with a strong chiefdom, opportunity may be limited and controlled by the chiefs, who may, however, avoid exposing their position by using hired orators to speak for them: "To speak persuasively to inferiors would imply that such individuals have or could have judgment, endangering the very basis of the dominance of nobles or chiefs" (Brenneis and Myers 1984:26). Orators sometimes also are the unacknowledged spokesmen for priests, who do not themselves enter into debates but wish to influence decisions.

Opportunities for speech by individuals are greater in those many native societies throughout the world described by ethnographers as "acephalous," that is those that have no official "head" and are nominally egalitarian. Age, comparative wealth, kinship ties, or shrewdness may give an individual higher social rank and greater private influence than others, but these are not necessarily the persons who play leading roles in public meetings. Much the same is true in Western society, where captains of industry only rarely seek public office, though they provide financial support for others who will speak in their interests. In this situation, artistic ethos comes to replace external authority.

In native egalitarian societies, where personal autonomy is valued, speakers generally avoid direct attack on other individuals, politeness prevails on the surface, and criticism tends to take the form of indirect and allusive speech with ambiguous references (Brenneis and Myers 1984:2). The West has inherited from the Greeks an acceptance of confrontation and personal invective (and, I might add, a tolerance of flattery) that has been rare in the rest of the world. I shall return to this in chapter 9. In all societies children have been indoctrinated in conventional politeness, in what they can say, when, to whom—especially to their elders—and how. In the modern West this has been modified as the child grows up and discovers social and political rights to challenge authority, and it has been eroded in urban conditions where the youth are alienated from authority beginning at an early age. Neither of these things has historically characterized societies in other parts of the world, but both have begun to emerge as contacts with outsiders increase.

Formal and Informal Deliberation

In most societies a distinction is drawn between formal and informal meetings for public discussion of important issues. In Polynesia, for example, the noun *fono* is widely used to mean a formal assembly of the people to receive a communication or to hold a discussion, and as a verb it means to address such a meeting (Firth 1975:29). Formal meetings often are accompanied by religious rituals, attract large attendance, and require the use of a special etiquette, designated seats by social rank, traditional rhetorical topics, and a special style of language and delivery. Informal meetings, on the other hand, are usually conducted in everyday language, and speakers are more often interrupted than in formal meetings. Aristotle (*Rhetoric* 1.4.7) identified the important subjects of deliberation in political life as he knew it as finances, war and peace, national defense, imports and exports, and the framing of laws. Traditional societies deliberate about these topics except for the last; proposals for constitutional change or new legislation are not to be expected in conservative traditional societies. A topic that should, however, be added is debate over whether or not some ritual should be performed. A western analogy is debate over the date of Easter, which vexed the Christian Church in the early Middle Ages.

The primary and explicit function of both formal and informal meetings in traditional societies is to achieve group consensus on some important issue. Even when a meeting is called and dominated by a chief who has already made a decision, the goal is public consensus that the chief's policy is the right one. A second, and tacit, function of speaking at public meetings is the converse of the primary function: The ethos of the speakers is usually the most important single factor in their success, but their success as speakers in turn is a significant element in establishing their ethos. Both in chiefdoms and in egalitarian societies, public speaking serves to establish and renew social ranking within the society and to reinforce traditional values.

Although formal oratory in most traditional societies avoids confrontation and emotionalism, there are exceptions. The Tiv people of northern Nigeria, the Eskimos, and some others are competitive and individualistic (Finnegan 1988:41). The Yanomami, who live in stone age conditions in southern Venezuela and northern Brazil, have often been regarded as especially aggressive and violent, but a recent study (Ferguson 1995) argues that this is a modern development resulting from competition for Western goods. Outside pressures or catastrophic changes in the environment often create internal dissension among traditionally peaceful people, though in some cases these occurred far back in time and are impossible to identify. The tribes that make up the Mauri of New Zealand, for some reason, were among the most aggressive and violent of native societies even before the arrival of Westerners. In intervals of peace, however, warfare was replaced by oratorical contests in which each speaker sought *mana*, or prestige, by his creativity, erudition, ability to introduce topical references, and dramatic or emotional power, and this tradition is still alive in rural areas (Salmond 1975). Speeches of greeting when representatives of different Mauri groups come together are the most formal and traditional. The speaker begins by claiming the right to the floor, and follows this with an initiatory chant, greetings to the dead, greetings to the living, and discussion of some issue of current interest, then closing with an ancient song in which the old women present stand and join. These speeches can be fiery, bitter, and cynical, but even so the best speeches are regarded as those that present the cultural unity of the people by the use of traditional proverbs, genealogy, myth, and history, and in more informal debates directly concerned with issues of the day a kind of consensus is achieved. No non-Western society, to the best of my knowledge, has traditionally used a system of votes and majority decision. This seems to have been a unique development of the Greeks in the classical period, used in both deliberative and judicial settings. It was copied by the Romans and from them became an inheritance of western national states. I shall return to this subject in chapter 9. Voting on Western models has been introduced into some traditional societies, but is often resented. Weiner (1984:178) describes the situation among the Trobrianders, where a call for a vote is regarded as leading to a fight, for voting establishes winners and losers, and losers must fight to preserve self-respect.

Maurice Bloch's study of village councils among the Merina of Madagascar furnishes a good example of the use of formal speech in a traditional culture (Bloch 1975:6–9). Although local councils have lost many of their functions to the central Malagasy government, they continue the forms of royal councils of the past and resolve local issues. Meetings are convened and organized according to fixed principles, participants sit in traditionally assigned positions, and the speakers, who are the village elders, observe exacting rules of rhetoric. According to Bloch, a Merina speech has four parts. A speaker begins quietly and hesitatingly with set phrases, standard examples, and proverbs expressive of humility as an apology for speaking at all. Ethos thus replaces authority. The second part of the speech thanks those in power for allowing him to speak, beginning with God and descending down through offices of state to the mayor and village elders, with a proverb attached to each in turn. The second part of a Merina speech ends with a statement of the value of unity. By now the orator is speaking somewhat more loudly and confidently, though at no point is personal emotion allowed to enter into the speech. The third part of the speech still abounds in proverbs and includes illustrations based on legend or incidents familiar to the audience and short poems, but it also contains the speaker's proposal to deal with the issue at hand. The final part returns to the quiet tone of the opening, consists almost entirely of thanks to everybody for listening, and ends with a blessing on all. Somewhat similar rhetoric can be found in other parts of the world, for example, in village meetings on the island of Bali in Indonesia (Hobart 1974).

Logical argument is often only a minor factor in the persuasive effect of a traditional formal speech. The evidence the speaker provides to support his position is its consistency with the traditional wisdom of the society, transmitted through proverbs and mythical or historical examples from the past. Although a Merina or Balinese speaker seemingly undermines his personal authority by his ethos of humility, he also implies authority by his ability to use the appropriate code. Such a speech is difficult to answer in any polite and acceptable terms: It has social power. Often, a speech is followed by silence, which effectively means agreement. In its most extreme form, by avoiding use of rational argument formal speech can forestall any potential logical objections, allegations of inconsistency on the part of the speaker, or attempts at rebuttal (Bloch 1975:21). There is nothing to rebut. Sometimes, however, another elder will speak in the same style with a somewhat different proposal, but aiming at compromise and consensus, which is likely to be accepted. On rare occasions someone will not allow the silence of consent to follow a speech and will even ridicule it. Bloch notes (1975:10) that the Merina take great pains to avoid being addressed in formal language, which is used on other occasions as well as in councils, if they are not willing to accept the results.

Formal Language

The use of "formal language" is a common feature of formal meetings in traditional societies. An example is the archaic language of Australian ritual and sacred song discussed in the previous chapter. Judith Irvine (1979) has identified four aspects of "formality" that apply cross-culturally.

First, in contrast to informal speech—story telling, conversation, gossiping, and the like—formal speech increases code structuring by imposing special rules of style and delivery on the speaker: A special dialect or an archaic or poetic form of the spoken dialect is often required. Individuals are referred to by title or complementary terms of rank rather than by personal name. There may be special conventions of pronunciation, including volume and speed of delivery. There may also be special conventions of turn-taking among speakers. The linguistic requirements can be very difficult to master, although a local audience may be satisfied with a bona fide effort to speak in the right way, even if less than perfect.

Second, the conventions of the appropriate code are consistently maintained. Code switching, such as lapsing into colloquial language, although it may secure identification with the audience, creates a distancing of the speaker (and sometimes the audience) from the subject, introduces irony, or otherwise undermines the seriousness of the occasion.

Third, formal speech involves a positional rather than a personal identity. The speaker speaks in a certain political or social role, performing a public function rather than advancing personal interest.

Fourth, a central situational focus emerges in formal speech: That is, it deals with important activities and the central actors within them, leaving aside trivial matters.

Irvine describes formal speech as found in the different settings of the Wolof of Senegal, the Marsi of Ethiopia, and the Ilongots of the Philippines. All three cultures distinguish between political meetings in which formal language is required and those in which it is not. Among the Wolof, political authority is centralized in the chiefs; there is a complex caste system and much emphasis on differences in rank. Any significant debate between the chief and his advisers takes place outside the public view, and the function of formal meetings is to announce decisions made by those in authority and to answer questions. The leaders, however, need to instill confidence that their decisions are the right ones, to demonstrate their wisdom and understanding of problems, and to answer questions with assurance. An effective presentation is a renewal of their political and moral authority. When persons of lower rank speak, their remarks are often loud, high-pitched, and repetitious, with key individual words or phrases given strong emphasis, while those of high rank speak softly, in lower pitch, with less repetition and emphasis. Examples of this could be cited from modern society in the West, for example, in altercations between management and labor. Shrillness is a way of seeking attention and expressing outrage, but also an expression of insecurity. It should be remembered that in animal communication loud, shrill calls can reflect fear or insecurity.

The Marsi live—if they have survived the recent droughts and turmoil in Ethiopia—in an egalitarian political system without official leaders and with no significant differences of rank except for age—retired elders, elders, junior elders, and the uninitiated—and sex (though women occasionally speak in meetings they have low status). The goal of their formal assemblies is to reach consensus on important matters, but there has usually been much preliminary informal talk, and the decision of a formal meeting is often a foregone conclusion, just as in Western deliberative assemblies the real differences are often debated in committee and when an item reaches the floor the decision may be inevitable. Formal assemblies among the Marsi as described by Turton (1975) usually take place when a group has come together for some other reason, such as a marriage, providing an opportunity also to discuss pressing issues, especially problems with neighboring tribes, and they are accompanied by the sacrifice of a stock animal and divination by inspection of its entrails, much as the ancient Romans and Chinese sacrificed and interpreted omens in advance of important actions. There is no chair of the meeting. Someone sets out his ideas and other individuals watch for an opportunity to enter the debate when a previous speaker seems to have made his point or the audience seems restive. The speakers pace back and forth before the group, holding a rifle, spear, or stick in their hands. Speakers in early Greek epic also often hold a staff. All formal speeches tend to begin with the same conventional phrases, including a promise to be brief. The latter is a common topos of public address, apparently more honored by the Marsi than by many others. Marsi speeches tend to be very allusive—that is, they assume knowledge on the part of the audience of persons, events, or customs without naming them—and some individuals particularly excel in their ability to employ allusions and images, thus achieving a terseness of style that is especially admired. Individuals who are acknowledged as orators usually enter the debate at a late stage when they can sum up the situation and make the best contributions to consensus. According to Turton (1975:174), "If one asks a Marsi for the meaning [of the term *jalaba*, "those skilled in speech"], one will be told that it denotes a man who speaks well in public, who is able to put together an argument fluently and forcefully, who never loses his temper or becomes excited at a meeting, who therefore has a way of enabling a meeting to reach a consensus, and who is an authority on the traditional norms and practices of the society."

"Formal speech" has had a history in the West; the most striking examples are the use of Attic Greek on public occasions and in literary composition in the time of the Roman and Byzantine empires and the use of Latin in the Western Middle Ages, but some vestiges of formal language still survive in modern deliberative assemblies where a speaker is expected to use polite, indirect references to others present: for example, "the right honorable member" or "the gentleman on the other side of the house."

A special language for formal occasions probably first came into use in imitation of the archaic and allusive language of ritual, which in turn probably derives from features of song, as distinct from ordinary language, and performative display in prehistoric times. Like ritual, from which it often borrows myths, formal speech carries cultural meaning for group identity and consensus, both may be open to allegorical interpretation, and both sometimes employ linguistic forms that are, or seem to be, archaic and thus a guarantee of the truth of the message. Both ritual and the language of formal oratory have to be learned; knowledge of the right forms is not available to everyone; to be able to perform in the approved way confers status on the practitioner. Conversely, the requirement of formal language is a form of social control of others exercised by those who occupy positions of power in the society.

Indirect Language and Allegory

The Ilongots of the Philippines traditionally admired orators who used "crooked speech," a highly allusive, metaphorical form of language in debate, for example, over retributions for killings or exchanges of a bride for property (Rosaldo 1973). The form was also used in songs, but not for narrative myth or story telling. Narrative characteristically seeks clarity. In the past, the Ilongots were a violent society in which at least one success in headhunting was a requisite for the status of a male adult. Their formal oratory was correspondingly more passionate than that of others I have discussed, asserting the anger of the speaker or his group in a debate with angry opponents, but both sides used indirection, veiled references, and metaphorical expressions that were admired for their aesthetic qualities. Indirection served to mediate differences as the anger of each side was ventilated and accepted by the other. By the 1970s, under the influence of evangelical Christianity and increased contacts with modern society, "crooked speech" became perceived as conducive of discord and characteristic of a rejected past, and it fell into decay (Rosaldo 1984). An interesting feature of the transitional period as described by Rosaldo was that orators were often moved to speak about speech, contrasting the older style with what had become acceptable.

A different form of indirect speech is found among the Bhatgaon, a community in the Fiji islands whose ancestors are immigrants from India. Formal meetings among the Bhatgaon as described by Brenneis (1984) are official assemblies of members of Hindu sects. Speakers are expected to use Hindi to the best of their abilities, and the ostensible subjects are religious themes, but often the speeches are veiled attacks in "sweet talk" directed against specific though unnamed opponents. This serves to bring the issue into the open, since the audience is usually aware of the persons involved. A different kind of meeting may then be held, conducted by an elected committee, in which "straight talk" is required, speeches are in the local dialect, evidence is taken under oath about the crucial issue from witnesses, and the whole matter laid out clearly. There is, however, no decision of responsibility on the part of the committee and no penalties are applied. The function of the meeting is not judgment, conviction, or confession, but clarification, catharsis, and peace in the community. The principals often shake hands at the end and try to make a new start in their relationship.

Allusive, indirect speech has long flourished in certain situations among traditional societies in Papua New Guinea. Strathern (1975) has described "veiled speech" (*el ik*) as practiced in judicial situations among five tribes in the Hagen subdistrict of the western highlands. When a delegation from one group seeks redress for the theft of a pig from a delegation of another group, neither directly accuses the other of theft or lying; instead, they recount experiences of their own relating to similar situations. At a formal meeting intended to renew amicable relations between two groups that had long been enemies, an orator offers compensation for past killings and implies but does not specify the need for compensation from the others in return. Sometimes veiled speech fails, insults follow, or even a fight.

Another group in New Guinea, the Tauade, "are notable for pride, self-assertion, envy, and for a capacity for tearful sentimentality and homicidal rage" (Hallpike 1977:80–81). The individual and particular are significant; the general and categorical of no interest to them. Their language lacks terms for time and for numbers larger than two. They have no word for the concept of peace and do not regard violence as disruptive of social order. Their culture lacks symbolism and has little ritual. Given these values and qualities one might not expect much use of oratory among them, but such is not the case: "Oratory is an integral part of peacemaking and organizing feasts and dances" (Ibid. 146). This requires an ability to use allegory (*manari tsinat*), especially on the part of chiefs or their spokesmen. From Hallpike's examples, however, it would seem that the allegory often has a bitter edge and that the use of indirect language instead of negotiating a settlement or smoothing over differences in the interest of community, as among the people described by Strathern, is a way of insulting enemies on occasions when open hostility is not good form. The allegory used is of a very simple sort and transparent to those present. "Sanza" as practiced by the Azande in central Africa is also indirect language used for insult, though there the speaker relies on the hope that the victim will not immediately understand what is meant (Evans-Pritchard 1962:221–22).

Much subtler is the metaphorical language used in *ha'a*, the term for allegorical speech among the Managalese, described by McKellin (1984). As an example, he quotes in its entirety a speech given by an "orator" to a local community early one morning when he has seen a young woman go to a young man's house in the night. The situation is deliberative rather than judicial in that the issue is whether or not the two should be allowed to marry despite family opposition. An outsider would never guess from the speech as taped and translated by McKellin (113–14) that it concerned this incident at all; it seems to be a narrative account of chasing a kangaroo up a tree, building a fence around the tree, and thus trapping and killing it. The audience, however, understood the allegory to describe the events of the previous night and a perceptive native explained that the speaker, an influential older man regarded as an especially fine orator, was trying to persuade the parents to agree to the marriage and avoid a quarrel. The parents also seem to have understood it in this way and were persuaded.

Annette Weiner (1984) has argued that the use of indirect language in traditional societies results from the desire to protect personal space in situations where everybody knows everybody else and often lives intimately with them and the resulting view that one cannot really know, or should admit knowing, what is in another person's mind. This view is doubtless increased by a belief in magic and the ever present danger that someone will secretly bring down a curse on yourself, your family, or your crops. In a later chapter I shall discuss the greater acceptance of direct language and confrontation in the West, beginning in classical Greece and Rome. One factor may have been the increased privacy in the home, greater personal security, and thus greater tolerance of differences and greater frankness. This is especially characteristic of urban living, which is more impersonal than village life and easily produces a lack of concern for the feelings of others.

Poetic Discourse

A striking feature of formal discourse common in traditional societies is the practice of casting thought into poetic forms. This can be inserted into a longer speech or can stand alone as an expression of thought. There is much diversity. A *kyori* as practiced in gatherings of men among the Wana in Indonesia is a two-lined rhymed stanza in "wrapped words," whose rhetorical function is to "encapsulate a state of affairs in a fitting image, express opinions or sentiments, pose questions, or propose a course of action" (Atkinson 1984:40). Kyori is thus a deliberative form, and collectively the poems reflect deliberation on the problems of the society. Speakers disguise their meaning, however, and say something indirectly in an elegant way to one who understands. Often the thought is criticism of the efforts of Indonesian officials to regularize native society, or of natives who cooperate with the government, and is supportive of local resistance. Kyori thus serves to protect the speaker from official criticism while communicating to his own group. The poems may be direct reflections of the speaker's feelings, or they may purport to come from dreams. Here is an example, expressing contempt for those who cooperate with the Indonesian officials and suggesting identification with the *totonsi majoli* bird of heroic myth:

> Eat, eat, you down there, cookies fried in coconut oil.
> We are the swift bird those flight turns back.
>
> (Atkinson 1984:46)

The Western counterpart of this form are the epigrams in elegiac couplets composed by participants at drinking parties in archaic and classical Greece, often containing some political comment. The verse epigram became a popular form in Latin as well and reappeared in seventeenth and eighteenth-century Europe, but the genre now seems moribund in the West.

A recurrent topic in Wana kyori is millenialism, the prophecy of a return of a happier age before the intrusion of Indonesian officials, with the reappearance of a dead leader of the past (Atkinson 1984:37–38, 51–68). Millenialism, with or without a messiah, has often emerged in societies under stress. The best known examples are in ancient Israel and among early Christians, but in the next chapter I shall describe its appearance among American Indians. A rationalized form of millenialism is utopianism, which is to be achieved by social or political reform. The thought of the Chinese philosopher Mencius has millenial features, and Plato's *Republic* is an influential Western example of utopianism.

Long speeches in poetic form are also a feature of some traditional societies and can be thought of as analogies to epideictic oratory or sermons. A good example are the chants of Cuna (or Kuna) chiefs, which have been studied by Sherzer (1974; see also Sherzer and Woodbury 1987:103–34). The Cuna live in the jungles and coastal islands of Panama. Every two or three days the men and women of a village gather in the "congress house" to discuss communal tasks and local problems. Individuals give speeches in colloquial Cuna but in a formal oratorical style, and chiefs give advice, which is usually elaborated and interpreted by their designated spokesmen (*arkars*). The central event, however, is a chant (*namakke*) by a chief, which may last as much as two hours. A second chief must be present and he acts as "responder," intoning the words "it is so" after each verse. The subject matter of the chant is the history, customs, and religion of the Cuna people, though some Christian elements occur. The major function of such a discourse is to encourage individuals to behave properly and in accord with tradition. The language of the chants differs significantly from the spoken dialect: It avoids eliding vowels, uses distinctive prefixes and suffixes, employs some vocabulary not found in colloquial speech or common words used metaphorically, and is characterized by grammatical parallelism through repetition of noun and verb phrases. For example,

This world / God / that sent us / for him banana root / in order to care for,
    (Responder) It is so.
For him / taro root / in order to care for,
    (Responder) It is so.
For him / yam living / in order to care for,
    (Responder) It is so. etc.

(SHERZER 1974:267–68)

At the end of the chant the chief's *arkar* gives an extended interpretation of the chant in colloquial language, ending with the words "You have heard."

The use of grammatical parallelism, combining similar or sometimes antithetical thoughts, is a common feature of formal language all over the world. When combined with alliteration and assonance it creates verse, and when the language is metaphorical the result can be called poetic. The most familiar example in the West is the language of Hebrew poetry found in the Book of Psalms and other parts of the Old Testament; for example, Psalm 70:1–2:

Be pleased, O God, to deliver me!
O Lord, make haste to help me!
Let them be put to shame and confusion who seek my life!
Let them be turned back and brought to dishonor who desire my hurt!

A good example of parallelism as a feature of formal discourse from the other side of the world are *bini* as composed among the Rotinese in Indonesia (Fox

1974). These may vary from two to a hundred lines and are used for greetings, farewells, petitions, courtship, negotiations, and ceremonies. Parallelism commonly takes the form of couplets, but sometimes a single thought may be extended to three, four, or five lines (see, e.g., Sherzer and Woodbury 1987:6–7, 70–72).

The use of poetry for political expression by public officials in the West had an abortive beginning in the elegies of Solon, who introduced the first steps toward democracy in Athens in the early sixth century BCE. A tradition of wisdom literature in poetry already existed, which Solon adapted to the purposes of describing his political program. Literature was still largely oral at that time; probably Solon performed his poems orally in public, and some manuscript copies may have been circulated to be read aloud by others. A century and a half elapsed before prose writings, including oratory and works of political philosophy, began to be circulated in writing in Greece. Although some classical and postclassical statesmen have played with verse in private, and many have used poetic language in formal oratory, no major public official in the West again, to the best of my knowledge, composed a speech in verse. Western orators from Demosthenes and Cicero to modern times have, however, often quoted famous passages of poetry in public speeches to illustrate a point and to give cultural authority to their views in an elegant form.

Metaphor, Proverbs, and Magic

Both public and private discourse in traditional societies make much use of metaphor and other tropes. These have been of great interest to ethnographers because they seem to offer an entré into particular values of the culture. One of the most often cited is a metaphor said to be current among the men of the Bororo in central Brazil: "We are macaws." This does not seem to reflect totemism or any sacred status of the macaw but to derive from the fact that these colorful birds are kept and tended as pets by women; it is thus a somewhat bemused statement of gender relationships in the culture (Crocker 1977). As I have argued earlier, troping was one of the ways that languages enlarged vocabulary; metaphorical uses were perhaps encouraged by dreaming and singing, thus their special use in poetry and ritual. Unlike synecdoche and metonymy, metaphor carries, or can carry, felt emotion. Simile would seem to be a rationalization of metaphor: that is, use of an explicit comparison when the speaker realizes a metaphor would not be literally true or would seem far-fetched. Proverbs function like metaphors; that is, they are substitutions or transferences of a traditional saying that takes the place of a more specific description of the immediate situation. Appeal to proverbs is often a feature of the code of politeness cultivated in traditional societies and thus a rhetorical strategy. An example is the proverb "One paddle leaves early," as used among the Haya of Tanzenia (Seitel 1977).

It provides a socially acceptable explanation of why an individual leaves a group earlier than others for whatever reason, even though the individual may not be literally paddling a canoe.

Magical practices, found throughout the world, are attempts to control or influence forces of nature, people, animals, or things—for example, to bring rain, make crops grow, cause someone's death, or induce love—by the recitation of certain formulas and performance of certain actions. Magical formulas are extreme forms of formal language. Some magic, especially sorcery, is performed in secret for private ends, but magical invocations are often a form of public address, used in many societies in public rituals relating to agriculture, trade, or war and difficult to distinguish from religious rites. Magical formulas clearly constitute a special code: They must be uttered in exactly the right words by the right persons, make frequent use of metaphor, are often not comprehensible to those who do not control the magic, and are usually repeated several times. The magical words, if properly recited, are thought to constrain the object of incantation so that it has no choice in its action. Magic claims to work through the intervention of spirits or the personification of objects; sometimes the formula is recited over some inanimate object, which is believed to be then impregnated with magical power and able to transmit this power to its destination. There is a large body of published research on magic, including some studies useful for understanding its rhetorical functions (e.g., Malinowski 1935; Evans-Pritchard 1963; Tambiah 1968; O'Keefe 1982; Weiner 1984:180–86; Ward 1988; Covino 1994). I shall return in my concluding chapter to the problem of how best to classify magic within a theory of general rhetoric.

Epideictic Rhetoric

Epideictic rhetoric in traditional, oral societies includes prayers, oral poetry recounting the myths of the people, performances like the chants of Cuma chiefs, speeches at weddings, funerals, and installation of chiefs, and other occasions. A Samoan *fono* for deliberation of some important issue by chiefs and orators representing villages begins with one or more epideictic speeches, called *lauga*, by the orators. Formal language is expected: turn taking, a special vocabulary, complete grammatical sentences, a serious attitude. Epideictic speeches often have traditional topoi that the orator is expected to touch on, and this is true of Samoan *lauga*, which have seven parts: introduction; reference to the kava ceremony, which has begun the meeting; thanksgiving to God; mention of the dignity of the chiefs; mention of some important events in the history of Samoa; statement of the reason for the meeting; and concluding wishes for good and long life for all. Each of these parts is made up of traditional expressions, mostly metaphors. Speakers are not allowed to take a position about the subject of the meeting; that follows in the *talanoaga*, which is a debate in somewhat less formal language (Duranti 1984:232).

Some societies have an epideictic tradition in which wealthy or influential individuals are praised by professional orators or singers in return for gifts. M.G. Smith (1957) has described in some detail *roko*, eulogy or praise-song, among the Hausa of northern Nigeria. *Roko* is practiced by professionals, mostly men but some women, and is often accompanied by drum music. Sometimes several singers work as a team praising a local ruler, but singers also seek out individuals for attention. The singer begins by rhythmically chanting the name of the addressee and calling for a gift. If an appropriate gift is forthcoming the singer announces it, gives thanks, and proceeds to praise the addressee; if there is no gift or an inadequate one, the singer may then deliver an invective.

The content of a Hausa eulogy consists of statements of the individual's ancestry, their notability, his prosperity and influence, the number of his dependents, his fame, and its range. If he has any well-known and important political connections, such as clientage with a senior official capable of protecting him, these are alluded to indirectly. If the declamation becomes hostile, the same themes recur, though with unfavorable emphases and connotations. Insinuations about the ancestry of the person addressed are made at this time. Unfavorable references to the individual's meanness, fortune, treatment of his dependents, occupation, reputation, and possible disloyalty to his community or political patrons are also liable to be made. The ultimate insult—imputation of ambiguous paternity—is never openly mentioned, but overshadows the process of increasing pressure (Smith 1959:39). Hausa *roko* well fits Aristotle's description of epideictic as praise or blame, but it is unusually frank in its public demand for and acknowledgment of payment for praise. A Western orator ordinarily seems to speak out of sincere admiration, untouched by thought of personal gain, whatever the true motives may be. *Roko* performs a specific regulative social function by publicly distributing praise and shame on individuals on the basis of traditional values.

Funeral orations in non-Western cultures sometimes include praise of the deceased, although they are more often expressions of grief or attempts to bring consolation to those who survive. It is not unusual for the dead person to be directly addressed. Helena Valero has provided translation of some short speeches at a Yanomami funeral on the upper Orinoco river (Ferguson 1995:ix), which can serve as an example:

> "Brother, you have gone away," said Shamawe. "I will stay. Remember that wherever you used to go, I would go too. I never left you alone. You guided us. Now we have no one to guide us. Why did you leave us alone?"
>
> Kumaiwe, embracing Miramawe, said: "The songs of the shaman that your father was going to teach you, you will never learn. His enemies consumed him. He always said that when you were bigger he would teach you to be a shaman. Now he has gone away. Who will teach you those songs?"

"Brother, brother," said weeping Nakisewe. "You went to the garden, went to hunt. We went with you. You never scolded me. You were good with everyone. Now you have left me. When our father died I did not suffer so because I knew I still had another father: you. Now you also have gone."

In a study of Greek and Roman consolatory rhetoric, viewed as the opposition of sets of symbols, Donovan Ochs (1993:45–57) has outlined a typology of symbolic behaviors in early Greek funeral rites. I hope that he or someone will undertake a comparison of these with practices elsewhere.

Judicial Rhetoric

Judicial rhetoric is the least developed in traditional societies. Some form of traditional understanding and practice of civil and criminal law can be found in every human society, although not codified or conceptualized (Malinowski 1926): It is instantiated in particular judgments made when the norms or postulates of the culture are violated (criminal cases) or in the determination of rights among individuals (civil cases). In hunter–gatherer societies, living in widely dispersed groups with no centralized authority, "might makes right" is the rule. The victim of a crime, or the victims' relatives in the case of murder, exact revenge with the tacit consent of the community, and quarrels among individuals over their rights take the form of insults and direct action on the part of the stronger party, with no appeal to any court. Sometimes judgment may be left to the gods. This is regularly the case in societies that admit the taking of an exculpatory oath by the accused. The article on "oaths" in the encyclopedia *Man, Myth, & Magic* (1995:1904–6) cites examples from the Comanche Indians and tribes in West Africa, New Guinea, New Zealand, and Samoa. Trial by ordeal has been practiced in some traditional societies; it was also a feature of early law in Mesopotamia and was practiced in medieval Europe. It presumably originated in allowing contestants to settle differences by a physical fight but became ritualized when the gods were called on to make judgment. In Mesopotamia, for example, the accused was thrown into a river and allowed to drown or survive as the gods will.

Traditional procedures among the Eskimo, living from Greenland across northern Canada and Alaska to eastern Siberia, may be taken as an example of judicial rhetoric in its simplest and perhaps archaic form. The best source of information about these practices as they existed before Western legal systems began to intrude are scattered through writings by the Norwegian traveler Knud Rasmussen in the early twentieth century, but a good summary of them can be found in E. A. Hoebel's *The Law of Primitive Man* (1964:67–99). Redress of wrongs lay with the individual or the individual's relatives, though when a group was affected a person who had prestige from his hunting ability might take direct action on behalf of the community. There are no private rights to hunting territory and quarrels between individuals primarily arose from rights to sexual intercourse with women. In a previous chapter I described the rhetoric of red deer stags in seeking rights to mate with females—vocal encounters, stalking, and fights with their horns if one animal does not give way. A similar sequence has characterized Eskimo quarrels over women: insults, threatening gestures, and fights in the form of butting or wrestling contests. An additional option, however, developed at some time in the past, reflecting nature's preference for speech over physical violence. These are the "song duels" in which the opponents challenge each other to a verbal duel before the community, which gives an informal judgment of the winner; the contestants are then expected to become friends (Hoebel 1964:93–98, with examples). The "songs" or "speeches" are usually characterized by boasts of power and insults of the opponent.

When a society lives permanently in a community of some size, compensation for wrongs, including a blood price for murder, can often be negotiated by a "go-between," a person not related to the opponents, a practice also often followed in arranging marriages. Hoebel (1964:114–16) describes the rhetoric of such a person among the Ifugao in the Philippines. Approaching the defendant,

> He scolds, wheedles, lashes with sarcasm, insinuates the ill-temper of the other side, exaggerates the ferocity of its warriors, blows up the number of kinsmen who have gathered at the call of the plaintiff, scoffs at the weakness of the defendant's supporters and at the thinness of his argument. Resentment of his remarks would render him no longer a go-between but an ally of the other family. He is also perfectly free to give the plaintiff the same treatment when he returns with the defendant's response. Since he knows the propensity of plaintiffs to overstate their grievances and expected damages, he works to whittle down the original demands to a point where in time an agreeable settlement is reached. (Hoebel 1964:116)

More elaborate judicial procedure in a formal court setting has developed among some African tribes. In a formal trial among the Ashanti in West Africa described by Hoebel (1964:246–49) two men have quarreled and have invoked a god by a forbidden name as an oath against each other. The crime is not the fight, but the violation of the taboo involved in uttering the god's name. There is then a trial before the chief. Each man is given an opportunity to state his case in his own words, ending with an assertion of innocence and a declaration of his willingness to bear the penalty if he has lied. An official then "corroborates" these statements by repeating them verbatim from memory. The elders cross-examine the principals; eventually, one claims to have a witness, who is produced, and this proves determinative to the court. In traditional societies, and as later chapters will reveal in courts in ancient literate societies, direct evidence is usually required for conviction; if lacking, the alternative is to seek some supernatural witness of the truth as in the procedure among the Australians described earlier, by ordeal, or by divination.

Admission of circumstantial evidence and the use of argument from probability, so characteristic of classical Greek legal procedure, has been slow to develop in traditional societies, but some evidence for it exists among relatively sophisticated tribes. Max Gluckman (1967) has described a large number of cases and speeches from among the Barotse when under British rule in Northern Rhodesia in the 1940s. Barotse trials admit circumstantial evidence and speakers employ argument from probability, which may be the result of the knowledge of procedures in British colonial courts. On the other hand, some understanding of motivation and thus admissibility of testimony about intent as a mitigating factor in criminal cases seems common in primitive law; Hoebel (1964:235, 239, 299) cites examples from the Ashunti in Africa and the Caribs in South America. It would seem a natural development to support an argument of lack of intent to commit a crime with a record of good character in the past, thus opening up the possibility of arguing that it is not "probable" that an individual would have deliberately acted criminally in the case alleged. The strong role of ethos in traditional deliberative rhetoric probably contributed to this development in judicial contexts.

Conceptualization of Rhetoric in Traditional Societies

As noted earlier, most traditional societies have some terms for orator, formal and informal speech situations, and some features of discourse. The degree to which individuals in an oral culture are consciously aware of rhetoric seems to vary with circumstances, as does the facility with which a language can coin abstract nouns. In many traditional societies there seems to be rather little reflection about language use and most thinking is cast in specific terms, as seen in myths or proverbs, without attempts at generalization as universal propositions. One factor that tends to encourage an awareness of language use is the familiarity of the group with speakers of a different language, people who often have different social and religious customs as well. A good example are the Limba in Sierra Leone as described by Finnegan (1988:45–88). The Limba are closely surrounded by speakers of different languages. They put a high value on speaking, are highly conscious of the differences between their language and that of others, like to talk about language use, and have a prefix, *hu*, that can be used to create abstract verbal nouns. They resemble many other cultures, however, in their belief that the primary function of formal speech is consensus, reconciliation, and the preservation of cultural identity. Abstract thinking about language and culture in ancient Greece also seems to have been encouraged by awareness of difference from others, seen for example in Herodotus's *Histories*, and in the facility of Greek for forming abstract nouns, whereas speculation about language and abstract thinking were somewhat slower to develop in other literate ancient cultures where these factors were less present.

Conclusion

Some general conclusions about public address in traditional, nonliterate societies seem possible, even though there are great differences in detail. The rhetoric of public address in traditional societies usually aims at consensus and the preservation of the values and traditions of the group. It is a conservative or corrective force, not an instrument of change. The primary means of persuasion is the authority or ethos of the speaker, deriving from such factors as age, experience, and skill at speaking, the latter partly derived from natural ability, partly from imitating effective speakers of the past. There is much repetition in most traditional speech and little in the way of explicit logical reasoning, though myth, legend, history, and proverbs supply evidence and statements sometimes take enthymematic form.

Traditional deliberative speech is usually polite, considerate of the feelings of others, and relatively unemotional. When attacks are made, veiled or indirect language is often used, which allows the victim to save face and protects the speaker from immediate reprisal. The authority of a speaker is increased in some contexts by an ability to use a special, formal language, which carries the collective values of the community and makes use of grammatical parallelism, alliteration, assonance, indirect allusions, and metaphor. The most common metaphors are personifications of forces of nature, animals, or physical objects. Members of a traditional society find a speech in formal language difficult to answer, since any response seems to reject communal values. Another speaker may, however, express a somewhat different point of view, usually in a respectful way, and seek compromise. When this process breaks down, as sometimes happens, it is apt to break down completely, with a quick resort to ridicule, insult, and even violence. Someone who is dissatisfied with an imposed consensus may resort to sorcery to counter its effects.

Sorcery and magic are rhetorical forms in traditional societies: The words of a magical incantation properly performed are thought to control and constrain the activities of a spirit, a force of nature, other people, or physical objects, and sorcerers can, by secret words and actions, bring disease and death upon others living at a distance.

Epideictic rhetoric is primarily practiced in religious and ritual contexts, often in poetic form, but public praise or blame of individuals exists in some cultures. Judicial rhetoric is least developed in traditional societies, but courts of law exist where there is an established framework of government including chiefs and councils. These courts admit argument of intent in criminal trials and even in some cases argument from probability. Judicial speeches are usually delivered in ordinary language, but there are some instances of the use of formal language in settling differences and achieving order and consensus in the society.

References

Atkinson, Jane M. (1984). " 'Wrapped Words': Poetry and Politics among the Wana of Central Sulawesi, Indonesia," in Brenneis and Myers (1984): 34–68.

Bauman, Richard, and Joel Sherzer, eds. (1974). *Explorations in the Ethnography of Speaking*. Cambridge: Cambridge University Press.

Bloch, Maurice, ed. (1975). *Political Language and Oratory in Traditional Society*. London: Academic Press.

Brenneis, Donald (1984). "Straight Talk and Sweet Talk: Political Discourse in an Occasionally Egalitarian Community," in Brenneis and Myers (1984): 69–84.

Brenneis, Donald, and Fred R. Myers, eds. (1984). *Dangerous Words: Language and Politics in the Pacific*. Reprinted with changes, 1991. Prospect Heights, IL: Waveland Press.

Covino, William A. (1994). *Magic, Rhetoric, and Literacy: An Eccentric History of the Composing Imagination*. Albany: State University of New York Press.

Crocker, J. Christopher (1977). "My Brother the Parrot," in Sapir and Crocker (see Bibliography) (1977): 164–92.

Duranti, Alessandro (1984). "*Lauga* and *Talanoaga*: Two Speech Genres in a Samoan Political Event," in Brenneis and Myers (1984): 217–42.

Evans-Pritchard, Edward E. (1962). *Essays in Social Anthropology*. London: Faber and Faber.

———(1963). *Witchcraft, Oracles, and Magic Among the Alzande*. Oxford: Clarendon Press.

Ferguson, R. Brian (1995). *Yanomami Warfare: A Political History*. Santa Fe: School of American Research Press.

Finnegan, Ruth (1988). *Literacy and Orality: Studies in the Technology of Communication*. Oxford: Basil Blackwell.

Firth, Raymond (1975). "Speech-Making and Authority in Tikopia," in Bloch (1975): 29–43.

Fox, James J. (1974). "'Our Ancestors Spoke in Pairs': Rotinese Views of Language, Dialect, and Code," in Bauman and Sherzer (1974): 65–85.

Gewertz, Deborah (1984). "Of Symbolic Anchors and Sago Soup: The Rhetoric of Exchange among the Chambri of Papua New Guinea," in Brenneis and Myers (1984): 192–213.

Gluckman, Max (1967). *The Judicial Process among the Barotse of Northern Rhodesia*, 2nd ed. Manchester: Manchester University Press.

Gumperz, John J., and Dell Hymes, eds. (1972). *Directions in Sociolinguistics: The Ethnology of Communication*. New York: Holt, Rinehart, and Winston.

Hallpike, Christopher R. (1977). *Bloodshed and Vengeance in the Papuan Mountains*. Oxford: Clarendon Press.

Hobart, Mark (1975). "Orators and Patrons: Two Types of Political Leader in Balinese Village Society," in Bloch (1975): 66–92.

Hoebel, E. Adamson (1964). *The Law of Primitive Man: A Study in Comparative Legal Dynamics*. Cambridge, MA: Harvard University Press.

Irvine, Judith T. (1979). "Formality and Informality in Communicative Events," *American Anthropologist* 81:773–90.

Malinowski, Bronislaw (1922). *Argonauts of the Western Pacific*. London: Routledge and Kegan Paul; reprinted, New York: E. P. Dutton, 1961.

———(1926). *Crime and Custom in Savage Society*. New York: Harcourt Brace.

———(1935). *Coral Gardens and Their Magic: Soil-Tilling and Agricultural Rites in the Trobriand Islands*. 2 vols. Bloomington: Indiana University Press.

Man, Myth & Magic (1995). Ed. by Richard Cavendisch and Brian Innes. 21 vols. New York: Marshall Cavendish.

McKellin, William H. (1984). "Putting Down Roots: Information in the Language of Managalase Exchange," in Brenneis and Myers (1984): 108–27.

Ochs, Donovan J. (1993). *Consolatory Rhetoric: Grief, Symbol, and Ritual in the Greco-Roman Era*. Columbia: University of South Carolina Press.

O'Keefe, Daniel Lawrence (1968). *Stolen Lightning: The Social Theory of Magic*. New York: Continuum Press.

Rosaldo, Michelle Z. (1973). "I Have Nothing to Hide: The Language of Ilongot Oratory," *Language in Society* 2:193–224.

———(1984). "Words That Are Moving: The Social Meanings of Ilongot Verbal Art," in Brenneis and Myers (1984): 131–60.

Salmond, Anne (1975). "Mana Makes the Man: A Look at Maori Oratory and Politics," in Bloch (1975): 45–63.

Seitel, Peter (1977). "Saying Haya Sayings," in Sapir and Crocker (see Bibliography) (1977): 75–99.

Sherzer, Joel (1974). "*Namakke, Sunmakke, Kormakke*: Three Types of Cuna Speech Event," in Brenneis and Sherzer (1974): 263–82.

———(1983). *Kuna Ways of Speaking: An Ethnographic Perspective*. Austin: University of Texas Press.

Sherzer, Joel, and Anthony C. Woodbury (1987). *Native American Discourse*. Cambridge: Cambridge University Press.

Smith, Michael G. (1957). "The Social Functions and Meaning of Hausa Praise-Singing," *Africa* 27:26–45.

Strathern, Andrew (1975). "Veiled Speech in Mount Hagen," in Bloch (1975): 185–203.

Tambiah, S. J. (1968). "The Magical Power of Words," *Man* 3: 175–208.

Turton, David (1975). "The Relationships between Oratory and the Exercise of Influence among the Mursi," in Bloch (1975): 163–83.

Ward, John O. (1988). "Magic and Rhetoric from Antiquity to the Renaissance: Some Ruminations," *Rhetorica* 6:57–118.

Weiner, Annette B. (1984). "From Words to Objects to Magic: 'Hard Words' and the Boundaries of Social Interaction," in Brenneis and Myers (1984): 161–91.

Bibliography

Hymes, Dell, ed. (1964). *Language in Culture and Society: A Reader in Linguistics and Anthropology*. New York: Harper & Row.

Richards, Audrey, and Adam Kuper, eds. (1971). *Councils in Action*. Cambridge Papers in Social Anthropology 6. Cambridge: Cambridge University Press.

Sapir, J. David, and J. Christopher Crocker (1977). *The Social Use of Metaphor*. Philadelphia: University of Pennsylvania Press.

Smith, Arthur J. (1971). "Markings of an African Concept of Rhetoric," *Communication Quarterly* 19:13–18.

Starosta, William J. (1979). "Roots of an Older Rhetoric: On Rhetorical Effectiveness in the Third World," *Western Journal of Speech Communication* 43:278–87.

CHAPTER 5

North American Indian Rhetoric

The rhetoric and traditional oral literature of Native Americans are naturally of special interest to those of us who live in North America. Most discussions of Indian rhetoric, however, have been by anthropologists or students of literature or have been written for a popular audience; in an article on Indian eloquence Edna Sorter (1972) called for more analyses by students trained in rhetoric and speech communication. Any generalization about the native population of North America, however, requires caution; though all were ultimately related and shared some cultural features, there were at the time of the first arrival of Europeans several hundred distinct groups, speaking different languages, leading very different lives: Some were hunter–gatherers, some agriculturalists, and some became pastoralists, and some Indian societies of the Southwest and Middle America can be described as urban. Although the Indians had been, like the Australians discussed in an earlier chapter, either completely or largely out of contact with the rest of the world for many millenia since their ancestors first entered Alaska from Asia, the Americans inhabited a much larger area with a greater diversity of natural environments and resources; they developed greater technological skills than did the Australians and lived in more diverse societies. It is reasonable to expect that their rhetoric would resemble traditional rhetoric in other parts of the world and also that some special features would have developed in some of their societies. Indian societies north of Mexico were basically egalitarian; as elsewhere in the world, men in the prime of life who were respected for their deeds had special prestige, but opportunity for leadership was open on the basis of perceived merit; in tribal conferences any man, and sometimes women, could speak, and a man might in time earn a leadership role. Chiefs were usually chosen on the basis of their successes in war and personal qualities of wisdom and eloquence, and the office was not usually inherited.

Indian Eloquence as Described by White Settlers

The earliest picture of Indian oratory in what is now the United States can be found in *The Florida* of "the Inca," Garcilaso de la Vega, written between 1567 and 1591 and published in 1605 (translation by Varner and Varner 1951). The work is a romanticized account of de Soto's explorations of the southeastern United States, intended to encourage Spanish settlement there, and largely based on what a member of the expedition recalled fifty years later. There are a number of speeches attributed to Indians, which were originally filtered through interpreters, nostalgically recalled later, and artistically composed by Garcilaso. The Spaniards came as conquerers and often evoked hostility but admired the courage, love of honor, and eloquence of the Indians, some of whom emerge as early instances of the "noble savage." In one passage Garcilaso complains to his informant that what he has reported cannot be the actual words of Indians, which prompts the following response:

> There are Indians of very fine understanding who in peace and war, and in adverse and prosperous times, are able to speak like the people of any nation of much wisdom. These Indians did answer in substance what I have told you, and furthermore they made many other magnificent speeches which I do not recall, but which I would not be able to repeat as they were said even if I should remember them. Nevertheless these speeches were so eloquent that the Governor (De Soto) and those who accompanied him were more surprised by the utterances of the Indians than they were by their having permitted themselves to swim almost thirty hours in the water. And when many Spaniards well read in history heard them, they asserted that the captains (i.e., chiefs) appeared to have been influenced by the most famous officers of Rome when that city dominated the world with its arms, and that the youths ... appeared to have been trained in Athens when it was flourishing in moral letters. (Varner and Varner 1951:160)

This reaction, and the comparison of Indian and classical rhetoric, will recur in later writers.

The English settlers of what became the United States created their own image of the Indians and a view of Indian discourse based on limited evidence. Most published speeches attributed to Indians in eastern North America in the seventeenth, eighteenth, and nineteenth centuries were addressed to whites and intended to influence whites; the speeches are known only in English translations or were spoken in English; they use features of European rhetoric, especially appealing to Christian values; some of the speakers were themselves Christianized. Reconstruction of native traditions is thus difficult. Modern Indian communities seek to preserve traditional ways, including deliberation among themselves, religious rituals, and the performance of oral literature, but in different circumstances and often in different places from their origins, affected by their experience over four centuries by contacts with Spanish, English, French, and other intruders, and often in a reconstructed form or one adjusted to contemporary needs. An example is the revival of the institution of the potlatch in the North West, but adapted to charitable purposes disguising its original function of personal enrichment and aggrandizement.

Colonial inhabitants of eastern North America commonly regarded the Indians as dirty, ignorant, and cruel savages, while at the same time they repeatedly commented on the eloquence of the natives, stressing their innate nobility, their dignity, their preference for brevity of speech. One nineteenth-century writer who tried to give an informed and balanced picture of the Indians of the North East was James Fenimore Cooper. In the "Author's Introduction" added in 1850 to *The Last of the Mohicans* Cooper described the Indian in war as "daring, boastful, cunning, ruthless, self-denying, and self-devoted"; in peace as "just, generous, hospitable, revengeful, superstitious, modest, and commonly chaste." He continues with a few remarks on Indian eloquence:

> The imagery of the Indian, both in his poetry and his oratory, is Oriental—chastened, and perhaps improved, by the limited range of his practical knowledge. He draws his metaphors from the clouds, the seasons, the birds, the beasts, and the vegetable world. In this, perhaps, he does no more than any other energetic and imaginative race would do, being compelled to set bounds to fancy by experience; but the North American Indian clothes his ideas in a dress which is different from that of the African, and is Oriental in itself. His language has the richness and sententious fullness of the Chinese. He will express a phrase in a word, and he will qualify the meaning of an entire sentence by a syllable; he will even convey different significations by the simplest inflections of the voice.

Like other traditional societies, the Indians encountered by the settlers valued politeness and sought consensus in debate, both among themselves and with whites. Benjamin Franklin noted that their politeness prevented them from directly contradicting what was said by others but made it difficult to know their minds or what impression others made on them (quoted in Murray 1991:39).

Logan's "Speech"

In Query VI of his *Notes on the State of Virginia*, seeking to refute the arguments of the French *philosophe* Buffon about the natural inferiority of the New World to the Old, Thomas Jefferson described the natives as intellectual equals to Europeans. He continued as follows:

> The principles of their society forbidding all compulsion, they are to be led to duty and to enterprize by personal influence and persuasion. Hence eloquence in council, bravery and address in war, become the foundations of all consequence with them.... Of their eminence in oratory we have fewer examples, because it is displayed chiefly in their own councils. Some, however, we have of very superior lustre. I may challenge the whole orations of Demosthenes and Cicero, and of any more eminent orator, if Europe has furnished more eminent, to produce a single passage, superior to the speech of Logan, a Mingo chief, to Lord Dunmore, when governor of this state.

He then describes the circumstances in which Logan became involved in 1774 and quotes a version of the speech in its entirety:

> I appeal to any white man to say, if ever he entered Logan's cabin hungry, and he gave him not meat; if ever he came cold and naked, and he clothed him not. During the course of the last long and bloody war, Logan remained idle in his cabin, an advocate for peace. Such was my love for the whites, that my countrymen pointed as they passed, and said, "Logan is the friend of white men." I have even thought to have lived with you, but for the injuries of one man. Col. Cresap, the last spring, in cold blood, and unprovoked, murdered all the relations of Logan, not sparing even my women and children. There runs not a drop of my blood in the veins of any living creature. This called on me for revenge. I have sought it: I have killed many; I have fully glutted my vengeance. For my country, I rejoice at the beams of peace. But do not harbour a thought that mine is the joy of fear. Logan never felt fear. He will not turn on his heel to save his life. Who is there to mourn for Logan?—Not one. (Jefferson 1984:188–89)

This became the most famous of all "speeches" attributed to an Indian in the colonial period. It was reprinted in grammar school readers in the nineteenth century and widely admired as an example of eloquence. There are, however, numerous problems in regarding it as an authentic example of Indian rhetoric: Jefferson seems to have edited the language somewhat (Sandefur 1960); the text is based on a letter sent by Logan to Lord Dunmore and is thus not a delivered speech; it is in English; in the first sentence it employs phraseology reminiscent of the English Bible. Certainly it is eloquent, noble, brave, and pathetic; O'Donnell (1979) has argued that Indian cultural values can be found in it. It is, however, also part of the construction by whites of the view of the Indian as "a noble savage" current in the Enlightenment in Europe, continued in the Romantic Movement of the nineteenth century as a tragic vision of a culture inevitably doomed by the advance of civilization (Camp 1978). David Murray (1991) has recently described in detail how this tradition was constructed and propagated to satisfy readers aesthetically and politically from the seventeenth to the twentieth century and its negative effect on understanding Indians.

Indian Response to Challenge

A basic principle in the history of rhetoric is that of challenge and response. Great oratory needs a cause and the greatest speakers have often emerged in response to some great and unexpected threat to their way of life or freedom: in Athens when confronted by Persia, Sparta, or Macedon; in the Roman republic of Cicero confronting the ambitions of Catiline, Caesar, and Mark Antony; Patrick Henry and other American leaders when oppressed by the mother country; Churchill and Roosevelt during World War II—all are examples. The phenomenon is consistent with my argument in earlier chapters that challenge sparks mental energy that is then transmitted by a code of signs, and rhetoric is in origin a conservative force whose natural sources lie in defense of the individual, the group, and the culture. Oratory had been an important feature of Indian councils and rituals, but with the threat to their way of life from white settlements and expansion Indian orators were faced with the greatest rhetorical challenge that could be imagined when they attempted to persuade the powerful intruders to fairness and consideration and their own people to a course of action, whether resistence, compromise, or surrender. For all their instinctive politeness, Indians were often impelled to disagree with whites, and in the process their orators developed topics dealing with the inconsistency, lack of logic, or hypocrisy of white demands, the deceitfulness that regularly characterized white offers of truce, and the unprincipled actions of many whites, especially in giving hard liquor to Indians.

The eighteenth and nineteenth centuries were also, of course, a major period in the history of American public address, beginning with the revolutionary orators and continuing in the political and social crises of the following century, but few Indians ever heard the great American orators or preachers of the time. No direct influence of them on Indian oratory is likely, though appreciation of oratory as an art form contributed to an interest in Indian orators among the general public. In 1880, Red Cloud and several other Oglala chiefs made a sensational appearance before a large white audience at the Cooper Institute in New York City. The report of the *New York Times* of June 17, 1880, includes the following description:

> No one who listened to Red Cloud's remarkable speech yesterday can doubt that he is a man of very great talents.... Although the audience labored under the disadvantage of not knowing what Red Cloud said, until his words were filtered through an interpreter ... still his earnest manner, his impassioned gestures, the eloquence of his hands, and the magnetism which he evidently exercises over an audience produced a vast effect on the dense throng which listened to him yesterday. (See further Ek 1966 and Balgooyen 1968:30.)

I shall return to Red Cloud later in the chapter. He comes relatively late in the history of Indian oratory and first I want to go back to some earlier sources.

Early Reports of Indian Speeches at Conferences with White Settlers

The earliest report of an Indian response to English settlers is that by Powhattan delivered in 1609 and recorded by Capt. John Smith:

> Why will you take by force what you may obtain by love? Why will you destroy us who supply you with food? What can you get by war?... We are unarmed, and willing to give you what you ask, if you come in a friendly manner.... I am not so simple as not to know it is better to eat good meat, sleep comfortably, live quietly with my women and children, laugh and be merry with the English, and being their friend, trade for their copper and hatchets, than to run away from them.... Take away your guns and swords, the cause of all our jealousy, or you may die in the same manner. (Armstrong 1971:1)

Powhattan appeals here to the best interest of his audience, the classic topic of deliberative oratory. Rhetorical questions and anaphora often appear in Indian speeches when arguing against whites and seem to be a natural feature of universal rhetoric; characteristic of Indian eloquence is the ethos of the speaker as a lover of peace and the clarity, dignity, and determination of the remarks, the last seen especially in the final phrase. Indian speeches at crucial times were often brief but could go on for hours in their own council meetings.

Major sources for what Indians said and how they said it when addressing whites in the seventeenth and eighteenth centuries are accounts of treaties between the colonists and Indians as white settlers sought to acquire new lands. The colonists broke terms of the treaties more often than did the Indians. Benjamin Franklin printed a series of accounts of treaties that include speeches by both the white and Indian representatives (Boyd 1938), and accounts were printed by others as well (examples in Armstrong 1971:6–16). Detailed records of speeches at the Councils of Greenville on the northwest frontier in 1790 and 1795 were prepared for the use of the U.S. Senate and published in *American State Papers (Indian Relations)* at the time. General "Mad" Anthony Wayne, who represented the federal government at the 1795 council, made a concerted effort to placate the Indian representatives, including adopting features of Indian rhetoric in his opening remarks: "I take you by the hand as brothers, assembled for the good work of peace. I thank the Great Spirit for his glorious sun.... The Great Spirit has favored us with a clear sky and refreshing breeze for this happy occasion..." (Jones 1965:73).

At the actual conferences the Indian chiefs usually spoke in their native language and their remarks were then translated by interpreters (Indians or half-breeds who lived with whites and were employed by them or whites who had lived with Indians and learned their language), written down, and later edited for publication. What we have may be faithful to the general thrust of Indian remarks but cannot be trusted as evidence for exactly how it was said. One In-

dian who made an effort to speak in English, while using imagery and wit native to an Indian, was Tammany, a Delaware chief who attended the signing of
a treaty with William Penn in Philadelphia in 1682. Penn was both the most
honorable of the colonial leaders in his dealings with Indians and also one of the
few to acquire some knowledge of the local Indian dialect. Tammany is reported
to have said, "We shall live as brothers as long as sun and moon shine in the
sky. We have a broad path to walk. If the Indian sleep and the Yengeesman (i.e.,
Englishman) come, he pass and do no harm to the Indian. If Yegneesman sleep
in path, the Indian pass and do him no harm. Indian say, 'He's Yengees; he loves
sleep' " (Armstrong 1971:6). In a speech attributed to Kanickhungo of the Iroquois Nation in Philadelphia in 1763 (Armstrong 1971:13) the imagery of a road
or path shared by whites and Indians recurs, together with the metaphor of a
campfire kept burning by the whites at which the Indians could warm themselves and the more European metaphor of a "chain" of friendship between the
two peoples. After the revolution the thirteen or more states were regularly referred to by Indians as "the fires." Indians were capable of irony. When Canasat-
ego rejected the invitation to send six Iroquois youth to the College of William
and Mary in 1744, he described contemptuously the education some Indians had
been given earlier in New England colleges, from which they returned ignorant
of every means of living the life of an Indian. He ended by saying, "We are,
however, not the less obliged for your kind offer, though we decline accepting
it; and to show our grateful sense of it, if the gentlemen of Virginia shall send
us a dozen of their sons, we will take great care of their education, instruct them
in all we know, and make men of them" (Armstrong 1971:16–17).

The Pan-Indian Movement in Indian Oratory

What is known about debates among eastern Indians in their own councils comes
largely from letters and records of missionaries and traders who witnissed the
proceedings. Gregory Dowd (1992) has published a detailed examination of the
struggle for unity among the Indians against white encroachment in the crucial
years 1745–1815. The most famous leaders in this policy are Pontiac in the eighteenth century and Tecumseh in the early nineteenth, but there were many others of considerable influence. Dowd gives an account of important pan-Indian
leaders and councils and, though he does not use the terminology of a student
of rhetoric, he identifies a number of recurring topoi. Indian resistance was largely
directed against Anglo-American settlers, for they were the ones who wanted
Indian lands. The French, in contrast, were primarily interested in hunting and
trapping, which was less disruptive of Indian culture and Indians often joined
with the French against a common enemy, but during the Revolution and the
War of 1812 some Indian federations cooperated with the British against the
United States.

According to Dowd, Indian policy toward Anglo-Americans can be divided into that of the "nativists" and that of advocates of accommodation with the settlers. He traces the partially successful efforts of nativists to unite the Indians from the Great Lakes to the Gulf of Mexico in a common policy. This involved communicating the magnitude of the threat to all, and necessarily stressed common religious and cultural practices, but the dislocation of Indian tribes from the eastern seaboard brought new rituals to the midwest, which were easily assimilated (Dowd 1992:129). Nativists regularly argued that the problems of the Indians resulted from their failure to perform the proper rituals for war, hunting, and agriculture, thus bringing down the anger of the Great Spirit. To succeed, Indians must first recapture sacred power; ritual cleansing by fasting and emetics was part of the procedure.

Anglo-American policy toward the Indians included conversion to Christianity, and pan-Indian rhetoric attempted to address the claims of evangelical missionaries to exclusive religious truth. In their discussions among themselves and in rejoinders to whites, this regularly took the form of the claim of separate creations. Christianity had perhaps been given by their god to the whites; however, the crucifixion of Christ was to many Indians a major objection to Christianity and they often taxed Christians with having killed the Christian god. Indians, in contrast, claimed they had been separately created by the Great Spirit, a more peaceful god, to whom they owed obedience. Since the Indians had also become aware of black slaves, they accorded them a third and separate creation (Dowd 1992:30–31 and passim). But Indian orators also adapted ideas from Christianity to native religion: Dowd (19, 126) suggests that the increasing importance given to the Great Spirit as a single god of the Indians and the introduction of the notion of Hell are Christian influences.

Indian nativism invoked a form of millenialism, the doctrine that the future will, or can under certain circumstances, bring a peaceful and prosperous time, a rhetorical topos that regularly appears in cultures under stress. In traditional societies, this Golden Age is often thought of as a return to an idealized past. Indian speakers, like those in other cultures, have often bolstered their authority by claims of divine inspiration. Popé, the leader of the Pueblo rebellion against the Spanish in the late seventeenth century, had done this, alleging that he had been commissioned by the Great Spirit to tell the Indians to drive out the invaders (Jones 1965:ix). In the eastern United States prophets played a major role in the nativist resistance to white intrusion. An early example is the Delaware prophet Neolin (Dowd 1992:33–40), who, about 1760, claimed to have had a vision in which a mysterious figure appeared and instructed him in religion. In his preaching he made use of a pictorial chart showing the path from earth to heaven, blocked by the white people. Horizontal marks along the side represented vices, including drunkenness, brought by Europeans, and Neolin taught that the Indians must find a difficult way through these to happiness. Dowd (129) insists that Indian preachers did not seek to revive a dead past, but this seems to me exaggerated: The idealized past, before the arrival of the whites, was the only model of happiness the Indians could conceive.

The most famous Indian claiming divine inspiration in the early nineteenth century was Tecumseh's brother, Tenskwatawa, widely known as "The Prophet" (Dowd 1992:124–46). He went about preaching union among all red men against the whites and expulsion of the white scourge. In 1806 he staged a clever ruse to demonstrate his divine authority. Having learned from some white sources that a total eclipse of the sun would occur at noon on June 16, he prophesied to the Indians that he would demonstrate his power by darkening the sun. He put on a dark robe, summoned his neighbors to his cabin, and commanded the sun to cover its face. Gradually the disk went dark as the Indians watched in amazement and fear. After an appropriate length of time The Prophet then commanded the sun to restore its light, which it did. As the eclipse ended, he called out, "Did I not prophesy aright?" (Jones 1965:80–82).

Indian messiahs later appeared in the western United States. The most influential in the late nineteenth century was Wovoka, a Paiute medicine man whose message combined the second coming of Jesus and the reawakening of the dead with elements of traditional Indian ritual in what is known as the Ghost Dance Religion about 1890 (Osterreich 1991). Wovoka's message counseled peace, but other members of the movement proclaimed the coming destruction of the whites and the return of the buffalo to the plains. Preachers brought hope and unity to Indians, but the movement was somewhat discredited by the efforts of a Kiowa medicine man named Apiatan who interviewed Wovoka and became disillusioned. For this, he was given a medal by President Benjamin Harrison (Balgooyen 1968:39). The federal government then took active steps to suppress the movement; in December 1890 over 300 Sioux men, women, and children gathered for a Ghost Dance ceremony at Wounded Knee, South Dakota, and were massacred by federal troups. Some elements of the Ghost Dance Religion were revived by Indian activists in the 1960s and 1970s (Morris and Wander 1990).

Red Jacket

The most eloquent Indian orator of the early federal period, at least as known to white readers, was probably Red Jacket (c. 1756–1830). He belonged to the Seneca tribe in western New York, which was one of the Six Nations of the Iroquois. His original name was Otitiani, "Always Ready"; when he was elected a chief he was given the name Sagoyewatha, "The Keeper Awake." The name "Red Jacket" is said to have been given him by the British when he served as a runner for them during the Revolution (Jones 1965:51–59). In 1866 William L. Stone published a life of Red Jacket containing versions of some of his speeches, and in 1886 J. Niles Hubbard published a second biography with additional information based on written records and reminiscences of those who had known

Red Jacket well. The most important of the latter was probably Horatio Jones who had lived near him and often acted as his interpreter. Apparently Red Jacket knew little English and could neither read nor write. He claimed to be a natural-born orator (Jones 1965:53), but according to Hubbard, when a young man he had heard Logan speak and modeled himself on Logan; he would "play Logan" by going off alone in the woods to practice oratory (Hubbard 1886:53). This is one of a number of ways in which Hubbard constructed a parallel between the Greek orator Demosthenes and Red Jacket.

Red Jacket apparently first received notice in his tribe when he unsuccessfully opposed their assistance to the British in the Revolution. As a result, he was charged with cowardice by other Indians. Demosthenes too met similar charges. After the Revolution, however, Red Jacket emerged as a leading figure in the councils of the Iroquois on the basis of his oratorical ability, he went on embassies to President Washington and other federal officials, and the fame of his eloquence spread widely through the country. Those who knew him personally always claimed that none of his speeches as published in translation really did justice to his powers, but the speeches we have do much to justify his great reputation. As in the case of many other native speeches, it is hard to know, however, how much they owe to their white translators and editors, for one reason they were admired by white readers is that they observe some of the conventions of Western literary rhetoric: They regularly contain a proemium, a narration, a proof that contains a serious of arguments, and an epilogue, and they are characterized by dignity, rationality, and wit.

The most famous of Red Jacket's speeches among white readers has been his reply to a missionary named Cram who was sent by the Boston Missionary Society to convert the Senecas to Christianity in 1806. Cram apparently spoke in a rather patronizing tone, announced that the gospel of Jesus Christ was the only true religion and that the Indians would never be happy without accepting it, but, in what proved a mistaken tactic of conciliation, invited the Indians to "reason" with him (for Cram's speech and Red Jacket's reply, see Velie 1991:136–39). Red Jacket's speech as we have it begins courteously:

> Friend and Brother, it was the will of the Great Spirit that we should meet together this day.... He has taken his garment from before the sun and caused it to shine with brightness upon us. Our eyes are opened, that we see clearly; our ears are unstopped, that we have been able to hear distinctly the words you have spoken.... You requested us to speak our minds freeely. This gives us great joy.... Brother, you say you want an answer to your talk before you leave this place. It is right that you should have one; as you are a great distance from home and we do not wish to detain you. But we will first look back a little, and tell you what our fathers have told us, and what we have heard from the white people.

This proemium is followed by a narration recounting the gifts of the Great Spirit to the Indians, the arrival of the whites who claimed to have come to America for religious freedom, and the Indians' hospitable treatment of the first settlers, but the passage ends with a sting that warns of what is to come: "We took pity on them; granted their request; and they sat down amongst us. We gave them corn and meat: they gave us poison [i.e., liquor] in return."

More settlers came, more land was demanded. "Our eyes were opened, and our minds became uneasy. Wars took place. Indians were hired to fight against Indians, and many of our people were destroyed. They also brought strong liquor amongst us. It was strong and powerful, and has slain thousands." The orator then sums up the situation and turns to the question of the moment: "You have now become a great people, and we have scarcely a place left to spread our blankets. You have got our country, but you are not satisfied; you want to force your religion upon us."

Red Jacket then enumerated a series of reasons why the missionary's demands should be rejected, utilizing some of the topos of separate creation developed by the nativists earlier: "You say that you are right and we are lost. How do we know this to be true?" If the Christian Bible was intended for the Indians, why did the Great Spirit not give that knowledge to the Indians? How can they trust those who have so often deceived them? If there is only one true religion, why are the whites divided into so many conflicting religious sects? "Why not all agreed, as you can all read the book?" The Indians' religion teaches them to love one another and be united. Since there are so many differences in race and customs between the whites and the Indians, why not conclude that the Great Spirit has given them different religions also? The missionary has claimed he does not seek land or money, but Red Jacket has seen collections of money taken at Christian meetings. "Perhaps you may want some from us."

The epilogue politely holds out some slender hope of future reconsideration, which, considering Indian experience as described, can best be read as irony:

> Brother, we are told that you have been preaching to the white people in this place. These people are our neighbors. We are acquainted with them. We will wait a little while, and see what effect your preaching has upon them. If we find it does them good, makes them honest and less disposed to cheat Indians, we will then consider again of what you have said. Brother, you have now heard our answer to your talk, and this is all we have to say at present. As we are going to part, we will come and take you by the hand, and hope the Great Spirit will protect you on your journey, and return you safe to your friends.

Cram refused to shake hands, "there being no fellowship between the religion of God and the devil." With traditional Indian politeness and dignity and forceful logic, Red Jacket had revealed the hypocrisy and bigotry of the missionary endeavor. Although Christian evangelism and religious bigotry were flourishing in nineteenth-century America, at the time of publication of this speech, more than thirty years after his death, Red Jacket's position would have sounded a sympathetic chord with readers familiar with the writings of Thoreau, Emerson, and other liberal thinkers.

Other Famous Indian Orators

Other famous Indian orators of the nineteenth century to whom published speeches are attributed include:

> Pontiac, a chief of the Ottawas (Jones 1965:43–45; Vanderwerth 1971:25–30; Dowd 1992:32–36)
>
> Red Jacket's rival among the Senecas, Cornplanter (Vanderwerth 1971:33–41; Sanders and Peek 1973:259–64)
>
> Joseph Brant the Mohawk, who unlike most Indian leaders read and spoke English fluently (Jones 1965:46–48; Vanderwerth 1971:49–53)
>
> Tecumseh, a Shawnee chief (Jones 1965:83–86; Armstrong 1971:43–47; Vanderwerth 1971:61–68; Velie 1991:148–51; Dowd 1992:passim)
>
> Geronimo, the Apache (Vanderwerth 1971:237–41)
>
> Chief Seattle of the Squamish and Duwamish (Jones 1965:98–100; Armstrong 1971:77–79; Vanderwerth 1971:117–22; Sanders and Peek 1973:282–85; Kaiser 1987)
>
> Chief Joseph of the Nez Percé (Jones 1965:109–11; Armstrong 1971:114–16; Vanderwerth 1971:129–30; Sanders and Peek 1973:295–311)
>
> Joseph's friend, Sitting Bull of the Sioux (Busell 1935; Armstrong 1971:83, 89, 112, 126–28; Vanderwerth 1971:227–34)
>
> and others quoted in Armstrong (1971) and Vanderwerth (1971).

Chief Joseph's final message to the federal commander, scrawled in English on paper at Eagle Creek, Montana, in 1877, has been one of the most famous examples of Indian pathos in defeat. Its effectiveness owes much to its simplicity and emphasis on family ties.

> I am tired of fighting. Our chiefs are killed. Looking Glass is dead. Toohulhulsote is dead. The old men are all dead. It is the young men who say yes or no. He who led the young men is dead. It is cold and we have no blankets. The little children are freezing to death. My people, some of them, have run away to the hills and have no blankets, no food; no one knows where they are—perhaps freezing to death. I want to have time for my children and see how many of them I can find. Maybe I shall find them among the dead. Hear me, my chiefs, I am tired; my heart is sick and sad. From where the sun now stands I will fight no more forever. (Armstrong 1971:115)

Although Indian rhetoric uses many common topics and motifs, individual Indian orators had their own distinctive styles, which white observers sometimes tried to describe by comparison to well-known white orators. The full and impassioned style of Sitting Bull was compared by those who heard him to the "silver-tongued" William Jennings Bryan, while the clear and logical oratory of the other leading orator of the Sioux, Chief Grass, was thought reminiscent of the style of Daniel Webster (Busell 1935).

There have been some Indian women famous for their eloquence. Sacajawewa, who acted as interpreter for Lewis and Clark during their exploration of the Northwest in 1804–6, was a woman with great verbal skills, as was Celsa Apapas, who interpreted in both English and Spanish for the Indians at conferences about landownership in California after the discovery of gold there in 1849. Sarah Winnemucca, a Piute, and Bright Eyes, a Pansa, toured the eastern United States between 1878 and 1884, lecturing in English to white audiences in protest at the resettlement of their tribes. They capitalized on the "noble savage" theme and presented themselves as "Indian maidens" to audiences familiar with Longfellow's recently published *The Song of Hiawatha* (Scholten 1977). There have also been a number of effective modern Indian spokeswomen (Jones 1965:xi, 113–20).

Indian Oratory in the Western United States

The best overall account of public speaking by Indians in the western United States in the nineteenth century is probably the 1968 article on the subject by Theodore Balgooyen. Since this may not be easily available to readers, I summarize here some of the main points. As in many other cultures, including the Greek, there were heralds or criers in Indian villages whose function was to summon people to public meetings. Chiefs had no tenure or immunity from criticism; they were respected for their achievements but anyone could and did speak, and sometimes new leaders emerged who led off a part of the group to form an independent faction. Individual Indians had their own relationship to the supernatural and not infrequently proclaimed divine inspiration as a basis of their authority. Even when speaking before a group, speakers tended to address their remarks to one person in the audience. Boys learned to speak by pretending they were adults in make-believe councils and clubs and describing their imagined experiences in battle in imitation of their elders. Recounting real experiences in battle, thus gaining the attention and good will of the audience, was the most common feature of any Indian speech, even speeches that were not directly concerned with war; thus, speeches at child-naming ceremonies, speeches honoring favorite sons, or ceremonies dedicating new lodges, of which Balgooyen quotes examples (1968:17–18). The speaker devoted most of his time to his own exploits, thus establishing his authority in other contexts. Speakers had to dramatize their exploits and their supernatural visions but at the same time try to project an image of modesty and keep fairly close to a conventional narrative pattern to be believed. The principal chiefs were usually spokesmen for peace, harmony, and the general welfare of the tribe. There were, however, also "war chiefs," individuals famous for bravery who took an aggressive posture against other tribes or whites. One such war chief was Red Cloud, who dedicated himself to keeping the whites out of the hunting grounds of the Black Hills in the 1860s and whose later appearance in New York has been mentioned earlier. When the tribe was on the war path the war chief was in command, gave pep talks to his men, explained his plans, and instructed them how to act. Medicine men were individuals who gained a reputation for being able to cure disease through a knowledge of the supernatural; they also acted as master of ceremonies at traditional rites and were expected to give speeches on certain occasions, for example, to address a war party before it set out and dedicate some implement that would bring special favor to the group. Generally, medicine men had little political influence, but there were occasional exceptions such as "The Gauche" among the Assiniboin who effectively combined the abilities of a medicine man and a war chief. Although age, sex, and experience gave status to Indian speakers as in other traditional cultures, among the Indians very old men were often suspected of being sorcerers; some old men gave speeches that put a hex on personal enemies. They were hated and feared, and medicine men were expected to combat their influence by curing illness and injury.

Descriptions of public address in Indian cultures of the western United States in the nineteenth century often show resemblances to traditional oratory in egalitarian oral cultures in other parts of the world as described in the previous chapter. Oratorical ability was widely respected. Buswell (1935) described the oratory of the Dakota Indians as usually courteous, simple, and clear; it was characterized by short sentences, constant use of the first person singular, and lack of adornment except for imagery from nature. The orators spoke in a smooth, "oily," voice and showed no nervousness. Philipsen (1972) has described Navajo discussions as aimed at consensus and characterized by politeness and endless repetition. Lindsay, who lived among the modern Navajo and understood the language, devoted her 1954 thesis to a study of Navajo public speaking as known from written records of nineteenth century orators and from speakers she had heard. She stresses the fact that traditional Navajo oratory, in both formal and informal meetings, was more a form of self-expression than a deliberate attempt to persuade others to some action or belief (Lindsay 1954:62). Speakers began with themselves and often devoted much of their remarks to explaining who they were and what they had experienced or felt, a feature that she found still characteristic of Navajo public address in the 1950s. Conversely, speeches ended abruptly without any summary or dramatic appeal when the speaker felt he had nothing more to say. In terms of rhetorical invention, the speaker's ethos, developed in the long introductory section, dominated the speeches. There was some use of emotional appeal. The Navajo had separate war chiefs and peace chiefs; the former often played on hatred of other tribes and the crimes of white soldiers against Indians, the latter appealed for pity and justice (64). Explicit logical argument was almost nonexistent except for analogies to the natural world to explain a point, another feature that continued in modern Navajo oratory (68). Speakers usually set out a series of facts about themselves and the issue and left members of the audience to draw their own conclusions.

When southwestern Indians were seeking to influence a white audience, however, their speeches resemble appeals by Indian orators elsewhere. The most famous Apache is probably Geronimo (1829–1909). His speech at a conference with federal authorities in 1886 (Vanderwerth 1971:238–41) asserts that he wished to live peaceably, objects to the treatment he has received, and justifies his actions. In doing so, he uses a striking example of argument from probability:

> To prove to you that I am telling the truth, remember I sent you word that I would come from a place far away to speak to you here, and you see us now. Some have come on horseback and some on foot. If I were thinking bad, or if I had done bad, I would never have come here. If it has been my fault, would I have come so far to talk to you? (Vanderwerth 1971:241).

Oratory was, and to some extent still is, a part of Indian ritual ceremonies, which "attempt to order [the tribe's] spiritual and physical world through the power of the word, whether chanted, spoken, or sung" (Ruoff 1990:19). The Iroquois "Ritual of Condolence" was performed to heal the grief caused in the Six Nations by the death of a member of the council of chiefs. Part of the ceremony was the "Requickening," where an orator delivered a speech to restore the people from the destructive nature of grief (example in Ruoff 1990:23). The *consolatio* genre of Greek and Latin literature is a European counterpart. Among the Pimas and Papagos of southern Arizona, ritual oratory was a part of war, rain, and harvest ceremonies, salt pilgrimages, and curing after war. A considerable body of Piman oratory from the late nineteenth and early twentieth centuries has been preserved in the original language. The speeches are narratives of the actions of a god in the legendary past, without explicit reference to the occasion of their delivery; an orator learned a speech by memorization of the speech of an earlier orator and was able to repeat it almost verbatim (Bahr 1988).

Distinctive Features of Indian Rhetoric

There are some differences between Indian oratory in the area that became the United States and traditional oratory in many other parts of the world. According to Jones (1965:24), North American Indians did not utilize oaths, either in speaking among themselves or in treaties with the whites; they regarded their word as sufficient testimony of their sincerity. This seems to be generally true, though Hoebel (1964:169) mentions exculpatory oaths as practiced among the Cheyenne. Possibly this is an imitation of customs among the whites. Another difference is that none of the Indian speeches I have read cite traditional proverbs as the basis of an argument for doing or believing something. Although a few proverbs have been collected from Indian oral tradition (Lowrie 1932), there was no rich proverbial tradition as is found in parts of Africa or the South Pacific or in the literate cultures of China, the Near East, and Europe. In this respect, the Indians resemble the Australians. Both cultures valued self-reliance, and neither was inclined to appeal to the authority of human individuals of the past, whether as named persons or in the form of anonymous sayings passed down by word of mouth. As among the Chamula Indians of southern Mexico studied by Gossen (1973), certain traditional sayings may have been used colloquially as a form of deliberately ambiguous criticism of individuals who broke taboos or social norms. Folklorists often associate proverbs with riddles, which were also unknown among the Indians.

Both proverbs and riddles function like metaphor and it seems to be generally recognized that North American Indian languages were weak in metaphor in comparison to linguistic traditions in other parts of the world. In a famous article on the Hopi language, Benjamin Whorf (1986:716) described the absence of metaphor in Hopi as "striking," and others have agreed that this applies to American Indian languages in general (Gossen 1973:206). True, descriptions of Indian speeches and oral literature often note the presence of metaphors drawn from nature, and some examples have been cited above, but the range of metaphor is rather limited and individual Indian speakers did not often develop new and original metaphors in their oratory. As I have noted in speaking of metaphor in earlier chapters, it seems likely that what to an English speaker seems a metaphor was to the native mind undifferentiated from literal reality. Similes are common in published nineteenth-century Indian speeches, but these are almost all translations of what was said, often showing signs of editing for publication to a white audience. Simile is not a regular feature of traditional Indian poetry. As in the case of English translations of Australian oral literature, similes in Indian speeches are often the contribution of the translator.

As in traditional cultures elsewhere, religious discourse among Native Americans sometimes required the use of an archaic, formal, or sacred language. The Sioux, for example, had two types of sacred language, one used by medicine men speaking to each other, which was translatable to the uninitiated, the other, untranslatable, was used by an individual medicine man when addressing spirits. One might compare "speaking in tongues" as practiced in some Christian groups. Most terms in these sacred languages were generated—by abbreviation, affixing elements, inversions, reduplication, etc.—out of familiar words that were given hidden meanings (Powers 1986:25–38). Among the Nez Percé, myths are distinguished from other tales by the use of a special vocabulary, which seems archaic but largely consists of loan words from other Indian languages (Aolei 1979:4). Something analogous to the use of dialect in modern fiction is also found in the Nez Percé tales: Fox speaks clearly and distinctly; Bear slurs his consonants; Skunk speaks with a nasal twang (Aolei 1979:5). For other features of special language in Indian discourse see Ruoff (1990:43).

Memory, the fifth canon of rhetoric, has not much entered into my discussions to this point. Ever since the time of Plato's *Phaedrus* the complaint has been made that the use of writing tends to undermine memory. A retentive memory of the wording of extensive oral texts is characteristic of high-status individuals in traditional cultures, the Brahmins in India, for example. Recomposition in performance on the basis of formulas and themes, best known from Serbo-Croatian epic poetry in modern times and regarded as the basis of composition of the Homeric poems in Greek, has been practiced by nonliterate bards in central Asia and Africa, but ritual literature has often been memorized; performances may be in longer or shorter versions or otherwise altered. Some American cultures exploited visual mnemonic devices. Indian tribes used wampum belts for this purpose. Strings of beads, like the background images in classical mnemonic theory, reminded the speaker of topics and the order in which they should be discussed; on one occasion in the eighteenth century the Indians postponed a treaty conference because they did not have the wampum strings and their speeches were in "disorder"(Jones 1965:27; Murray 1991:21, 25, 38). Pictographs were also sometimes used to remind singers of the contents of ceremonial songs (Ruoff 1990:29). Among the most detailed Indian pictographs are those that shamans of the southern Ojibway wrote on birchbark scrolls, creating mnemonic devices to assist initiates in learning sacred lore (Dewdney 1975). In the more complex cultures of Mexico and Peru there was further development from mnemonic devices in the direction of written scripts. The knotted cords called "quipus" used by the Incas carried a mnemonic technique almost to the stage of writing (Brotherston 1992:77–81), and Mayan hieroglyphs were capable of phonetic transcription.

The Rhetoric of Indian Poetry

As discussed in the last chapter, traditional myth and legend is often transmitted in poetic form. Surprisingly, the poetic form of some Native American oral literature has only recently been recognized. For long, traditional texts were regarded and printed as prose in scholarly reports. Recent studies by Dell Hymes and others reveal a complex poetics that adds some aesthetic merit to composition. This is part of the project known as the "ethnology of communication," developed in recent years by Hymes and his students; there is a thoughtful review of research on the subject by Leeds-Hurwitz (1990) (see also the discussion of ethnographic studies by Philipsen and others, 1991). Hymes himself has worked on Chinook texts (1981) and has also published (1987) a text, translation, and linguistic analysis of the narrative of "Coyote and Eagle's Daughter" as transmitted in Tonkawa, a now-extinct Indian language of Texas, using typographical format to indicate the form of the verse. He includes a section (49–52) on "rhetorical coherence," by which he really means poetic structure, for he does not make any use of rhetorical terminology. The narrative makes no apparent use of metaphor or simile or rhetorical figures other than anaphora (a common device in oral composition everywhere). Cultural symbolism is certainly present in the actions attributed to the characters: When the roguish folk hero Coyote belittles his wife and boasts she will give him water—an indication that she acknowledges him as her husband—she refuses to do so (Hymes 1987:53–54). Both Coyote, who prefers gambling to women, and the unnamed wife can be viewed as cultural types. No overall conclusion or moral is made explicit. No reasons are given for actions by the characters; these have to be induced by the audience. A supporting reason for a statement by one of the characters is sometimes added, creating what I have called enthymeme by juxtaposition. For example, Coyote four times repeats the statement "Quick!" (or "Hurry!") "This camp is on fire," the first three times to no effect, the fourth successfully. A feature of the narrative is its constant repetition of "it is said," asserting its validity in the oral tradition. Except for this usage, the rhetoric of the poetic myths of Indian cultures in Oregon and Alaska as described by Virginia Hymes and by Anthony Woodbury in the same volume of studies seems quite similar (Sherzer and Woodbury 1987:62–102, 176–239) and is relatively undeveloped in comparison with what can be found in oral cultures elsewhere. The Indian myths described by Dell and Virginia Hymes are told informally in colloquial language. Except for their poetic form, they do not show the characteristics of formal language as discussed in the last chapter.

Features of traditional Indian rhetoric, often in connection with native religion, continue to be employed by Native Americans in their contemporary fiction, memoirs, and poetry. Analysis of these usages is beyond the scope of my book, but John Lame Deer's memoirs, *Lame Deer, Seeker of Visions*, provides some particularly good examples, especially the section entitled "Talking to the Owls and Butteflies," in which he argues in favor of the Indian's understanding of nature and against the values of white society (Lame Deer 1972; Velie 1991:188–95).

Aztec Rhetoric

The most sophisticated rhetorical forms developed by Native Americans are to be found in the records of oratory as practiced in Mexico at the time of the arrival of Spaniards in the sixteenth century. Although a writing system was in use among the Aztecs, it had severe limitations: The pictographs represented actions, facts, ideas, or concepts, not specific words, and were not used for recording speeches. For knowledge of these we are indebted to transcriptions by Spanish missionaries who learned native languages. The most important was Bernardino de Sahagún (c. 1499–1590), a Franciscan friar who arrived in Mexico in 1529, learned Nahuatl, the language of the Aztecs, and taught natives at the College of the Holy Cross in Tlatelolco. Between 1547 and 1562 Sahagún compiled a vast encyclopedia of Aztec society known in English as *General History of the Things of New Spain*. The original version was in Nahuatl, but later in life Sahagún translated the work into Spanish. A manuscript in Florence, Italy, first published in 1929–30, is the major authority for both the Nahuatl and Spanish text; the standard English translation is that of Anderson and Dibble (1950–82). Sahagún describes his methods and objectives in the prologue to book two; he claims here that he regarded the native culture as a creation of the devil and that he was seeking to provide an understanding of the language, religion, and customs of the natives in enough detail to alert Catholic leaders to any heretical ideas that might creep into native understanding of Christianity (Edmonson 1974). This was perhaps in part an apology to the Church for his fascination with the native culture and admiration for many of its features, including its oratory.

With the help of a native informant, Sahagún transcribed some eighty-nine orations known as *huehuetlatolli*, or "speeches of the elders," regularly practiced by educated natives; others are quoted in writings by Andres de Olmos and other missionaries (Sullivan 1974; Blythin 1990:15–26; Abbott 1996:24–40). The speeches reveal the great importance of formal speech in Aztec culture, both in public and in private life. At some time in the past there had apparently been a creative period in oratory in which new speeches were composed; by the sixteenth century, examples of each form had been canonized and were memorized for verbatim delivery on appropriate occasions, though the traditional style was apparently sometimes adapted to new situations. As noted earlier, the Pimas in Arizona also had a tradition of memorized oratory, but Aztec speeches are far more sophisticated. This doubtless reflects the more complex level of their civilization, which included a system of schools for training the priestly and warrior classes, something not found elsewhere in North America; memorization of speeches, but apparently not original composition, was a part of the curriculum. Sahagún says (Anderson and Dibble III:64) that the boys "were thoroughly instructed in good speech [and] he who did not speak well, who did not greet people properly, they pricked [with maguey thorns]." In the prologue to book six, which is entitled "Rhetoric and Moral Philosophy," he says that "wise, superior, and effective rhetoricians were held in high regard. And they elected these to be high priests, lords, leaders, and captains, no matter how humble their estate." There is no reason to doubt that the speeches he records constitute a genuine, traditional body of oratory that was an important vehicle of religious and ethical thought. That does not mean, of course, that the speeches were always given on the prescribed occasions and exactly in the form Sahagún recorded. In particular, the many speeches for family occasions, some quite long and complex, may well represent a cultural model of what ideally should be said rather than evidence for what was actually said in Aztec homes.

Aztec *huehuetlatolli* clearly fall under the category of "formal language" used on ceremonial occasions, as discussed in the last chapter. They are distinguished from ordinary discourse by the dignity of the composition and formulaic phrases; probably there were also special conventions of voice and gesture in delivery. They also clearly fall within the category of epideictic oratory as understood in the West, for their major function is to exhort and admonish an addressee to act in a way deemed appropriate in the culture in certain standard situations. They are somewhat comparable to the epideictic forms taught in Greek rhetorical schools of the Roman period, used in political and social settings, and described in the handbooks of Menander Rhetor. Two sophisticated cultures, Greek and Aztec, in a relatively late period of development canonized comparable models of polite discourse. An important difference, however, between the Greek and Aztec forms is that Greeks learned rhetorical techniques from written texts and practiced its application in original speeches adapted to specific occasions, whereas the Aztecs learned the proper modes of speaking from an oral tradition and, to judge from Sahagún's account, delivered the same speeches verbatim on each prescribed occasion; however, the speech attributed to Moctezuma, quoted below, shows that the *huehuetlatolli* style could be employed in speeches for which the tradition provided no specific model. As in most other traditional cultures, formal oratory was a conservative force, preserving the moral and political values of the past and reinforcing class distinctions. As León-Patilla (1985:40) observes, "In many of the *huehuetlatolli* we find attempts to inculcate in the people that it is the destiny of the nobles to keep and transmit the ancient wisdom, to carry the people on their shoulders, and to feed the gods with the blood of captives seized in the sacred war. Such ideas confirm not only that these discourses were the speeches of nobles but also that among their aims was the reinforcement of the status of the ruling group." The tone of Aztec epideictic differs greatly from that of Greek, reflecting differences between the two cultures: Aztec speeches are often very critical of the addressee, whereas Greek epideictic is more often given to flattery; Aztec oratory is harsh, austere, and fatalistic, whereas Greek is frequently playful and humane.

The addresses transcribed by Sahagún in book six include prayers to the gods, speeches given by and to a king at the time of his election, speeches of parents to children, and speeches given on the occasion of a pregnancy, birth, the entry of a child into school, and death; in book nine is a series of speeches to a merchant on departure and return from a trading expedition.

The speeches by and to the king at his installation (Anderson and Dibble VII:41–85) make up a ritual sequence of unusual rhetorical interest. As noted in the last chapter, a traditional orator in an oral society characteristically begins in a quiet and modest way, though as in the case of some American Indian speeches described earlier this may be followed by an account of the speaker's deeds that is anything but modest. It is also conventional in many cultures for a person chosen for some honor to protest somewhat or seek exemption from a duty on the ground that others are more qualified. This has largely disappeared from Western political life but still exists in some religious and social contexts where it is deemed inappropriate to seem ambitious, however much the honor is sought. The rhetorical technique of protesting selection was carried to an extreme in the Aztec ritual of a newly chosen king. In his first speech the new king utterly debases himself as "filth" and "excrement" and totally unqualified for the position to which the god has called him. Perhaps a mistake has been made? Perhaps he is dreaming? What is he to do? Gradually, however, he begins to show some acceptance of the situation: "Howsoever thou wilt require of me, that I shall do, that I shall perform. Whichsoever road thou wilt show me, that one I shall follow; whatsoever thou wilt reveal unto me, that I shall say, that I shall pronounce" (Anderson and Dibble VII:44).

The king's speech is followed by an address delivered by a priest or other dignitary that accepts the god's decision on behalf of the people and exhorts the king to his difficult task. Shagún comments, "These words are very admirable and the metaphors are very difficult" (Ibid. 47). The speech begins as follows:

> O master, O ruler, O precious person, O precious one, O valued one, O precious green stone, O precious torquoise, O bracelet, O precious feather, thou art here present; the lord of the near, of the nigh, he by whom we live, hath set thee here. Now, in truth, thy progenitors, thy great-grandfathers, have departed, have gone to rest. Our lord hath destroyed, hath hidden those who already have gone to remain beyond.... For they departed placing, they departed leaving the bundle, the carrying frame, the governed—heavy, intolerable, insupportable. (Ibid.).

This is the characteristic style of *huehuetlatolli*: constant amplification with synonyms, often metaphorical, and redundancy of formulaic expression. Emphasis is put on the great burden of the office. A dire fatalism runs throughout the speech, repeating some of the language the king had used earlier:

> Perhaps thou canst for a time support the governed. And perhaps also for a time, for a day, the city will dream—will see in dreams—that perhaps it will borrow thee. Do not reflect upon thyself; our lord knoweth, seeth, heareth the things within the rocks, within the wood. He will know thy secrets. Soon he will dispose something upon thee, for, in truth, he acteth of his own volition; he mocketh. Thou wilt become as smut, and he will send thee into the vegetation, into the forest. And he will cast thee, push thee, as is said, into the excrement, into the refuse. And also something evil, filthy, will come upon thee. And also some filth, vice, contention, discord will develop, will move upon thee. (Ibid. 49)

The predominant means of persuasion in Aztec oratory is ethical and pathetical. Speakers usually proclaim a thought authoritatively and provide no supporting reasons. This passage, however, shows some incipient logical argument: The king should not reflect upon himself (because) the lord knows all things; the god will cause something to happen for (the word in Nahuatl is *ca*) he does what he pleases and mocks everyone. Some interesting examples of argument also occur in the prayers preserved by Sahagún when the speaker suggests reasons why the god should alleviate suffering: "a certain pattern of interplay between man and diety emerges in these supplications, with the burden placed on the god" (Sullivan 1974:86).

The speaker continues with advice to the king: "Cause no one to weep, cause no one sadness, cause no one to cry out. Injure no one. Do not manifest thy fury, thy anger; do not address anyone in fury; do not frighten, do not scandalize. Again, do not speak in vanity, in ridicule; [do not] ridicule; for vain words, mockery are no longer thy office" (*Anderson and* Dibble VII:52). The speech ends with a brief epilogue:

> However, thereby the motherhood, the fatherhood is satisfied, is complied with. And furthermore, in like manner, this is all with which I pray to the master, our lord. He taketh it, he heareth it. I give it to him, I offer it to him in his presence. O master, O our lord, O ruler, perform thy office, do thy work. (Ibid. 54)

A secondary dignitary then speaks briefly. The tone shifts to a more positive view of the future as the speaker expresses the people's joy at the king's accession. Sahagún, in an introductory comment, says that the speaker wishes the king a long life, certainly a common topos in addresses to kings in other cultures, but what the Aztec orator actually dwells on (Ibid. 58) is the possibility of an early death and apotheosis.

The fourth speech in the ritual is the ruler's brief reply to the previous speakers. He still protests that there is some mistake, that he is unworthy, but he accepts the office: "May I try to be worthy of the word or two thou bringest forth" (Ibid. 61).

The fifth speech envisions the situation in which the chosen king has refused to speak and seeks to abdicate his responsibility. The orator prays to the god for help and exhorts the people not to lose faith.

The sixth speech is the longest. At this point the king still insists on his unworthiness but has accepted his office, and he now uses his new authority to admonish the people to live more virtuous lives, in particular to avoid drunkenness, thievery, and adultery, and to serve the gods.

Finally, two dignitaries of state praise the king and support the advice he has given. The ritual of installation has thus completed its movement from the trauma of change in ruler through an emotional catharsis of the city in the person of the new king, to the establishment of orderly government and the restoration of ordinary life.

From the examples cited, the style of traditional Aztec oratory should be evident. It is an extreme version of "formal" or "sacred" language found elsewhere as discussed in the last chapter, characterized by repetition and metaphor. Andrés de Olmos made lists of the metaphors in speeches he heard (Maxwell and

Hansen 1992). The use of this language imparts authority. The ritual for the new king and some other *huehuetlotolli* make great use of metaphor, but that seems an aspect of the religious nature of the occasion. If one turns to the speeches to merchants where the situation is entirely secular, the same redundancy of expression is found but there is little or no metaphor. Here is part of a speech in which the senior merchant of a city gives advice to a younger merchant who is about to set out (what in classical rhetoric is called a *propemptikon*):

> It is well that thou art here. For we have accepted, taken, and heard thy discourse. Be careful in taking to travel, for already thou wilt meet One Serpent, the straight way. Thou mayest somewhere set foot on the rocky way, the mountain trail, with the gods of the road. Travel with care in the plain, in the desert, lest our lord, the protector of all, the master of the heavens, of the earth, will somewhere destroy thee.... But if the master, our lord, indeed should nowhere destroy, slay thee, endure the unseasoned, the saltless, the briny [food]; the dried tortillas, the coarse pinole, the wretched, soggy maize. And likewise nowhere cast slander, aspersions at one; make thyself reverent, respectful, to others. If thereby the protector of all should entrust thee something of his riches, his wealth, do not let thyself be arrogant....
> (Anderson and Dibble X: 13)

The primary means of persuasion is the authority of the speaker, who is regularly an older individual of high status, wise in the ways of the culture. As in the passage quoted above, an emotional element is often present. Rhetorical questions are common and give some vigor to the speech. There is little use of logical argument. Advice by a father to a son contains some remarks about appropriate speech that is consistent with values in traditional cultures described in the previous chapter and resembles what we shall find in Egypt and China:

> Thou are to speak very slowly, very deliberately; thou art not to speak hurriedly, not to pant, not to squeak, lest it be said of thee that thou art a groaner, a growler, a squeaker. Also thou art not to cry out, lest thou be known as an imbecile, a shameless one, a rustic, very much a rustic. Moderately, middlingly art thou to carry, to emit thy spirit, thy words. And thou art to improve, to soften thy words, thy voice. (Anderson and Dibble VII:122)

In book twelve of the *General History* occurs the one example of a speech attributed to a named individual on a specific occasion: Moctezuma's address of greeting to Cortés on the latter's first entry into what is now Mexico City, November 8, 1519. Moctezuma—known also as Montezuma—was an intelligent and educated man; in the earlier part of his reign he had been a successful military leader but he became arrogant and oppressive in later years. Much of the success of Cortés in overthowing the empire of Mexico with a small band of Spanish soldiers of fortune was due to the willingness of native states subject to the Aztecs to cooperate with the Spaniards against their oppressors.

Moctezuma long refused to meet with Cortés; he was eventually forced to do so when the Spaniards arrived at his capital. By this time Moctezuma was thoroughly frightened and demoralized, partly by the success of the Spaniards, more perhaps by prophecies and omens of disaster awaiting him. The most important of the prophecies was probably the tradition that the white-faced god Quetzalcoatl, who had appeared in the distant past and was regarded as the ancestor of the Aztec noble class, would reappear and claim his rights, a millenial topos. The sudden arrival of the comparatively light-skinned Spaniards bringing with them the advantages of steel, cannons, and horses, all unknown to the Aztecs, seemed to fulfill this prophecy. Sahagún quotes the speech in Nahuatl and does not identify his source; if the speech is genuine, perhaps it was transmitted by an oral tradition from Merina, the remarkable Mexican woman who learned Spanish and acted as translator for Cortés during his expedition. There seems to me at least the possibility that the speech was created after the fact as a piece of Spanish propaganda and taught to the natives to aid in their acceptance of Spanish rule. Sahagún may not have realized this. The speech is in the formal style of *huehuetlatolli* but with the content adapted to the occasion. There is constant repetition, a rhetorical question, and use of formulaic phrases. Moctezuma's greeting according to Sahagún was as follows:

> O our lord, thou hast suffered fatigue, thou hast endured weariness. Thou hast come to arrive on earth. Thou hast come to govern thy city of Mexico; thou hast come to descend upon my mat, upon my seat, which for a moment I have watched for thee, which I have guarded for thee. For the governors are departed—the rulers Itzcoatl, Moctezuma the Elder, Axayacatl, Tizoc, Auitzotl, who yet a very short time ago had come to stand guard for thee, who had come to govern the city of Mexico. Under their protection thy common folk came. Do they yet perchance know it in their absence? O that one of them might witness, might marvel at what to me now hath befallen, at what I see quite in the absence of our lords. I by no means merely dream, I do not merely see in a dream, I do not see in my sleep; I do not merely dream that I see thee, that I look into thy face. I have been afflicted for some time. I have gazed at the unknown place whence thou has come—from among the clouds, from among the mists. And so this. The rulers departed maintaining that thou wouldst come to visit thy city, that thou wouldst come to descend upon thy mat, upon thy seat. And now it hath been fulfilled; thou hast come; thou hast endured fatigue, thou hast endured weariness. Peace be with thee. Rest thyself. Visit thy palace. Rest thy body. May peace be with our lords. (Anderson and Dibble XIII:44)

Aztec ideas of courtesy, like those of other traditional cultures, required politeness in addressing visitors, even potentially hostile visitors, but it is difficult to imagine an Indian chief in what became the United States humiliating himself in public in this way. That it was possible in Aztec culture is, however, clear from the first speech of a new king discussed earlier.

There are other sources in native languages and Spanish that can be used for a more detailed study of traditional Mexican rhetoric as practiced in the sixteenth and seventeenth centuries (for a survey see Edmonson 1985). For example, *The*

Chronicles of Michoacán, written in Spanish about 1540 and attributed to Fr. Martín de Jesús de la Coruña, give an account of the society and history of the Tarascans, who lived west of the Aztecs and reached to the Pacific coast (translation by Craine and Reindorp 1970). The work contains short speeches attributed to named individuals and summaries of debates that illustrate rhetorical praxis of the time. *The Bancroft Dialogues* (translation by Kartturen and Lockhart 1987) consist of models for polite conversation in colloquial Nahuatl. They were composed in the mid-seventeenth century to instruct Jesuits in the language and its social uses. The contents are somewhat analogous to Western medieval models of letter writing (the *dictamen*), which also stress formal courtesy in address.

Don Abbott (1989) has identified three phases in the history of rhetoric in Mexico. The first, which is the one most relevant to my discussion, is that in which Sahagún and others observed and appreciated native eloquence. By the mid-sixteenth century the Spanish had begun to teach some features of European rhetoric to Christianized natives so that they in turn would apply it in preaching. The third phase began with the founding of the University of Mexico in 1553 and continued through the colonial period; it consisted in the academic study of the liberal arts, including the classical tradition in rhetoric, as taught in Europe, without consideration for native traditions. Although the early Spanish missionaries, especially Diego Valadés, recognized the need to adapt Western rhetorical practice to the understanding of the native population throughout Spanish America, their successors abandonned this experiment in cross-cultural communication in favor of a dogmatic, and often unsuccessful, imposition of European rhetorical theory (Abbott 1996:112–17).

I cannot close these comments on Mexican rhetoric without some mention of what is to me one of the greatest works of nineteenth-century American literature and scholarship, but one that seems rarely read by students today: *The Conquest of Mexico* by William H. Prescott, first published in 1844. Why I happened to look into it many years ago I do not recall, but I remember vividly the excitement with which I followed Prescott's eloquent, dramatic, and, as he acknowledges, romantic account of the world of the Aztecs and the expedition of Cortés. I mention Prescott's work here because it can be read as a study in comparative rhetoric, that of the Spanish invaders and that of the Mexican natives as they negotiated and fought with each other. Prescott was still working in the grand tradition of narrative historiography derived from Herodotus, Thucydides, Livy, and Tacitus; he did not hesitate to attribute thoughts and words to his characters as the dramatic situation seemed to require. He knew and used Sahagún's *General History*, but his description in chapter 9 of the meeting of Moctezuma and Cortés is drawn from other sources, which he documents, and is much more sympathetic to the Mexican emperor. Prescott describes how Moctezuma—or Montezuma as he calls him—hung a gorgeous collar around the conqueror's neck, saying: " 'This palace belongs to you, Malinche,' (the epithet by which he always addressed him) 'and to your brethern. Rest after your fatigues, for you have much need to do so, and in a little while I will visit you again.' So saying, he withdrew with his attendants, evincing, in this act, a delicate consideration not to have been expected in a barbarian."

Conclusion

Generalization about traditional North American Indian rhetoric is difficult because much of the evidence comes from white sources or from speeches intended to influence whites and because of differences among Indian cultures. Except in Mexico, Indian societies were usually egalitarian; any man and sometimes women could speak in their assemblies, where the object of deliberation was consensus. Judicial rhetoric seems not to have been developed. Epideictic forms were practiced when war parties were sent out, at funerals, and on some ritual occasions, and myths, story telling, and songs, as elsewhere, transmitted cultural values. "Formal language" was employed by medicine men and in religious rites, but was not a distinguishing feature of other public address except in Mexico.

As in nonliterate societies elsewhere, effective oratory depended heavily on the ethos of the speaker and was often polite, restrained, and dignified. Although Indian discourse made use of traditional analogies from nature and everyday life, neither oratory (except again in Mexico) nor oral literature was strikingly metaphorical, nor did Indians traditionally use proverbs or oaths as a basis of argument. Wampum and pictographs were sometimes used as mnemonic devices by speakers.

White settlement of the United States created a crisis for the Indians who responded by seeking unity among themselves and creating new topoi relating to a "separate creation" from the whites and millenial hopes. Some Indian orators claimed inspiration by the Great Spirit and became famous as prophets.

Some Indians of the southwestern United States have had a traditional form of epideictic that was memorized and redelivered over several generations. Aztec society developed memorized epideictic genres, in "formal language," to a remarkable degree, and in general constitutes a special case in the study of Indian rhetoric. Aztec epideictic was repetitive, highly metaphorical, and emotional.

Rhetoric among the Indians, as in other traditional societies, was largely a conservative, defensive force in transmitting and preserving the independence, way of life, and values of the cultures.

References

Abbott, Don P. (1987). "The Ancient Word: Rhetoric in Aztec Culture," *Rhetorica* 5:251–64.

———(1989). "Aztecs and Orators: Rhetoric in New Spain," *Texte: Revue de Critique et de Théorie Litteraire* 8/9:353–65.

————(1996). *Rhetoric in the New World: Rhetorical Theory and Practice in Colonial Spanish America*. Columbia: University of South Carolina Press.

Anderson, Arthur J. O., and Charles E. Dibble, eds. (1950–82). *Florentine Codex: General History of the Things of New Spain*, by Fray Bernardino de Sahagún. Thirteen parts. Santa Fe: School of American Research and University of Utah Press.

Aolei, Haruo, ed. (1979). *Nez Percé Texts*. University of California Publications in Linguistics 90. Berkeley: University of California Press.

Armstrong, Virginia I., ed. (1971). *I Have Spoken: American History Through the Voices of the Indians*. Chicago: Swallow Press.

Bahr, Donald M. (1988). *Pima and Papago Ritual Oratory: A Study of Three Texts*. San Francisco: Indian Historical Press.

Balgooyen, Theodore (1968). "The Plains Indian as a Public Speaker," in *Landmarks in Western Oratory*, ed. by David H. Grover. University of Wyoming Publications 34, 2:13–43.

Blythin, Evan (1990). *Huei Tlatoani: The Mexican Speaker*. Lanham, MD: University Press of America.

Boyd, Julia P., ed. (1938). *Indian Treatises Printed by Benjamin Franklin 1736–1762*. Philadelphia: Historical Society of Pennsylvania.

Brotherston, Gordon (1992). *Book of the Fourth World: Reading the Native Americans Through Their Literature*. Cambridge, England: Cambridge University Press.

Busell, Lois E. (1935). "The Oratory of the Dakota Indians," *Quarterly Journal of Speech* 21:323–27.

Camp, Charles (1978). "American Indian Oratory in the White Image: An Analysis of Stereotypes," *Journal of American Culture* 1:811–17.

Craine, Eugene R., and Reginald C. Reindorp, trans. and eds.(1970). *The Chronicles of Michoacán*. Norman: University of Oklahoma Press.

Dewdney, Selwyn (1975). *Sacred Scrolls of the Southern Ojibway*. Toronto: University of Toronto Press.

Dowd, Gregory Evans (1992). *A Spirited Resistance: The North American Indian Struggle for Unity, 1745–1815*. Baltimore: Johns Hopkins University Press.

Edmonson, Munro, ed. (1974). *Sixteenth Century Mexico*. Albuquerque: University of New Mexico Press.

————, ed. (1985). *Supplement to the Handbook of Middle American Indians*, Vol. III: *Literature*. Austin: University of Texas Press.

Ek, Richard A. (1966). "Red Cloud's Cooper Union Address," *Central States Speech Journal* 16:252–62.

Gossen, Gary H. (1973). "Chamula Tzotzil Proverbs: Neither Fish Nor Fowl," in *Meaning in Mayan Languages: Ethnolinguistic Studies*, ed. by Munro S. Edmonson, pp. 205–33. The Hague: Mouton.

Hoebel, E. Adamson (1964). *The Law of Primitive Man: A Study in Comparative Legal Dynamics*. Cambridge, MA: Harvard University Press.

Hubbard, J. Niles (1886). *An Account of Sa-Go-Ye-Wat-Ha, or Red Jacket, and His People*. Albany, NY: Munsell; reprinted New York: Burt Franklin 1971.

Hymes, Dell (1981). *"In Vain I Tried to Tell You": Essay in Native American Ethnopoetics*. Philadelphia: University of Pennsylvania Press.

————(1987). "Tonkawa Poetics: John Rush Buffalo's 'Coyote and Eagle's Daughter,' " in *Native American Discourse: Poetics and Rhetoric*, ed. by Joel Sherzer and Anthony C. Woodbury, pp. 17–61. Cambridge, England: Cambridge University Press.

Jefferson, Thomas (1984). "Notes on the State of Virginia," in *Writings*, pp.123–325. The Library of America. New York: Literary Classics of the United States.

Jones, Louis T. (1965). *Aboriginal American Oratory; The Tradition of Eloquence Among the Indians of the United States.* Los Angeles: Southwest Museum.

Kaiser, Rudolf (1987). "Chief Seattle's Speeches: American Origin and European Reception," in *Recovering the Word: Essays in North American Literature*, ed. by Brian Swan and Arnold Krupat, pp. 495–536. Berkeley: University of California Press.

Karttunen, Frances, and James Lockhart, eds. (1987). *The Art of Nahuatl Speech: The Bancroft Dialogues.* Los Angeles: UCLA Latin American Center Publications.

Kroeber, Karl, ed. (1981). *Traditional Literatures of the American Indian: Texts and Interpretations.* Lincoln: University of Nebraska Press.

Lame Deer, John, and Richard Erdoes (1972). *Lame Deer, Seeker of Visions.* New York: Simon and Schuster.

Leeds-Hurwitz, Wendy (1990). "Culture and Communication: A Review Essay," *Quarterly Journal of Speech* 76:85–95.

León-Portilla, Miguel (1985). "Nahuatl Literature," in *Supplement to the Handbook of Middle American Indians*, ed. by Munro S. Edmonson, vol. III, pp. 7–43. Austin: University of Texas Press.

Lindsay, Janet P. (1954). *Navajo Public Speaking.* Master's Thesis, Colorado State University.

Maxwell, Judith M., and Craig A. Hansen (1992). *Of the Manners of Speaking the Old Ones Had: The Metaphors of Andrés de Olmos in the TULAL Manuscript.* Salt Lake City: University of Utah Press.

Morris, Richard, and Philip Wander (1990). "Native American Rhetoric: Dancing in the Shadows of the Ghost Dance," *Quarterly Journal of Speech* 76:164–91.

Murray, David (1991). *Forked Tongues: Speech, Writing and Representation in North American Indian Texts.* Bloomington: Indiana University Press.

O'Donnell, James H., (1979). "Logan's Oration: A Case Study in Ethnographic Authentication," *Quarterly Journal of Speech* 65:150–56.

Osterreich, Shelley Anne (1991). *The American Ghost Dance, 1870 and 1890: An Annotated Bibliography.* New York: Greenwood Press.

Philipsen, Gerry (1972). "Navajo World View and Cultural Patterns in Speech," *Speech Monographs* 39:133–35.

———, ed. (1991). "Writing Ethnographies," *Quarterly Journal of Speech* 77:327–42.

Powers, William K. (1986). *Sacred Language: The Nature of Supernatural Discourse in Lakota.* Norman: University of Oklahoma Press.

Ruoff, A. LaVonne Brown, ed. (1990). *American Indian Literatures: An Introduction, Bibliographic Review, and Selected Bibliography.* New York: Modern Language Association.

Sanders, Thomas E., and Walter W. Peek, eds. (1973). *Literature of the American Indian.* Beverly Hills, CA: Glencoe Press.

Sandefur, Ray H. (1960). "Logan's Oration: How Authentic?" *Quarterly Journal of Speech* 46:289–96.

Scholten, Pat Creech (1977). "Exploitation of Ethos: Sarah Winnemucca and Bright Eyes on the Lecture Tour," *Quarterly Journal of Speech* 41:233–44.

Sherzer, Joel, and Anthony C. Woodbury, eds. (1987). *Native American Discourse: Poetics and Rhetoric.* Cambridge, England: Cambridge University Press.

Sorter, Edna C. (1972). "The Noble Savage," *Ethnohistory* 19:227–36.

Stone, William L. (1886). *The Life and Times of Sa-Go-Ye-Wat-Ha*. Albany, NY: Munsell.

Sullivan, Thelma D. (1974). "The Rhetorical Orations, or *Huehuetlatolli*, Collected by Sahagún," in *Sixteenth Century Mexico*, ed. by Munro S. Edmonson, pp. 79–109. Albuquerque: University of New Mexico Press.

Vanderwerth, W. C., ed. (1971). *Indian Oratory: Famous Speeches by Noted Indian Chieftains*. Norman: University of Oklahoma Press.

Varner, John G., and Jeanette J. Varner, trans. (1951). *The Florida of the Inca*. Austin: University of Texas Press.

Velie, Alan R., ed. (1991). *American Indian Literature: An Anthology*, revised edition. Norman: University of Oklahoma Press.

Whorf, Benjamin L. (1986). "The Relation of Habitual Thought and Behavior to Language," in *Critical Theory Since 1965*, ed. by Hazard Adams and Leroy Searle, pp. 709–23; originally published in *Language, Culture, and Personality: Essays in Memory of Edward Sapir*. Menasha, WI: Sapir Memorial Fund, 1941.

Bibliography

Arias-Larretta, Abraham (1964). *Pre-Columbian Literatures*. State College, MS: published by the author.

Bierhorst, John, ed. (1971). *In the Trail of the Wind: American Indian Poems and Ritual Orations*. New York: Farrar, Strauss, and Giroux.

Holder, Preston, ed. (1966). Franz Boas, "Introduction" to *Handbook of American Indian Languages* and J. W. Powell, *Indian Linguistic Families of American North of Mexico*. Lincoln: University of Nebraska Press.

Merritt, Frank W. (1955). "Teedyuscung—Speaker for the Delawares," *Communication Quarterly* 3:14–18.

Morris, Mabel (1944). "Indian Oratory," *Southern Speech Communication Journal* 10:29–36.

Strickland, William M. (1982). "The Rhetoric of Removal and the Trail of Tears: Cherokee Speaking Against Jackson's Indian Removal Policy, 1828–1832," *Southern Speech Communication Journal* 47:292–309.

Swan, Brian, ed. (1983). *Smoothing the Ground: Essays on Native American Oral Literature*. Berkeley: University of California Press.

Witt, Shirley H., and Stan Steiner, eds. (1972). *The Way: An Anthology of American Indian Literatures*. New York: Alfred Knopf.

Part II

RHETORIC IN ANCIENT LITERATE CULTURES

CHAPTER 6

Literacy and Rhetoric in the Ancient Near East

The first people known to have developed a system of writing were the Sumerians in Mesopotamia some time before 3000 BCE in response to the needs of what was probably the earliest commercial society. In Mesopotamia, as in India and Greece, the predecessor of writing seems to be marks put on objects to identify ownership and "readable" only to the owner. These developed into seals, impressed on clay or wax by rings or cylinders. Writing in this sense was more a form of identification than of communication. In Mesopotamia these were followed by simple pictographs, used as mnemonic devices to record the number of objects received, on hand, payed out, or due to temples, palaces, or merchants. Pictographs were gradually stylized into cuneiform ideographs—wedged-shaped marks on clay tablets—and these then took on phonetic values. During the third millenium writing developed in Mesopotamia to the degree that extensive historical, religious, legal, and literary texts could be written and preserved indefinitely. Many thousands of such tablets have been found in archaeological excavations throughout the Near East; the majority are administrative records and contracts. The Sumerian experiment probably provided the Egyptians with the idea of writing, which appears suddenly soon after the first stages of writing in Mesopotamia (Postgate 1992:56). It may also be the precedent for writing in north India, which had begun by the second millenium.

The invention and development of writing in Mesopotamia seems to have reflected the needs of societies that had moved from the hunter–gatherer way of life of primitive human beings to the cultivation of crops and systematic irrigation of land in what is known as "the Fertile Crescent." Efficient use of land and water required planning and discipline, thus the development of central government, taxation, bureaucracies, and record keeping. Mesopotamian written texts often reflect a rigidity and impersonal quality in a society where everything was recorded and individuals, other than great kings, were only parts of a vast social machine. Professional scribes were trained in schools where the course lasted for several years; something is known about the educational methods and the life of students from surviving tablets, which include classified vocabulary lists and school exercises (Kramer 1981:3–17). Among the exercises practiced in Mesopotamian schools were imaginary disputes between two "speakers," each of whom asserts superiority over the other, often indulging in belittling of the opponent (Kramer 1981:132–40). These early rhetorical exercises in amplification of a topic were written compositions, not oral debates, though perhaps they were read aloud after composition. One of the best examples is a dispute between the tamarisk tree and the date palm as to which gives the greatest benefits to human beings (Pritchard 1975, II:142–45). The "argument," if it can be called that, is simply an assertion of benefits.

Effects of the Invention of Writing in Mesopotamia

The invention of writing was a major technological event that had important results in cultural history, including the history of rhetoric. Writing communicates across time and across distance. A writer can correct and revise a text, creating an authoritative statement that can be read, re-read, and studied by someone else. Laws can be written down and consistently applied. Writing opens up the possibility for scholarship and new opportunities for interpretation. Writing makes a more efficient use of language than does speech; it discourages irrelevancies and encourages grammatical regularity, systematic thought, and analysis of complex ideas. Writing made possible the conceptualization, standardization, and teaching of grammar. Rhetorical structure is more easily observed in writing than in speech. So is style; the artistry of the author can be studied and imitated. Although public speaking was learned in nonliterate societies by imitation of older speakers, with written texts students could also study speeches of the past. Writing and reading had to be learned; they created the need for teachers and schools, and in the Near East created a scribal class. The scribes might reasonably be regarded as the first intellectuals, for they could master a body of texts not available to others and create new texts. In the process, writing created an elitism separate from traditional social hierarchies: the class of writers, readers, and thinkers. Over the millenia this has prompted greater freedom of thought. Writing also created personal authorship; writers began to identify themselves in contrast to the impersonality of oral transmission. Written words are a physical object, seen on the page. They give substance to abstract ideas. History can be recorded and continue to live; scientific phenomena can be recorded, categorized, studied, and predicted. Writing probably contributed to the development of logical reasoning and explanations of causes and results (Goody 1987:74–77). Technical manuals, including treatises on rhetoric, could be created; eventually metarhetoric came into being.

Written texts were a new category of "formal language" as discussed in chapter 4. Writing was a *code* in which there were conventions of word choice, spelling, grammar, structure, and style. A writer was expected to observe these conventions *consistently* within the context of the composition. A writer of a literary, scholarly, legal, or scientific text spoke with *positional authority* and provided a *focus* on a central issue. As literacy has become more common over the millenia, writing has often become more informal, but it remains a code that cannot be entirely discarded without inviting incoherence, and students continue to be taught how to write, as they are taught how to speak, a "standard" form of language. The formal nature of Sumerian cuneiform is especially seen in the second millenium and later when Sumerian had ceased to be a spoken language and was replaced by Akkadian; but Sumerian continued to be studied, taught, and used for special purposes, much as Latin was in the western Middle Ages. Other features of formal language in Mesopotamia are analogous to those found elsewhere; they include parallelisms (Segert 1984), archaisms and obscurities in ritual, poetic forms in praises, laments, and epic literature, and the elaboration of formulas of respect in addressing gods and humans of high rank. Some examples will be noted later in this chapter.

Some of the potentials of writing were realized in ancient Mesopotamia; others have taken thousands of years to develop. A factor that inhibited understanding of causation in Mesopotamia was the universal belief that human events were determined by the gods and were often arbitrary and inexplicable. A dialectic of written signs emerged in place of oral amplification: Jean Bottéro (1992:87–102) has shown how the polyphony of cuneiform writing, in which ideograms may represent a variety of signifieds, further enhanced by the use of Sumerian script to write Akkadian, created a kind of hermeneutics in which multiple ideas could be induced in theological texts from the written symbols of a divine name. Writing sometimes imposed new restraints on society. The publication of law codes—that of Hammurapi (c. 1792–1750 BCE) is the most famous, though not the earliest—probably encouraged reliance on the letter of the law at the expense of discussion of its intent or wider considerations of justice in the courts. Hammurapi's Code (Pritchard 1958:138–70) is an instance of formulary law: Its provisions are largely cast in the form "if such and such has happened, then such and such a judgment shall be given." The function of the court seems limited to determining the facts.

The extensive records of the culture of the Sumerians and their Semitic successors in the Near East have been studied as literature and as a source for knowledge of politics, social and religious practices, and history. Good translations exist of major works. Except for an article by John Wills (1970), which provides a useful introduction, the material has been little studied from the point of view of rhetoric. The Mesopotamian cultures seem consistently to privilege writing over speech; doubtless oral traditions lie behind their myths and legends, but writing incorporated and erased them. While other cultures, even after attaining literacy, have honored oral skills, eloquence, and the figure of the orator, Mesopotamian literature, so far as I have found, never did so. The scribes triumphed over the speakers. Even the gods wrote letters (Grayson 1984), something unknown in other cultures. There is a considerable body of proverbs, fables, and wisdom literature (Gordon 1968; Kramer 1981:116–31) in which one might expect to find some reference to effective speech, as in the biblical book of Proverbs to be discussed later. What is found, and this can be paralleled elsewhere though often accompanied by its opposites, are warnings against unnecessary or thoughtless speech:

> Let your mouth be restrained and your speech guarded; that is a man's pride. Let what you say be very precious. Let insolence and blasphemy be an abomination for you. Speak nothing profane nor any unjust report. A talebearer is looked down upon. Do not set out to stand around the assembly. Do not loiter where there is a dispute, for in the dispute they will have you as an observer; then you will be made a witness for them, and they will involve you in a lawsuit to affirm something that does not concern you. In case of a dispute, get away from it, disregard it. If a dispute involving you should flare up, calm it down. (Adapted from Pritchard 1975, II:145–46).

Mesopotamian poetry, like poetry in most cultures, is highly metaphorical, but the Sumerian word *gim*, "like," is used to create similes (Kramer 1969), which seems to reflect a rationalism of differentiating what can be identified with something else from what is in some way like something else. It is possible that this is a result of the greater self-consciousness of written composition. How simile came to be distinguished from metaphor is, however, a difficult question, on which I have found no good discussion. I noted in chapter 3 that simile does not occur in aboriginal Australian poetry and in the next chapter I shall note that it is not a feature of the earliest Chinese poetry. On the other hand, it is found in early Indian and early Greek poetry, both products of an oral tradition that were eventually written down. In Sumerian and Indian poetry similes are generally short—e.g., "like a lion"—and only in Greek are found the long similes that became a traditional feature of Western epic. I shall return to this subject in later chapters.

Public Address in Mesopotamia

Opportunities for public address existed in early Mesopotamia (Wills 1970). Sumerian society in its prehistoric and preliterate state seems to have resembled others throughout the world where older, experienced, or wealthier individuals function as a deliberative and judicial council while the adult male population as a whole makes or confirms major decisions such as the appointment of a war lord and declaration of war. As urbanization developed, individual Sumerian leaders made themselves into powerful kings, first in their own states, then in larger areas; the political history of Mesopotamia is a movement from participatory polity to autocracy. Efficiency suppresses liberty. At the beginning of the historical period individual Sumerian cities had a council of elders (not necessarily old men, but heads of families and wealthy merchants) and an assembly of male citizens that made major political and military decisions (Jacobsen 1943; Evans 1958; Postgate 1992:80–81). This system was projected onto the divine realm— the Sumerians would probably have said copied from it—where the gods in epic poems are described in council and assembly, debating issues before implementing important actions, such as sending the Deluge.

Gilgamesh and Agga, an epic poem written many centuries later, is regularly cited as preserving a picture of early Sumerian deliberation (translation by Kramer 1963:187–90; reprinted in Kagan 1975:4–6). Agga, ruler of Kish, has sent an ultimatum to Gilgamesh, ruler of Erech (also transliterated Uruk). Gilgamesh convenes the council and speaks as follows:

> To complete the wells, to complete all the wells of the land,
> To complete the wells, the small bowls of the land.
> To dig the wells, to complete the fastening ropes—
> Let us not submit to the house of Kish, let us smite it with weapons.

The style—especially the parallelism and repetition—will be familiar to the reader from discussion of other cultures in earlier chapters. The argument seems to be that the economic prosperity of the city, dependent on irrigation, cannot be insured unless independence is preserved. The elders respond by repeating the statement about the wells and coming to the opposite conclusion, "Let us submit to the house of Kish, let us not smite it with weapons." Probably we can envision individual speakers expressing their views and a consensus emerging that economic prosperity is best served by avoiding war and thus accepting the demands of Kish. Gilgamesh, however, was not pleased. He convened the "men" of the city, the full assembly, and repeated his speech. They believe that the honor and greatness of Erech demands a warlike response; perhaps they prefer the excitement of an expedition to digging wells. No debate is mentioned; probably, as in other such assemblies, we should envision approval by acclamation (voice vote or show of hands). The assembly's decision prevails, war follows, with victory to Erech.

In the Babylonian period, which followed the conquest of the Sumerian cities by Sargon the Great around 2350 BCE and led to the replacement throughout Mesopotamia of Sumerian by Akkadian, a Semitic language, assemblies continued in existence as courts of law. The court of first resort was the local council of elders; from them appeal was possible to professional judges appointed by the king or to the king himself, who might refer important cases to the assembly (Postgate 1992:275–91). Oral and written evidence was taken under oath. In the absence of direct evidence, a defendant could take an oath of purgation, swearing that he had not committed the alleged act; refusal to do so sometimes occurred and was regarded as acceptance of guilt. The possibility of perjury, however, was recognized and if in doubt the judges could order the "river ordeal," in which a defendant was thrown into the river and judgment of the gods shown by death or survival. Mesopotamian courts do not seem to have allowed for circumstantial evidence of guilt or innocence, which becomes the basis for argument from probability, characteristic of Greek and later Western judicial rhetoric and a major opening for eloquent amplification. There is, however, some evidence of the occasional use of an incipient form of argument from probability in nonjudicial Mesopotamian texts, which I shall discuss later in this chapter.

Sumeria, like Greece, consisted of numerous small city-states engaged in rivalries for economic and political power, territory, and hegemony over the region as a whole. Embassies were regularly sent by the king of one city to the king of another to make demands or negotiate differences. The surviving account of one such embassy in the third millenium BCE provides some evidence for what was persuasive to Sumerian leaders (Kramer 1981:18–29). Enmerkar, king of Erech, determined to subdue the city of Aratta and require it to send precious metal and stone and to build a temple to the goddess Inanna in Erech. He prays to the goddess, who approves, and tells him to send a herald to Aratta with his demand. The king of Aratta initially refuses, but negotiations continue and eventually Aratta brings tribute to Erech. What persuaded the ruler of Aratta to accede to the demand? There were two main practical reasons, what can be called "nonartistic" means of persuasion: Aratta was dependent on grain from Erech, and Enmerkar threatened to destroy Aratta if his demand was not met. Nothing is said about justice or rights deriving from historical precedent or advantages Aratta may receive. Much of the negotiation is carried out in terms of the favor of the goddess, which symbolizes at the divine level the rivalry between the two kings. "Symbolize," however, is too rationalizing a word, since the participants almost certainly believed that the real decision was that of the goddess. Enmerkar claims her authority from the start: He has been chosen king by her, she tells him to send the herald, and the threat to Aratta is conveyed in her name, together with the claim that the god Enki has cursed the place. In reply, the king of Aratta claims that he too was installed by the goddess and enjoys her favor, but when the herald reiterates the demand the king becomes depressed and gives way. Kramer entitles the incident "The First War of Nerves." He also says (22–23) that the herald carries the message inscribed on a tablet because Enmerkar thought the herald "heavy of mouth," though in the text the herald is repeatedly described as "speaking." A written text would be consistent with the greater trust the Sumerians put on writing in contrast with speech.

Rhetoric in The Epic of Gilgamesh

The greatest literary work from ancient Mesopotamia is *The Epic of Gilgamesh*, the story of the adventures of the king of Erech (Uruk) in his quest for fame and immortality. The best of several available translations are those of Kovacs (1989) and Ferry (1992). The fullest version of the text was found on eleven clay tablets in Akkadian from the palace of Assurbanipal at Nineveh and dates from the seventh century BCE, but portions of the poem are also found in earlier versions from elsewhere (Tigay 1982). If there was a bardic tradition of oral poetry in early Mesopotamia—something one would expect from comparison with other cultures—no evidence for it seems to have survived. The epic as we know it was a written composition; according to the narrator the story was originally engraved in stone on the walls of Erech, but the earliest versions known from tablets are a series of separate incidents in Gilgamesh's career, written in Sumerian in the third millenium. At some point these incidents were edited into a unified poem that included a version of the story of the Deluge sent by the gods, the probable source of the story of Noah as found in the biblical book of Genesis (Kramer 1981:148–53). *Gilgamesh* is a noble work, of great imaginative power, and deserves study for its literary, religious, and historical qualities. My comments here, however, will be limited to identifying certain of its rhetorical features.

The poem begins with praise of Gilgamesh, his wisdom, strength, physical beauty, and achievements as builder of the walls and temple of Erech, and it ends with a briefer encomium of the hero. Since it is praise poetry it can easily be assigned to the epideictic species of rhetoric. As the poem unfolds, however, it is clear that Gilgamesh's rule is unpopular in Erech. A king should be "shepherd of his people" (Tablet 1, column 2), but Gilgamesh does not measure up to this requirement: He is egotistical, arrogant, and acquisitive. In particular, he offends the populace by his demand for the king's right to the first night with any bride he lusts after. The people pray to the gods, who hear their lament and create a distraction for the king that turns him from self-indulgence to heroic deeds. The poem thus carries a cultural message to future kings about how they should act and asserts the efficacy of prayer and the justice of the gods. For a wider audience it carries the message that human beings, however great their deeds or determined their efforts, cannot expect to live forever.

In response to the people's prayers, the gods create Enkidu to be a companion for Gilgamesh in heroic deeds that he is inspired to undertake. Originally Enkidu is a creature of the wild, entirely uncivilized. He pulls up traps and hunters thus lose their prey. One hunter appeals to Gilgamesh for help. The king suggests sending a temple prostitute out into the woods to lure, seduce, and civilize Enkidu, which is successfully accomplished (Tablet 1, column 4). The offer of sexual favors is one of the oldest and most effective forms of nonartistic rhetoric, here described in erotic detail.

A recurring narrative device in the poem are the dreams Gilgamesh has at crucial times. These come from the gods and provide knowledge, but only when correctly interpreted. The interpretation of dreams is a common phenomenon in many traditional cultures and a recurring incident in literature. Interpretation of dreams or other omens is a rhetorical act in that the interpreter induces and communicates meaning from the visions or actions seen in a dream and uses the dream to accomplish some purpose. Though not mentioned in *Gilgamesh*, a common form of interpretation of omens in Mesopotamia, practiced also in Greece, Rome, and other societies, was the inspection by priests of the entrails of sacrificial animals; this provided the priestly cast with some control and influence over secular events.

Consistent with what has been said about the political structure of Sumerian cities, before going out on his first adventure, the cutting down of the great cedar and killing of the giant Humbaba, Gilgamesh consults the elders of the city (Tablet 3, column 5). As in the case of war with Agga described above, they see the dangers more clearly than the advantages and are opposed to the expedition. Gilgamesh persists, however, not by appealing to the people but by turning to his mother who successfully prays to the sun god, Shamash, for help. The elders accept the decision, bless Gilgamesh, and send him and Enkidu forth with parting advice, the form of discourse known in classical rhetoric as a propemptikon.

After the successful expedition, which includes killing the Bull of Heaven, Enkidu has a dream about a council of the gods (Tablet 7, column 1). This is unfortunately only briefly described. Anu, father of the gods, demands that either Gilgamesh or Enkidu die because of killing Humbaba and the bull. Shamash opposes this and says they acted with his authority. Enlili, god of earth, wind, and air and the administrator of divine affairs, is angry at Shamash for identifying himself with the actions of human beings in a way inappropriate for a god. The consensus of the council is that revenge is necessary, and Enkidu is made the scapegoat. Councils of the gods are one of several similarities between Sumerian and Greco-Roman epic; others include the role of Enkidu in *Gilgamesh*, which might be compared to that of Patroclus, who dies for Achilles in the *Iliad*, and some similarities between the wanderings of Gilgamesh and those of Odysseus. Both archaeological and mythological evidence supports the conclusion that Greek bards of the early first millenium BCE are likely to have had some knowledge of Mesopotamian epic (Burkert 1992:88–127). The debate of the gods, which is really a trial of the two warriors, shows some awareness of what in Western rhetorical theory is called "stasis theory," the determination of the question at issue. The fact of the heroes' killing the giant and the bull is not denied. Their right to do so is in question. Shamash seeks to transfer responsibility to himself, but his right to do so is denied by the court.

The Bull of Heaven was sent by Anu in revenge for Gilgamesh's rejection of the erotic advances of Ishtar (Sumerian Inanna), goddess of love and Anu's daughter. At the beginning of Tablet 6, moved by Gilgamesh's beauty, she invites him to become her husband. He rejects her in one of the two rather long speeches in the poem, setting out probable arguments based on their respective status and her character. How can they live together as equals? What can he give her in return? Moreoever, which of her lovers has she ever loved for long? He catalogues her previous lovers and her bad treatment of them in some detail. It is this that she finds most offensive, though she admits the truth of his remarks and her father initially tells her she has brought the rebuke on herself. The other rather long speech is Gilgamesh's lament on the death of Enkidu in Tablet 8. Lamentation is a rhetorical form practiced at funerals in many cultures and developed as a literary genre in Sumeria (Kramer 1981:270–76), in the Hebrew bible, and in Greek and Indian literature.

Some use of argument from probability can also be found in Tablet 10 where Gilgamesh is on his journey to Utnapishtim, the Sumerian Noah who alone has been given immortality by the gods and from whom Gilgamesh hopes to learn its secret. He encounters a young woman named Siduri, to whom he identifies himself and from whom he seeks help, and then the ferryman Urshanabi, to whom he also identifies himself. Both initially reject his claim because of his sad, emaciated appearance. Thus they appear to reason on the basis of the signs visible to them that it is not probable that he really is Gilgamesh as he claims.

Rhetorical Features of Letter-Writing in the Near East

The development of writing facilitated communication over distance for the first time through the sending of letters written on clay or wooden tablets, parchment, or papyrus. Numerous official, business, and personal letters have survived in the ancient Near East, especially in Egypt, showing features of rhetorical invention, arrangement, and style that also characterize epistolography in the Greco-Roman and later periods in the West and are described in numerous medieval and renaissance dictaminal treatises. Among the most interesting early epistles are the "Amarna Letters," dating from the fourteenth century BCE (translation by Moran 1992). Although found on papyrus in Egypt, they are written in Babylonian cuneiform, which was the *lingua franca* of the time, and come from the archives of letters received by the Egyptian king from independent rulers in Mesopotamia and subordinate officials in Syria and Palestine. There are also a few copies of letters sent from the Pharaoh to these correspondents. The letters are of great importance for an understanding of international relations in this period. As usual, my discussion will be limited to identifying some of the more significant rhetorical features.

The letters begin with an address to the scribe who will receive the letter and translate it for the Egyptian king and his staff. Addresses take two different forms: If the writer names himself first, he is asserting that he is the superior or equal of the addressee; if the writer recognizes his own inferior position or is trying to be especially polite, the name of the recipient goes first. A similar conventional etiquette was required in Western medieval correspondence. There follows a salutation, of which the first part, sometimes omitted, reports the writer's state of health (e.g., "For me all goes well."), while the second part is an expression of good will for the recipient. Here is an example of a complimentary address and salutation:

> Say to Nimuwareya, the king of Egypt, my brother: Thus Kadashman-Enlil, the king of Karaduniyash, your brother. For me all indeed goes well. For you, your household, your wives, and for your sons, your country, your chariots, your horses, your magnates may all go very well. (Moran 1992:7)

There then follows the body of the letter, which varies greatly with the circumstances. Some letters include a considerable amount of narrative; previous good relations are sometimes cited and compared to recent neglect. Complaints are common. The correspondence between kings often deals with dynastic marriages or the exchange of gifts, sometimes with the treatment of their representatives. The letters to the king of Egypt from his officials in Syria and Palestine report on their problems and ask for help such as additional troops. Letters end abruptly without any complimentary close, but sometimes there is a postscript in which the sender's scribe sends a message to the addressee's scribe: for example, "You, scribe, write well to me; put down, moreover your name. The tablets that are brought here always write in Hittite!" (Moran 1992:103).

Ethos, pathos, and logical argument are all used as means of persuasion in the letters. The conventions of the address and salutation suggest the good will of the writer and references in the body of the letter portray his character by citing honorable actions of the past. Pathos is most evident in the letters of the Egyptian officials in Syria and Palestine, who often seem to be in terrible situations, even besieged in their cities, as the result of local uprisings and the lack of adequate military forces. Nonartistic logical argument occurs in the form of listing services and good deeds of the writer to the addressee. A good example of enthymematic argument occurs in an amusing letter from an Eastern ruler to the King of Egypt of which the beginning, and thus the name of the writer, is lost:

> You, my brother, when I wrote about marrying your daughter, in accordance with your practice of not giving a daughter, [wrote to me] saying, "From time immemorial no daughter of the king of Egypt is given to anyone." Why not? You are a king; you do as you please. Were you to give a daughter, who would say anything? Since I was told of this message, I wrote as follows to my brother, saying "Someone's grown daughters, beautiful women, must be available. Send me a beautiful woman as if she were your daughter. Who is going to say, 'She is no daughter of the king'?" But holding to your decision you have not sent me anyone. Did not you yourself seek brotherhood and amity, and so wrote me about marriage that we might come closer to each other, and did not I, for my part, write you about mar-

riage for this very same reason, i.e., brotherhood and amity, that we might come closer to each other? Why, then, did my brother not send me just one woman? Should I, perhaps, since you did not send me a woman, refuse you a woman, just as you did to me, and not send her? But my daughters being available, I will not refuse one to you. (Moran 1992:8–9)

Argument from probability also can be found in some letters, based on the ethos of the writer. Abdi-Heba, a vassal of the Egyptian king, was slanderously (he says) accused of rebelling against his master. In his defense, he argues that it is improbable he would do so: "Seeing that, as far as I am concerned, neither my father nor my mother put me in this place, but the strong arm of the king brought me into my father's house, why should I of all people commit a crime against the king, my lord?" The letter ends with a postscript: "To the scribe of the king, my lord: Message of Abdi-Heba, your servant. Present eloquent words to the king, my lord. Lost are all the lands of the king my lord" (Moran 1992:326).

Eloquence in Egypt

As this postscript suggests, eloquence seems to have been more highly valued in Egypt and its dependencies than in Mesopotamia. The most striking evidence is probably the story of "The Eloquent Peasant" (Simpson 1972:31–49; Lichtheim 1973, I:169–74). It was written during the "Middle Kingdom," between 2000 and 1800 BCE, which is the most creative period of Egyptian literature. Lichtheim (169) has described the story as "a serious disquisition on the need for justice, and a parable on the utility of fine speech." The narrative frame describes how a peasant from the desert is taking animal skins, birds, and plants to a city on the Nile to trade for food. He is stopped on the way by Nemtynakht, a subordinate of the high steward Rensi, and robbed of his goods and donkeys. When he appeals to Rensi, the case is first referred to the local magistrates, who suspect that the peasant has earlier run away from Nemtynakht and dismiss the incident as trifling. The peasant then appeals again to Rensi in a speech that combines ordinary prose with "formal language" as used in ancient Egypt for important subjects, a register of rhythmical prose more elevated than what is commonly used in narrative or letter writing but not quite so elevated or metaphorical as that found in hymns and lyric poetry. This eloquence is apparently a natural gift, not something learned by imitation or study. The high steward is so impressed that, without making any response to the peasant, he pays a visit to King Nebkaure and tells him about this remarkable speaker. The king is much interested and tells Rensi to keep the peasant talking, making no response to him but providing for his needs and those of his family, and to have his speeches written down so that the king can read them. Rensi follows this advice, which results in an additional eight eloquent appeals of increasing despair, until finally the peasant is exhausted. The written copies are sent to the king: "They pleased his majesty's heart more than anything in the whole land" (Lichtheim 182). Rensi is then told to make judgment, and all of the property of Nemtynakht is transferred to the peasant as retribution for his loss and reward for his eloquence.

Throughout his speeches the peasant does not argue about his own case: He does not demand that witnesses be heard, as he was probably entitled to do; he does not argue that it is improbable that he would have stolen the goods; his speeches are pathetical appeals to the judge's sense of justice. The argument, for there is an argument, is sustained at a general level in the series of examples of prevailing conditions: the loss of goodness and mercy and official neglect of duty. It may be that this argument stirred the conscience of the high steward, but we are not told so; it was the peasant's remarkable control of style that is stressed as winning his case. As an example of the peasant's argument and style, here is his fourth petition to Rensi. The passages printed as poetry are in the formal, rhythmical style.

O praised one, may [the god] Harsaphes praise you, from whose temple
   you have come!
Goodness is destroyed, none adhere to it,
To fling falsehood's back to the ground.
If the ferry is grounded, wherewith does one cross?...
Is crossing the river on sandals a good crossing? No! Who now sleeps till day
   break? Gone is walking by night, travel by day, and letting a man defend
   his own good cause. But it is no use to tell you this; mercy has passed
   you by. How miserable is the wretch whom you have destroyed!
Lo, you are a hunter who takes his fill,
Bent on doing what he pleases;
Spearing hippopotami, shooting birds,
Catching fish, snaring birds.
(But) none quick to speak is free from haste,
None light of heart is weighty in conduct.
Be patient so as to learn justice,
Restrain your [anger] for the good of the humble seeker.
No hasty man attains excellence,
No impatient man is leaned upon.
Let the eyes see, let the heart take notice. Be not harsh in your power, lest
   trouble befall you. Pass over a matter, it becomes two. He who eats
   tastes; one addressed answers. It is the sleeper who sees the dream; and a
   judge who deserves punishment is a model for the (evil)doer. Fool, you
   are attacked! Ignorant man, you are questioned! Spouter of water, you
   are attained!
Steersman, let not drift your boat,
Life-sustainer, let not die,
Provider, let not perish,

Shade, let one not dry out,
Shelter, let not the crocodile snatch!
The fourth time I petition you! Shall I go on all day?

(LICHTHEIM 1973, I:177–78)

Throughout his petitions the peasant coins what in the Western rhetorical tradition are called *sententiae*, gnomic utterances or maxims of general application, resembling proverbs. These, and the examples of injustice and neglect he cites, are his major rhetorical techniques. The maxims associate the story with the genre of Egyptian wisdom literature, to which I shall return below, but the peasant's maxims are more metaphorical than is usually found in other Egyptian wisdom literature. If the translation can be relied on, some of the images in the sixth petition are expressed as similes. Apostrophe and rhetorical questions are frequent. The passages in the high style fall into two line couplets, exhibiting the parallelism that is characteristic of poetic language in the Near East. The speeches also employ a version of a topos that becomes common in late Middle Kingdom didactic works and is also found in the Hebrew prophets and elsewhere (Luria 1929; Lichtheim 1973, I:149–50). This is the idea of social chaos when rulers fail to perform their proper functions and traditional values are turned upside down.

Egyptian Society

The oldest Egyptian texts are funerary inscriptions on stone from the third millenium BCE, the period called "The Old Kingdom." These consist of prayers and lists of the virtuous accomplishments of kings and aristocrats, and were intended to persuade the gods to grant immortality to the deceased and to persuade readers to honor the dead. Threats against those who would desecrate or rob tombs were also inscribed and were at times efficacious, though in some periods tomb robbery was a major problem for Egyptian officials (Montet 1958:260–67).

Throughout its history, Egyptian government was autocratic; so far as I know, there is no evidence for popular assemblies such as those found in Mesopotamia and elsewhere. The Egyptian kings were surrounded by an elaborate court of secular and religious officials headed by the vizier. The Pharoahs certainly consulted senior officials and received advice from them. Some hints of this are found in the story of Joseph in Egypt in the book of Genesis (41:37; 50:4–6). But advising Pharoah was a delicate matter, especially in the case of a proud and arrogant king like Ramesses II (reigned 1298–1235 BCE). When he consulted his high officials, they were expected first to prostrate themselves before him, and tact required that they not give straightforward answers or seem to display their own wisdom. Instead, they eulogized the king and advised him to do what he seemed intent on doing (Montet 1958:201). As in Mesopotamia, schools existed for the training of scribes, merchants, and the civil service; these seem to have been open to any boy whose family could afford instruction, and persons of humble origin sometimes rose to high rank (Kaster 1968:188–99). Most of the students' time was initially devoted to learning the complex system of hieroglyphic writing and the somewhat simpler cursive script derived from it. As in Mesopotamia and in Greece, students copied out texts from which they learned grammar and style as well as religious and historical lore. Imitation of canonical models was regarded as the source of rhetorical skill: "One will do all you say if you are versed in writings; study the writings, put them in your heart, then all your words will be effective," writes the scribe Any (Lichtheim 1976, II:140). Egyptian education also had a practical side, lacking in Western schools of the classical and medieval period: Students familiarized themselves with laws, regulations, geography, and the technology of building, transportation, and agriculture (Montet 1958:256). Numerous school exercises on papyri have been found in Egypt. There are many fine works in English about life in ancient Egypt, often beautifully illustrated with drawings and photographs. A classic example is J. Gardner Wilkinson's *The Manners and Customs of the Ancient Egyptians* (1837, often reprinted); Murray's *Splendour That Was Egypt* (1963) is a useful introduction; two recent books are those by Kemp (1989) and Strouhal (1992).

The Instruction of Ptahhotep:
The Earliest Rhetorical Handbook?

Wisdom literature in Egypt began in the time of the Old Kingdom and continued in later periods. It usually takes the form of instructions by a father to a son about the appropriate way to act, to earn respect, and to succeed in life. Unlike other Egyptian literature, where the author is usually anonymous, instructions were attributed to named, identified sages of the past; the attribution, however, may be a way of giving authority to texts that were actually written somewhat later. The most important of these texts for the history of rhetoric is what is known as *The Instruction* (or *Maxims*) *of Ptahhotep*, a vizier under King Isesi in the late Old Kingdom; the oldest papyrus of the text dates from the early second millenium BCE. This can perhaps be regarded as the oldest known rhetorical handbook, though it only deals with certain features of the subject; for example, it says nothing about style, even though we know that there were different stylistic registers that had to be mastered by an effective speaker. There are translations of the work by R. O. Falkner in Simpson (1973:159–76), reprinted in Blythin (1986), and by Lichtheim (1973, I:61–80).

After an address to the king and a prayer for his own son by Ptahhotep, the text continues with the following statement by the scribe:

> Beginning of the formations of excellent discourse spoken by the Prince,
> Count, God's Father, God's beloved, Eldest Son of the King, of his body,

Mayor of the city and Vizier, Ptahhotep, instructing the ignorant in knowledge and in the standard [*tp-ḥsb*] of excellent discourse [*mdt-nfrt*], as profit
for him who will hear, as woe to him who would neglect them. He spoke
to his son. (Lichtheim 1975, I:63).

Ptahhotep's ethos is indicated by listing his titles. There follow thirty-seven separate pieces of advice and a long epilogue, all stated simply but using parallelism
and rhythm, which doubtless facilitated memorization of the instructions. Although the scribe's statement describes the work as concerned with "excellent
discourse," much of the advice deals with social and family relationships rather
than with speech. The writer jumps from topic to topic without any clear sequence of thought; possibly the scribe has collected precepts from different
sources. Speech is, however, an important consideration and the writer begins
with advice about speech, but it is not differentiated from moral philosophy. The
first four maxims are translated by Lichtheim (1975, I:63–64) as follows:

1. Don't be proud of your knowledge,
    Consult the ignorant and the wise;
    The limits of art are not reached.
    No artist's skills are perfect;
    Good speech is more hidden than greenstone,
    Yet may be found among maids at the grindstones.

2. If you meet a disputant in action,
    A powerful man, superior to you,
    Fold your arms, bend your back,
    To flout him will not make him agree with you.
    Make little of the evil speech
    By not opposing him while he's in action;
    He will be called an ignoramus,
    Your self-control will match his pile (of words).

3. If you meet a disputant in action
    Who is your equal, on your level,
    You will make your worth exceed his by silence;
    While he is speaking evilly,
    There will be much talk by the hearers,
    Your name will be good in the mind of the magistrates.

4. If you meet a disputant in action,
    A poor man, not your equal,
    Do not attack him because he is weak,
    Let him alone, he will confute himself.
    Do not answer him to relieve your heart,
    Do not vent yourself against your opponent;
    Wretched is he who injures a poor man,
    One will wish to do what you desire,
    You will beat him through the magistrates' reproof.

The modesty, restraint, and courtesy here recommended is consistent with the practice of most nonliterate societies as described in chapter 4, and a more thoughtful amplification of Mesopotamian warnings about the dangers of speech. Ptahhotep's instructions emphasize ethos as basis for authority in speech. Within the hierarchical distinctions of the powerful, the equal, and the poor a person can achieve success in speech whatever his rank in society. No precepts for logical argument are offered. The instructions are perhaps consistent with the actions of the high steward in the story of the eloquent peasant, but the peasant seems quite ignorant of them. Clearly, the Egyptians thought that there was an appropriate form of public discourse, but they were also on occasion able to admire exceptions to the conventions. The higher a person's rank, the more need for him to observe the conventions.

The maxims of Ptahhotep were first drawn to the attention of Western speech students by an article by Giles W. Gray (1946). The best account of rhetoric in ancient Egypt is an article by Michael V. Fox (1983), which discusses the instructions of Ptahhotep and other sages and the story of *The Eloquent Peasant*. Fox identified five "canons," or rules, of rhetoric in Egypt: keeping *silent*; waiting for the *right moment* to speak; *restraining* passionate words; speaking *fluently* but with great deliberation; and keeping your tongue at one with your heart so that you speak the *truth*. Silence is the initial calmness that listens to what others say and shows respect for them and self-dignity. The value put on silence is not a denial of the power of words; Fox quotes (1983:14) a maxim from the instructions of Merikare, "Speaking is more powerful than any fighting," a principle I found even in animal communication in chapter 1. (On silence as a rhetorical tactic, see Scott 1972 and 1993.) The "right moment" resembles the concept of *kairos* in classical rhetoric, the need to judge what to say and when; no rules are adequate to teach this, but it can be learned by observation. Restraining passionate words in the course of a speech is the counterpart of the original silence and the way ethos is maintained. Fluency was learned from the study of texts. It gives the impression of security and knowing what you are talking about. Yet the reference to good speech as "found among maids at the grindstone" in section 1, quoted above, seems to suggest that it may also be a natural gift, as it was in the case of the Eloquent Peasant. Truthfulness is the most important canon and is obedient to the will of the gods. There is throughout the instructions an assumption that the truth will emerge from discussion, that falsehood will be detected, and that justice will prevail.

This summary gives a somewhat misleading picture of the *Instruction of Ptahhotep* in that it is not at all systematic. Advice about speech is combined with more general advice, in an apparently random sequence, about how an official, a subordinate, a husband, a father, a son, a neighbor, a rich man, and a poor man should conduct himself. In all ways, Ptahhotep strongly recommends conformity to social norms, obedience to superiors and fathers, listening to others, patience, good will, forebearance, and cheerfulness even in difficulty. Through these qualities a man will achieve a character that gives weight to his speech. Of the five canons Fox identifies, silence, restraint, and truthfulness are repeatedly stressed. There is only a single mention of finding the right opportunity to speak (section 24) and fluency (section 15). The former passage does advise waiting for the right moment, but that moment comes "only when you have discovered your solution.... It is only a craftsman who can speak in council." The speaker should know what he is talking about.

Fox concludes his article with the following characterization of Egyptian rhetoric, which seems to me a fair statement:

> Egyptian rhetorical thought differs most sharply from the Greek in not be-
> ing analytical and introspective. It does not examine exemplars of rhetoric
> in an attempt to isolate forms of argumentation, organization, or style, nor
> does it look within itself to find ways of generating new rules from existing
> principles. Lacking its own procedures for expansion and internal critique,
> Egyptian rhetoric could not become an independent discipline. It had to re-
> main a variety of rules scattered among general moral and practical counsels
> ... But we should recognize that Egyptian rhetorical theory is highly suited
> to its purposes, not trying so much to teach the techniques of a craft as to
> inculcate an attitude or moral posture which will make one's verbal craft-
> manship effective. It does not teach how to formulate arguments because it
> is not argumentation but rather the ethical stance of the speakers that will
> maintain harmony in the social order, and that is the ultimate goal of Egypt-
> ian rhetoric. (For 1983:21–22)

This is, of course, also the goal of rhetoric in most societies outside the West-ern tradition, as has emerged from discussion in previous chapters. Egyptian thinkers articulated principles and functions of speech that are inherent in rhetor-ical practice in traditional societies all over the world. We shall see that a simi-lar development occurred independently in China.

Debate in Egyptian Literature

One should not assume from this that Egyptians did not sometimes engage in debate or that they did not seek to support statements with reasons that might help to persuade a listener, though I have not found any good examples of ar-gument from probability. Neither in Egypt nor elsewhere outside classical Greece are full syllogisms stated, but enthymemes, as early chapters have indicated, are ubiquitous. In an Egyptian tale in simple style (Lichtheim 1976, II:204) an el-der brother says to a younger brother, "Have a team made ready for us for plow-ing, for the soil has emerged and is right for ploughing. Also, come to the field with seed, for we shall start plowing tomorrow." The autobiographic inscrip-tions of the Old Kingdom, as noted earlier, provide reasons why the dead de-serve immortality. In one of the early pyramid inscriptions (Lichtheim 1973, I:33) the sky goddess says to the dead king "Make your seat in heaven, among the stars of heaven, for you are the Lone Star, the comrade of Hu!" In the parallelism of the high style, which initially seems more assertive than logical, the second clause may only reinforce the first by repeating the thought with a different image, but it may also explain the assertion or give a reason for believing it. Thus, in the second maxim of Ptahhotep quoted above, advising silence in response to the attack of a powerful man, the reader is told, "Fold your arms, bend your back, [for] to flout him will not make him agree with you." Dispute among the gods is dramatized in the myth of Horus and Seth, which includes a trial scene (Lichtheim 1976, II:214–23). *The Dispute Between a Man and His Ba* (Lichtheim 1975, I:163–69) is a debate between a man tired of life who wants to die and his soul, which objects. Among other things, the *ba* argues, "Are you not a man? Are you not alive? What do you gain by complaining about life like a man of wealth?" There are some Egyptian counterparts to the disputations practiced in Mesopotamian schools. The instructions of the scribe Nebmarenakht to his apprentice praises the life of a scribe and then compares it favorably to all other occupations (Lichtheim 1976, II:168–75). Another work is an allegorical tale about Truth and Falsehood in which Truth has been denounced by Falsehood before the gods for stealing a wondrous dagger; Truth is punished by blindness but eventually is vindicated by his son (Lichtheim 1976, II:211–14).

The Propaganda Program of Akhenaton

Egyptian civilization gives an initial impression of great continuity over thousands of years. There were, however, recurrent crises, economic distress, civil wars, and foreign invasions that sometimes created serious disruptions; there were also times of reform, renewal, and change. As in other times and places where historical records survive, it is possible to trace an official rhetoric by which those in power sought to solidify their position, not only by means of spoken and written words, but by calling on the aid of art, architecture, and religious institutions. The most remarkable period in Egypt in this respect was the reign of Akhenaton (sometimes transliterated Ikhnaton) in the fourteenth century. As archaeological evidence about Akhenaton and his queen, Nefertyty, was revealed in the late nineteenth and early twentieth century, some historians glorified him as the first "monotheist" and the first "individual" in history (see the articles reprinted in Kagan 1975:36–68). Akhenaton's reign—the time of the Amarna letters discussed earlier—was a political disaster, and it is questionable whether he can be regarded a monotheist (Murray 1963:38; Kastor 1968); perhaps "henotheist" would be a better description, the term sometimes used to describe religion in Vedic India and early Israel, when a single god was elevated to supreme position without necessarily denying the existence of other divinities. Akhenaton was intensely hostile to the influence of the priests of Amon in Thebes, the capital city, and sought to replace dominance of Amon with worship of Aton, the sun's disk. What can be viewed as a rhetorical or propaganda program to mark a dramatic change in political, religious, and cultural traditions was undertaken that included the change of the king's name from Amonhotep ("Amon Is Satisfied") to Akhenaton ("He Who Serves Aton"), the founding of a new capital, far from Thebes, the encouraging of naturalistic art, and the composition of poetry celebrating Aton. The program was a failure. With Akhenaton's death the priests of Amon reasserted their power, the capital returned to Thebes, and Egyptian art returned to a traditional style.

The Failure of Language as Seen by an Egyptian

Mention was made earlier of the theme of national distress in Egyptian literature. In my reading I was particularly struck by *The Complaints of Khakheperre-Sonb*, which begins with an unusual passage in the parallel style on the failure of traditional language to express what the author feels. The passage seems to me a good conclusion to this brief discussion of Egyptian rhetoric.

> [O that I had] unknown phrases, sayings that are strange,
> novel, untried words, free of repetition;
> not transmitted sayings, spoken by the ancestors!
> I wring out my body of what it holds in releasing all my words;
> for what was said is repetition, when what was said is said.
> Ancestor's words are nothing to boast of,
> they are found by those who come after.
> Not one speaks who spoke, there speaks one who will speak,
> may another find what he will speak!
> Not a teller of tales after they happen, this has been done before;
> nor a teller of what might be said, this is vain endeavor, it is lies,
> and none will recall his name to others.
> I say this in accord with what I have seen:
> from the first generation to those who come after, they imitate what is past.
> Would that I knew what others ignore, such as has not been repeated,
> to say it and have my heart answer me, to inform it of my distress,
> shift to it the load on my back, the matters that afflict me,
> relate to it of what I suffer, and sigh "Ah" with relief!
>
> (ADAPTED FROM LICHTHEIM 1973, I:146–47)

Rhetoric in the Biblical Book of Proverbs

Palestine was within the Egyptian sphere of influence and sometimes under Egyptian rule in the second and early first millenium BCE. Egyptian sources lie behind some of the material in the Hebrew bible. This is especially true of the book of Proverbs, which is indebted to Egyptian wisdom literature. Proverbs is actually a collection of four distinct works with appendices; it probably did not take its present form much before 300 BCE but considerable portions go back to earlier times. Like traditional rhetoric everywhere, the teaching of Proverbs is highly conservative, for it consistently reinforces respect for kings, fathers, husbands, and traditional values. Parallelism, as in Mesopotamia and Egypt, is used as a "formal" style to supplement admonitions and render them memorable. Except in the third of the four "books" (i.e., 22:17–24:22), the speaker, whether the allegorical figure of Wisdom or King Solomon, imagined as the source of the proverbs, often refers to speech. (The historical Solomon may have coined proverbs but according to 1 Kings 4:32–33 they were concerned with nature, not with human actions.)

The majority of the references to speech in Proverbs, consistent with what can be found in Mesopotamian and Egyptian literature, are warnings against its misuses—against scoffers, gossips, liers, and false witnesses—but all five of the canons of Egyptian rhetoric as defined by Fox and discussed earlier in this chapter can be found in the book. Among examples that could be cited are the following: "A man of understanding remains *silent*" (11:12). "A soft answer turns away wrath, but a harsh word stirs up anger" (i.e., use *restraint*) (15:1). "A word *fitly* spoken is like apples of gold in a setting of silver" (25:11) (compare Ecclesiastes 3:7, "A time to keep silence and a time to speak"). "The words of a man's mouth are deep waters; the fountain of wisdom is a gushing stream" (*fluency*) (18:4). "He who speaks the *truth* gives honest evidence, but a false witness utters deceit" (12:17). Special care is needed in addressing kings, but "with patience a ruler may be persuaded" (25:15). Examples of bad and of good rhetoric are offered: the description of the harlot and her speech in chapter 7 can be contrasted to the invitation to dinner in the house of Wisdom in chapter 9.

Chapter 16 of Proverbs is especially interesting for an idea not found in Egyptian wisdom literature and which may be regarded as an additional "canon" of Hebrew rhetoric. This is the belief that God will provide the words needed by the speaker who trusts Him: "The plans of the mind belong to man but the answer of the tongue is from the Lord.... Commit your work to the Lord and your plans will be established" (16:1–3). Later in the chapter (16:10) inspiration is referred to as especially a feature of the discourse of kings. Belief in inspiration is basic to Hebrew prophecy (e.g., Jeremiah 1:4–8); the prophet is a vehicle for a divine message. It can also be illustrated in contexts such as the account of plans to secure release of the Children of Israel from Egypt in Exodus, where Moses protests to God that he is not eloquent. This is metaphorically restated in Exodus 6:12 and 30 as "I am uncircumcised of lips," which has traditionally been understood to refer to a stutter. God replies "I will be with your mouth and teach you what you shall speak" (Exodus 4:12). Moses begs for some other person to be sent and the Lord names Aaron to be the orator of the Jews; the content of speeches to the people will be given by the Lord to Moses and by him to Aaron: "you shall be to him as God." Aaron will then cast this into effective words and their authority will be demonstrated by the miraculous signs Moses has been taught to use (4.14–17). Eloquence is apparently a natural gift that Moses lacks, though one of my students suggested to me that Moses' close association with the Pharonic court might make him suspect in the eyes of some Jews. The belief that a speaker can rely on inspiration from God is continued in Christianity: in Mark 13:11, Jesus tells his disciples to take no thought of what they are to say if brought to trial, "but say whatever is given you in that hour, for it is not you who speak but the Holy Spirit."

Although Ptahhotep's "canons" did not include eloquence, we know that was valued highly in Egypt, and the importance for persuasion of a pleasing style is also stressed in chapter 16 of Proverbs: "pleasant speech increases persuasiveness" (16:21); "pleasant words are like a honeycomb, sweetness to the soul and health to the body" (16:24). The scribes who added the orthodox appendix to the somewhat heretical teaching of Ecclesiastes say of him "The Preacher sought to find pleasing words..." (Ecclesiastes 12:9). Approval of "honeyed" words might encourage use of flattery, but Proverbs warns against this: "It is not good to eat much honey, so be sparing of complimentary words" (25:27). If we try to define more specifically what is meant by a honeyed style in the Bible, other than the use of complimentary words, the answer probably is euphonic and harmonious language; the use of metaphor or other tropes, chiefly from nature, the pastoral life (e.g., "the Lord is my shepherd"), or agriculture; and parallelism in composition, as well as such figures of speech as simile, anaphora, and rhetorical question. On some of the pitfalls in understanding figures of speech in the Old Testament see the remarks of Brichto (1992:37–44).

Persuasion in the Old Testament

Judaism and its offsprings, Christianity and Islam, have historically accepted the doctrine of creation as found in the first chapter of Genesis, where God's initial acts are accomplished by speech and accompanied by naming. It is interesting to contrast the tradition in China: according to Confucius, "Heaven does not speak" (*Analects* 17.19). In Judaism, Christianity, Islam, and also in Buddhism, preaching has had a major role, while in paganism, ancient and modern, priests do not preach at all. The Lord, the patriarchs, and the prophets in the Bible speak authoritatively, but to their injunctions they not infrequently add a reason, thus creating enthymemes. The most striking instance in the Old Testament are the reasons added in support of the first six of the Ten Commandments in Exodus 20:2–17: In the first commandment, for example, God supports his claim that no other gods should be honored before him among the Israelites by reminding them that he was the God "who brought you out of the house of bondage," and the commandment against making graven images is supported by a threat and a promise, "for I am a jealous God, visiting the inquity of the fathers upon the children to the third and the fourth generation of those who hate me, but showing steadfast love to thousands of those who love me and keep my commandments." The most characteristic form of public address in the Old Testament is the "covenant speech," built on the assumption of a covenant between God and the people of Israel. The general pattern is, first, to strengthen the authority of the Lord by reminding the audience of what He has done; second, to add new commandments; and third, to conclude with a warning of what will happen if the commandments are disregarded. Deuteronomy is made up in large part of three covenant speeches (1–4, 5–28, and 29–30), each containing a narrative of what has happened in the past, commandments, and warnings against disobedience or promises of blessings of obedience. Other good examples are found in Joshua 24 and 1 Samuel 12.

Although Saint Augustine, Martin Luther, and other theologians of the past who had been trained in rhetoric often used that knowledge in interpreting the Old Testament, twentieth-century biblical scholars rarely showed any awareness of rhetoric until James Muilenberg raised the need to do so in his 1969 Presidential Address to the Society of Biblical Literature. Since then, numerous studies of rhetoric in the Old Testament have appeared (e.g., Jackson and Kessler 1974; Medhurst 1991). I say nothing here of rhetorical interpretations of the New Testament, on which I have written a separate book (Kennedy 1984). An article of special relevance for my discussion here is that by Margaret D. Zulick (1992a) on the Hebrew language of persuasion. She begins by noting that though there are many words for eloquence, speaking, and persuading in the Hebrew text of the Old Testament, there is no Hebrew transitive verb to express the thought "He persuades someone" in a positive sense. The closest is the verb *pātâ*, which carries the connotation of enticement, seduction, and deception. Even the Lord is said to engage occasionally in this kind of rhetoric (1 Kings 22:20–22; 2 Chronicles 18:19–21; Ezekiel 14:9). Active persuasion in this sense is generally thought of as negative. Hebrew describes active, ethically positive persuasion, according to Zulick, in terms of audience reception by words meaning "hear, listen, pay attention to." "The effect of the idiom," she says, "is two-fold. In the first place, it throws responsibility to the respondent, making the hearer rather than the speaker the deciding figure in a rhetorical act. In the second place, it strengthens the medium, the word itself, by removing any suggestion that true words might fail to persuade" (Zulick 1992a:377). She ends her article by raising questions about how the rather different Greek view of persuasion came into existence, the view that persuasion is a competitive art, that rhetoric has the power to compel, and that such a gift is admirable. It is, however, perhaps worth pointing out that the power of words to compel is a common belief in most cultures in the case of magical spells, and that sorcerers compete with each other for power. The Jewish religion was exceptional in its hostility to witchcraft and magic as a necessary corollary to its acceptance of the power of a single god, which was also an exception to the religious views of the rest of the world. In a pagan pantheon, the gods too compete for honor and power by speech and action, a process which both reflects and is reflected by the activities of mortals.

Lamentations and prophecies are found in Mesopotamian, Egyptian, and other cultures, as noted earlier, but the texts of the Hebrew prophets exhibit a far more complex rhetorical invention than is found elsewhere. This results primarily from two factors, the nature of Jewish religion and the editing and publication of written texts. In polytheism, human suffering can easily be projected into rivalries between different gods, as the Greeks did in the case of the Trojan war; powerful contending forces are thought susceptible to the performance of the proper ritual and sacrifice; and suffering is often accepted as the lot of mortals without deep theological speculation on why this should be so. The religion of the Jews as it developed into monotheism, with all power assigned to a god who claimed to bestow special favor on his chosen people, created an unprecedented theological and rhetorical problem when that favor seemed to be withheld. The crisis of understanding and explanation became intense with the Assyrian occupation of the two kingdoms of Israel, culminating in the destruction of Jerusalem and dispersal of the Jews in 587 BCE. This is the problem with which Jeremiah, Isaiah, and other prophets contended. In the text of Jeremiah, in particular, many different voices are heard, including that of God and Jeremiah himself, in bitter contention (Zulich 1992b). Prophets may be assumed to have gone about the countryside claiming inspiration and crying "woe," but the dramatic synthesis into a dialogic frame, as found in our texts, can only be imagined as a product of written composition, drawing on varied sources, and subject to scribal editing. Hebrew prophecy, through Christian canonization of the Old Testament, has contributed a distinct tradition of invention and style to both religious and political discourse in the West, which continues vigorously at the present time.

Conclusion

Unlike what is found in nonliterate cultures and other literate cultures of antiquity, Mesopotamian scribes show no inclination to celebrate speech or to honor the role of an orator. Writing, first developed there in the fourth millenium, is privileged over speech. Writing should be regarded as a kind of "formal language." Written texts in the Near East were canonized, studied, and imitated by students. The effect of written law codes in Mesopotamia was to limit judicial decisions to the question of whether an act met the conditions prescribed by a legal formula. Deliberative oratory in public assemblies existed in early times in Mesopotamia, but waned with autocratic government. *The Epic of Gilgamesh* describes assemblies and councils, and contains instances of argument from probability. Rhetorical conventions appear in letter-writing in the Near East, including formulas of salutation, ethical and pathetical appeals, and argument from probability.

In contrast to Mesopotamian scribes, Egyptian writers often celebrated eloquence. Several registers of formal language are found in Egyptian texts. *The Instructions of Ptahhotep* may be regarded as the earliest known rhetorical handbook and sets out canons of silence, choosing the right moment to speak, facility, restraint, and truthfulness. An official rhetoric is expressed in Egyptian inscriptions and highly developed during the reign of Akhenaton.

The biblical book of Proverbs contains advice about speech resembling that of Ptahhotep, but adds to it a theory of inspiration and recommendations for the use of "honeyed" words. The former is found also in Exodus and in writings of the prophets and is continued in Christianity. Judaism created special conditions for rhetoric; among the results are covenant speeches and a dialogic technique found in the writing of the prophets.

The introduction of writing facilitated conceptualization, and thus writing about rhetoric first appears in the ancient Near East, though rhetoric was never regarded there as a distinct discipline; it was always an aspect of political, religious, or moral philosophy. As in nonliterate societies, rhetoric in the ancient Near East was primarily a tool of transmitting and defending traditional political, social, and religious values.

References

Blythin, Evan, ed. (1986). *The Maxims of Ptahhotep.* Annandale, VA: Speech Communication Association.

Bottéro, Jean (1992). *Mesopotamia: Writing, Reasoning, and the Gods,* trans. by Zainab Bahrani and Marc Van De Mierop. Chicago: University of Chicago Press.

Brichto, Herbert C. (1992). *Towards a Grammar of Biblical Poetics: Tales of the Prophets.* New York: Oxford University Press.

Burkert, Walter (1992). *The Orientalizing Revolution: Near Eastern Influences in the Early Archaic Age,* trans. by Margaret E. Pinder and Walter Burkert. Cambridge, MA: Harvard University Press.

Evans, Geoffrey (1958). "Ancient Mesopotamian Assemblies," *Journal of the American Oriental Society* 78:1–11; reprinted in Kagan (1975): 20–29.

Ferry, David, trans. (1992). *Gilgamesh: A New Reading in English Verse.* New York: Farrar, Strauss and Giroux.

Fox, Michael V. (1983). "Ancient Egyptian Rhetoric," *Rhetorica* 1:9–22; reprinted in Blythin (1986): 21–34.

Goody, Jack (1987). *The Interface Between the Written and the Oral.* Cambridge: Cambridge University Press.

Gordon, Edmund (1968). *Sumerian Proverbs: Glimpses of Everyday Life in Ancient Mesopotamia.* New York: Greenwood Press.

Gowen, Herbert H. (1968). *A History of Indian Literature.* New York: Greenwood Press.

Gray, Giles Wilkinson (1946). "The 'Precepts' of Kagemni and Ptah-Hotep," *Quarterly Journal of Speech* 32:446–54.

Grayson, A. Kirk (1984). "Literary Letters from Deities and Divities," in Sasson (1984): 143–48.

Jackson, Jared J., and Martin Kessler, eds. (1974). *Sacred Eloquence: Essays in Honor of James Muilenberg*. Pittsburgh: Pickwick Press.

Jacobsen, Thorkild (1943). "Primitive Democracy in Mesopotamia," *Journal of Near Eastern Studies* 22:159–72; reprinted in Kagan (1975): 6–13.

Kagan, Donald, ed. (1975). *Problems in Ancient History, Volume One: The Ancient Near East and Greece*. New York: Macmillan.

Kaster, Joseph (1968). *The Wings of the Falcon: Life and Thought of Ancient Egypt*. New York: Holt, Rinehart and Winston.

Kemp, Barry J. (1989). *Ancient Egypt: Anatomy of a Civilization*. London: Routledge.

Kennedy, George A. (1984). *New Testament Interpretation through Rhetorical Criticism*. Chapel Hill: University of North Carolina Press.

Kovacs, Maureen G., trans. (1989). *The Epic of Gilgamesh*. Stanford: Stanford University Press.

Kramer, Samuel N. (1963). *The Sumerians*. Chicago: University of Chicago Press.

——— (1969). "Sumerian Similes: A Panoramic View of Man's Oldest Literary Images," *Journal of the American Oriental Society* 89:1–10.

——— (1981). *History Begins at Sumer: Thirty-Nine Firsts in Man's Recorded History*. Philadelphia: University of Pennsylvania Press.

Lichtheim, Miriam, ed. (1973, 1976). *Ancient Egyptian Literature*: I: *The Old and Middle Kingdoms*; II: *The New Kingdom*. Berkeley: University of California Press.

Luria, S. (1929). "Die Ersten werden die Letzten sein," *Klio* 22:405–31.

Medhurst, Martin J. (1991). "Rhetorical Dimensions in Biblical Criticism: Beyond Style and Genre," *Quarterly Journal of Speech* 77:214–26.

Montet, Pierre (1958). *Everyday Life in Egypt in the Days of Ramesses the Great*, trans. by A. R. Maxwell-Hyslop and Margaret S. Drower. London: Edward Arnold.

Moran, William L., ed. (1992). *The Amarna Letters*. Baltimore: Johns Hopkins University Press.

Muilenberg, James (1969). "Form Criticism and Beyond," *Journal of Biblical Literature* 88:1–18.

Murray, Margaret A. (1963). *The Splendour That Was Egypt*. New York: Hawthorne Books.

Postgate, J. N. (1992). *Early Mesopotamia: Society and Economy at the Dawn of History*. London: Routledge.

Pritchard, James B., ed. (1958, 1975). *The Ancient Near East: Volume I, An Anthology of Texts and Pictures*; Volume II: *A New Anthology of Texts and Pictures* Princeton: Princeton University Press.

Sasson, Jack, ed. (1984). *Studies in Literature from the Ancient Near East Dedicated to Samuel Noah Kramer*. New Haven: American Oriental Society.

Scott, Robert L. (1972). "Rhetoric and Silence," *Western Speech* 36:146–58.

——— (1993). "Dialectical Tensions of Speaking and Silence," *Quarterly Journal of Speech* 79:1–18.

Segert, Stanislav (1984). "Parallelims in Ugaritic Poetry," in Sasson (1984): 295–306.

Simpson, William K., ed. (1972). *The Literature of Egypt*. New Haven: Yale University Press.

Strouhal, Evzen (1992). *Life of the Ancient Egyptians*. Norman: University of Oklahoma Press.

Tigay, Jeffrey H. (1982). *The Evolution of the Gilgamesh Epic*. Philadelphia: University of Pennsylvania Press.

Wilkinson, J. Garner (1837). *The Manners and Customs of the Ancient Egyptians*. London: J. Murray.

Wills, John W. (1970). "Speaking Arenas of Ancient Mesopotamia," *Quarterly Journal of Speech* 56:398–405.

Zulick, Margaret D. (1992a) "The Active Force of Hearing: The Ancient Hebrew Language of Persuasion," *Rhetorica* 10:367–80.

———(1992b). "The Agon of Jeremiah: On the Dialogic Invention of Prophetic Ethos," *Quarterly Journal of Speech* 78:125–48.

CHAPTER 7

Rhetoric in
Ancient China

The earliest surviving Chinese writing is found on bones and bronze vessels dating from the second millenium BCE when pictograms, the ancestor of Chinese characters as known today, were used to record omens and prophecies (an example in Mair 1994:3–4). It is probable that writing on bamboo or other perishable substances was in use by the same time, perhaps primarily for religious texts; there is, so far as I know, no evidence of the early use of writing in China for commercial purposes, which was the main impetus for its development in Mesopotamia. Writing was being used to record poetry and the teachings of philosophers by at least the sixth century BCE, about the same time as in India and Greece. Although facility in Chinese writing and reading requires memorization of thousands of characters, the system has the advantage that these are ideograms with semantic signification; as a result, a single system of writing can be read in different spoken dialects. Readers, however, constituted only a small fraction of the population in ancient China; the texts to be discussed in this chapter were written by and for the intellectual and political élite.

Early Chinese Literature by Burton Watson (1962) provides a readable introduction to classical Chinese language and literature. The earliest Chinese texts, according to Watson, are extremely lapidary and difficult; much was required of the reader in the way of supplying contexts and references. Although the accuracy of the written language had developed greatly by the third century, brevity and simplicity of composition remained characteristic of literary style. Classical Chinese, the language of literature as developed between the sixth and third centuries BCE, gradually ceased to be the spoken language but was canonized, much as was Attic Greek and classical Latin in the West, and remained in use for serious and elevated written discourse up to modern times. It is thus a "formal language" as that term has been employed in earlier chapters of this book. Among its formal characteristics are archaism, parallelism, and indirection. Ancient Chinese texts avoid indirect discourse, preferring instead to quote, or seem to quote, the actual words of a speaker. A result is hundreds of formal speeches attributed to rulers, officials, and philosophers, providing a body of rhetorical texts unmatched even in Greece and Rome.

China was, and to a considerable extent remains, a land of small agricultural villages. Urban centers, however, had developed in the valley of the Huang (or Yellow) river and its tributaries in north China by the third millenium BCE. About 1040 BCE this area was conquered by people who came from the plateau to the west, and what is known as the Chou dynasty was founded, which lasted until the middle of the third century. Beginning in the eighth century, however, powerful feudal lords often asserted their independence. Further political disintegration occurred in the fifth, fourth, and third centuries, known as "the Period of the Warring States," but this was also the time of major developments in Chinese philosophy and literature. In 221 BCE the classical period was brought to an abrupt end by the establishment of the autocratic Ch'in dynasty, which proceeded to unify the country—the Great Wall was begun at this time—and to destroy influences of the past by a wholesale burning of books, censorship of thought, and execution of scholars. Ch'in rule, however, lasted only briefly and was succeeded by the Han dynasty from 206 BCE to 220 CE; study of older traditions then revived and new literary and rhetorical forms were created. This chapter will be primarily concerned with the period of the Chou and the Ch'in.

An important rhetorical topos in ancient Chinese politics was *t'ien ming*, "the mandate of Heaven" (Watson 1962:27–34). This is the claim by a new emperor or king that because of his justice and virtue he has been commanded by the spiritual power that rules the universe to establish a new dynasty. He and his successors then take the title "Son of Heaven." This rule was in theory absolute, reaching down through hierarchies of society modeled on the structure of a family, though philosophers often emphasized that rule was also dependent on popular support resulting from just and benevolent policies. All Chinese thinkers explicitly or implicitly accepted an authoritarian society as the only reasonable and stable political structure. Emperors were, however, occasionally overthrown by force; the legitimacy of the new dynasty was then based on the claim that the previous ruler had forfeited the mandate of heaven (Graham 1989:1). The imperial court and the courts of local rulers exercised control through bureaucracies, including law courts under judges appointed by the ruler, and standing armies. A preoccupation with holding office—when it should be accepted or rejected and who deserved appointment—is noticeable in philosophical texts (Graham 1989:3). Public address and discussions of rhetoric in China before the third century BCE are almost totally concerned with efforts to restore order to society, to induce rulers to act wisely, justly, and compassionately toward the people, to encourage the public to respond with loyalty to the regime, and to perpetuate ancient traditions in ritual and social relationships. The mythical past down to the time of the early Chou dynasty was often idealized into a Golden Age of peace, order, prosperity, and happiness for all, which should be a model for more troubled contemporary times. Like traditional rhetoric in other parts of the world, Chinese rhetoric as we see it in the earliest texts was conservative, even reactionary, aimed at consensus, and sought to reaffirm social and political hierarchies, modeled on family relationships in which great emphasis was put on the authority of a father over his sons and the respect of a son for a father.

As elsewhere outside the Greco-Roman tradition of the West, rhetoric was not a distinct discipline in ancient China. The traditional Chinese arts were six: ceremony, music, archery, charioteering, writing, and mathematics (Graham 1989:31), making an interesting comparison with the "seven liberal arts" of the West: grammar, rhetoric, dialectic, arithmetic, geometry, astronomy, and music. In classical Chinese, the word *pièn*, literally "to till apart," thus "to distinguish," "to argue," or "argument," (many Chinese words can be used both as a noun and a verb) is probably the closest approximation to "rhetoric" as understood in Greece: It can refer to an art of persuasion including understanding of audience psychology, as well as moral and rational actions in the interest of social order (Lu 1991), but it lacks the connotation of artistic composition or style, which "rhetoric" often carries in the West. "To speak" or "speech" in classical Chinese is *shuo*; "to persuade" or "persuasion" is *shùei*. Effective public and private formal address was highly prized, and texts of speeches were created or preserved from early times, but discussion of speech and rhetoric is found in connection with political and ethical teaching or, after the second century BCE, in literary criticism by scholar-poets. The view of rhetoric reflected in early writings resembles the standards for effective speech that are inherent in traditional cultures as discussed in previous chapters, especially consensus-seeking, reinforcement of traditional custom, courtesy, and respect for authority. Chinese thinkers, however, often emphasized a need for frankness and sincerity in political contexts to a degree not found elsewhere, and during the long history of China rhetorical teaching was given considerably greater depth and detail than is found in the Near East. This is primarily because of the rich philosophical traditions, especially Confucianism, that came to dominate Chinese thought. Neither Confucius nor most other Chinese thinkers held a very high opinion of the intelligence of the general public; what they have to say about speech, persuasion, and other aspects of rhetoric is addressed to rulers or to their own philosophical students and does not consider techniques of addressing a mass audience. It is equally true that most ancient Chinese speeches are addressed to a single individual, a ruler or one of his ministers, or to a small group of political advisers (Garrett 1993b:22–23). After the introduction of Buddhism in the early centuries of the common era examples of public address to a general audience become more common.

The Chinese themselves would probably never have distinguished rhetoric as an art or discipline distinct from politics, ethics, or literary criticism if it had not been for Westerners who had been trained in classical rhetoric and applied that knowledge to the analysis of Chinese practices. The first to do so were French Jesuits of the seventeenth century; their reports were the basis of a chapter on rhetoric in *A Description of the Empire of China* by P. F. B. DuHalde, published in London between 1738 and 1741. DuHalde stressed that eloquence in China at that time was primarily based on imitation of canonical texts and that it was characterized by lively phrases, metaphor, comparison, and maxims taken from ancient sages. The modern study of early Chinese rhetoric was greatly advanced by the research of Robert T. Oliver of Pennsylvania State University, culminating in his fine book, *Communication and Culture in Ancient India and China* (1971). This remains the single best introduction to the subject, but published research grows steadily. In June 1988 Kathleen Jamieson organized a conference on "Rhetoric: East and West" at the University of Hawaii, which brought together those known to have an interest in the subject from the United States and Asian countries. I was one of the participants and in this chapter draw on some of the discussion there. The proceedings as a whole were not published but some of the papers delivered at the conference have been published separately and will be mentioned below. As in the case of many other parts of this book, I have to rely on information from those who have a knowledge of the original language, which is essential for significant new contribution to the subject. Chinese terms are differently transliterated in the discussions on which I draw. I have usually thought it best to keep the transliterations of my source, even though knowing that sometimes these are not in the form currently used by sinologists.

The Book of Songs

Evidence for rhetoric in very early China comes from several literary works, of which the most famous is the *Shih Ching*, in English *Book of Songs* or *Book of Odes*, a collection of 305 lyric and narrative poems dating from the seventh century or earlier (Ch'ên 1961:15–32; Watson 1962:201–30). The collection derived its authority in large part from the tradition that it was edited by Confucius (c. 551–479 BCE). Confucius probably did not prepare an edition but he certainly studied and discussed the songs frequently: He said that they stimulated the mind, were useful for self-contemplation, taught sociability and the duty of serving one's father and one's prince, showed how to regulate feelings, and acquainted the student with the names of birds, beasts, and plants (*Analects* 17.9). His interest in the songs was almost entirely limited to how passages could be used for moral instruction, often entirely out of context, not in their literary qualities (Holzman 1978). The poems have been studied, memorized, and appealed to as an authority throughout Chinese history. Allusions to them were sometimes made as an indirect form of persuasion in political contexts, as when the Duke of Lu, who had taken refuge in a foreign land, was encouraged to return home by intonation of a poem containing the refrain "let us go back." Arthur Waley, who made major contributions to translation amd interpretation of classical Chinese, comments, "The emotional effect of the familiar poem is greater than that of any direct appeal" (Waley 1960:335). Extensive Chinese commentaries have been written on the collection since ancient times, moralizing them under Confucian influence and often interpreting poems allegorically in the interest of contemporary political application.

Good English translations of the *Shih* are those by Karlgren (1950), Legge (reprinted 1960:I), and Waley (1960); selections are translated by Riegel in Mair (1994:149–69). Ezra Pound's *Cathey* is probably the most famous version, but its rhetoric is more that of Pound than that of the originals. There is a good discussion of the problems of translating Chinese poetry, with comparative examples, by Eoyang (1993). Waley rearranged the traditional order to group the poems by theme, and his headings give a sense of the subjects: courtship, marriage, warriors and battles, agriculture, blessings, welcome, feasting, sacrifice, music and dancing, dynastic songs and legends, building, hunting, moral pieces, and lamentations. Although many songs are simple reflections on nature or human situations, they also have the characteristic of "formal language" as found elsewhere. The language of the poems is conventional. Each line ordinarily consists of only four words; ideas and lines are constantly repeated, and a rhyming scheme employed in most poems (in a quatrain the second and fourth line rhyme and sometimes all four lines rhyme). Rhyme is found in religious poetry in nonliterate societies and in magical formulas, but the Chinese were the first to perfect rhyming verse in literary composition, something not found in the West before the medieval period. Although metaphor is constantly present, imagery is not rationalized as simile: "Early Chinese songs do not as a rule introduce a comparison with an 'as if' or 'like,' but state it on the same footing as the facts they narrate" (Waley 1960:13). This is consistent with the treatment of metaphor in traditional oral cultures as I have described it in earlier chapters.

The Chinese had no great early epic like the *Gilgamesh* or the *Iliad*, nor was any national epic like the *Aeneid* created in their later literary history. The *Shih*, however, performed some of the functions of epic elsewhere (Ch'ên 1961:23). Its 305 songs collectively express traditional religious and social values in a form accessible to a popular audience. What principles governed the original formation of the collection are unknown; perhaps these poems were regarded as the most beautiful or most popular. All the songs are anonymous. Another way in which the collection performed a function of epic is that some of the poems narrate dynastic legends using folk-tale motives and reflect the existence of myths of gods and heroes that resemble those in other cultures (Waley 1960:239–80). These are, however, short separate poems, scattered through the collection and only brought together by modern scholars to form a cycle, much as Elias Lønnrot in the nineteenth century created the Finnish epic, *Kalevala*, from individual shorter ballads. The Chinese collection as a whole does not reflect any strong idealization of heroic values; rather it is more concerned with the experience of ordinary people living ordinary lives and giving expression to their feelings.

The Book of History

Although the Chinese thus had no tradition of heroic epic, they had from very early times an historiographic tradition, reflecting fascination with narrating events as models, precedents, or warnings for the present and future. The classic example of this is the *Shu Ching* or *Shoo King*, known in English as the *Book of Historical Documents* or *Book of History* (late nineteenth-century translation by Legge, reprinted 1960:III). The *Shu* is an account, incompletely preserved, by anonymous authors or editors of events involving kings who allegedly reigned from around 2200 to 628 BCE (later Chinese scholars constructed a traditional chronology that may not be trustworthy, although archaeological discoveries provide some confirmation). Into this outline are inserted some fifty speeches by emperors, generals, and officials of state. The earliest ones are unlikely to be entirely authentic and even the later ones may be the composition of scholars who sought to recreate an historical situation known from oral tradition. There is thus some analogy to the speeches found in Thucydides and other Greek and Roman historians. But if the speeches do not represent an entirely authentic earlier rhetorical tradition they were decisive in establishing the model for what rhetoric at its best should be throughout the later history of China. The collection as a whole, perhaps as a result of Confucian influence, is remarkably consistent in its assumptions about appropriate and effective speech and in rhetorical technique. In the first century BCE the *Shu*, like the *Shih*, became one of the textbooks of formal education and later a subject for examinations for the civil service (Chaffee 1995).

Robert Oliver (1971:102–20) has given an excellent account of rhetoric as found in the *Shu*. He states (102) that the overall message of the work is that "to rule well meant to communicate honestly, intelligently, and effectively.... Ministers must be courageous in speaking with utmost frankness to their monarchs; and kings must make unmistakably clear what responsibilities and duties they expect their ministers, generals, and officials to exercise. Social harmony and individual dignity ... could not be attained by evasive speaking, by false flattery, or by curbing honest criticism. The kind of speech repeatedly recommended was that which aimed to achieve the speaker's goal through means that would enhance rather than undermine communal contentment. Disruptive personal attack or appeal to self-interest in persuasive appeals was always to be condemned.... The best speaking was that which showed that the good of each one inhered within what was good for all." With the exception of the need for frankness, this is the view of speech found in many traditional cultures.

The speeches in the *Shu* are all examples of "deliberative" oratory, aimed at persuading an individual or audience to undertake an action or act in a certain way. There are some nine speeches attributed to a ruler, high official, or general exhorting troops to battle, a form also found in Greek and Latin historiography (Oliver 1971:104–6). The earliest (Legge 1960, III:64–65) is attributed to Yu, minister to the emperor Shung, who according to tradition reigned from 2254 to 2204 BCE. The arrangement is a simple address to those present, then a justification of the war in the form of an invective against the wickedness of the enemy, and a call to fight bravely. The authority and confidence of the speaker are the major means of persuasion, but the list of the enemy's vices provides reasons why the war is morally justified and introduces an emotional element. Mary Garrett (1993b) has explored in some detail ancient Chinese views of the emotions, their implication for Chinese rhetoric, and their possible contributions to Western theories of rhetorical pathos. It sometimes happened that a general addressing his troups was in revolt against the legitimate ruler, in which case the "mandate of Heaven" becomes an issue; for example, General T'ang in a speech traditionally dated to 1765 BCE (Legge III:173–75) rejected the legitimacy of the emperor because of his crimes, claimed for himself the authority of Heaven, and revealed his own ruthless character by promising death to anyone who disobeys him. The inclusion of the speech doubtless results from the fact that T'ang was successful in overthrowing the emperor and establishing a dynasty that, according to traditional Chinese chronology, lasted for over 600 years.

A second category of speeches, numbering about a dozen, are "announcements" by a ruler or other high official that lay out public policy or deal with some serious problem. Most are addressed to assembled officials, a few to the people brought together to hear the ruler's words. A long announcement by the King of Chou (Legge III:525–43), traditionally dated about 1100 BCE, is of special interest in that it lists the titles and duties of the leading officials of state; these include the prime minister, the minister of religion, the minister of war, the minister of crime, the minister of works, and "the Grand Tutor," but many other functionaries are mentioned elsewhere including a minister of communication (Legge III:49) and "the Grand Historian" (Legge III:353 and 557). There is no specific reference to a council of state, but the emperors were encouraged to consult widely: with their own heart, their nobles and officers, with the masses of the people, and with the diviners (Legge III:337).

Perhaps the most interesting of the announcements is the series of speeches by King Pwan-kang (traditionally ruled 1407–1400 BCE) when he sought to move the capital to the south bank of the Huang river, where flooding would be less of a problem (text in Legge III:220–47; discussion by Oliver 1971:113–17). There was much opposition, both within the court and from the inhabitants who were being asked to leave their homes and the graves of their ancestors. In the first speech, apparently addressed to a large group of officials and leading citizens, the king began by acknowledging that the present capital had been founded by his ancestors with good intentions, but, he adds, it was no longer suitable. No specific problems are cited. He has posed the question of what to do to the gods by divination and the oracular response is "This is no place for us." Given the belief among ancient Chinese in divination, this is a strong argument in support of his decision to move. He goes on to argue that the capital has at different times been in five different places; to refuse another change is to reject the will of Heaven, to destroy the dynasty, and to abandon the precedent of former kings. He concludes with an image, intended to encourage the people: "As from the stump of a felled tree there are sprouts and shoots, Heaven will perpetuate its decree in our favour in this new city; the great possession of the former kings will be continued and renewed; tranquillity will be secured to the four quarters of the empire" (Legge III:223).

The king then became aware that members of the court were encouraging popular opposition to moving the capital, and he summoned them to his presence for a second speech, which I quote in its entirety in the translation of James Legge as a good example of early Chinese official eloquence. The king does not seek to justify his decision: that he has done before on the basis of the will of Heaven and his own careful assessment of the situation. He speaks with authority and sternly rebukes, even threatens, the dissidents. His emphasis throughout is on the need for consensus, loyalty, and obedience, in accord with tradition. As is to be expected in deliberative rhetoric, the overall topic is the advantage to the hearers of the announced policy. The speech falls clearly into the four parts that are familiar from Western rhetorical theory: proemium, narration, proof, and epilogue.

> (proemium) Come, all of you; I will announce to you my instructions. Take counsel now to put away your selfish thoughts. Do not with haughty disregard of me follow after your own ease.
>
> (narration) Of old, our former kings had it as a principal object in their plans to employ the men of old families to share in the government. When they wished to proclaim and announce what was to be attended to, those did not conceal the imperial views, and on this account the kings greatly respected them. They did not exceed the truth in their communications with the people, and on this account the people became greatly changed. Now, however, you keep clamouring, and get the confidence of the people by alarming and shallow speeches. I do not know what you keep wrangling about. In this movement I am not myself abandoning my proper virtue, but you conceal the goodness of my intentions, not standing in awe of me, the one man. I see you as clearly as one sees fire; but still by my undecided plans I have produced your error.

The king thus begins by indicting the conduct of his officials, reminding them of their traditional duty and its good results, contrasting that with their present conduct, and asserting his authority and the rightness of his plan, but then softens the rebuke by taking some of the responsibility himself: He has not been as decisive as he should have been. "The one man" is a phrase often used by Chinese rulers to refer to themselves and their authority. He continues into the main body of his speech, beginning with two comparisons with everyday life and reminding his hearers of the advantages of his plan:

> (proof) When the net has its line, there is order and not confusion; and when the husbandman labours upon the fields, and spends his strength in reaping, there is then the abundant autumn. If you can put away your selfish thoughts, you will bestow real good upon the people, reaching to your relatives and friends, and may boldly venture to make your words great, and say that you have accumulated virtue. You do not fear the great evils which are far and near. You are like the husbandman who yields himself to ease, and is not strong to toil and to labour on his acres, and who in such a case cannot have either rice or millet. You do not use friendly and good words to the people, and are only producing suffering for yourselves. As destroyers and calamities, villains and traitors, the punishment shall come on your persons. You set the example of evil, and must feel its smart,—what will it avail you then to repent? Look at the poor people;—they can still consult together about remonstrances which they wish to address to me, but when they begin to speak, you are ready with your extravagant talk:—how much more ought you to have me before your eyes, with whom it is to make your lives long or short! Why do you not report their words to me, but go about to excite one another by empty speeches, frightening and involving the multitudes in misery? When a fire is blazing in the plains, so that it cannot be approached, can it still be beaten out? Thus for you to cause dispeace in this way:—it is not I who am to blame.
>
> Ch'e Jin has said, "In men, we seek individuals of old families; in vessels, we do not seek old ones, but new." Formerly, the kings, my predecessors, and your forefathers and fathers, shared together the ease and labours of the State;—how should I dare to lay undeserved inflictions on you? For generations the toils of your families have been approved, and I will not conceal your greatness. Now when I offer the great sacrifices to my predecessors, your forefathers are present to share in them. They observe the happiness I confer and the sufferings I inflict, and I cannot dare to reward virtue that does not exist.
>
> (epilogue) I have announced to you the difficulties of the present enterprise. My will is that of an archer. Do not you despise the old and experienced, and do not make little of the helpless and young. Seek everyone long continuance in your new abode; exert yourselves to listen to the plans of me, the one man. There is with me no distinction of distant and near. The criminal shall die the death; and the good-doer shall have his virtue displayed. The prosperity of the country must come from you all. If it fail in prosperity, that must arise from me, the one man, erring in the application

of punishment. All of you be sure to make known this announcement. From this time forward attend respectfully to your business; have the duties of your offices regularly adjusted; bring your mouths under the rule of law:—lest punishment come upon you, when repentance will be of no avail. (Legge III:225–31).

The king seems to have been successful in his appeal, for the work of moving the capital went forward. After the crossing was completed, however, the people indulged themselves rather than settling down to hard work, and the king had to continue to exhort them to their duty.

The speeches showing the most characteristic features of the earliest Chinese rhetoric are the "instructions," especially those by a minister of state to a ruler, for it is here that the speaker is expected to be honest, sincere, and forthright, to preserve his own dignity, to avoid flattery, and at the same time to show respect for the ruler and keep from antagonizing him. There are examples of addresses to rulers by Greek sophists in the time of the Roman empire with which these speeches can be compared (Kennedy 1994:230–56); the Greek examples are more epideictic than deliberative in that they praise the addressee for his past actions and only occasionally or by implication give advice for the future, and they often make much use of exaggerated flattery. The many warnings by Chinese thinkers against flattery are doubtless evidence that it was very common, and probably often effective; it was not, however, socially approved to the extent that it was in the West from the late classical until the early modern period.

"Announcements" and speeches of "instruction" sometimes overlap, making a clear-cut distinction impossible—the speech of Pwan-kang quoted above combines the two—but there are about twenty speeches in the *Shu*, some of considerable length, that are primarily instructions, some by a king to his ministers, some addressed to a king by one of his leading ministers, and some by a minister to a subordinate. Among the most famous instruction speeches were those of the Duke of Chou (in Legge's transliteration Chow), who is a major figure in the fifth and last part of the *Shu*.

I have not found any examples of judicial rhetoric from early China, but a speech attributed to the emperor Muh (traditionally reigned 1000–945 BCE) gives an account of the system of criminal justice in early times (Legge III:602–10). Judges appointed by the emperor or his officials heard all cases. Prosecution and defense made opening statements and introduced documents and witnesses. The judges were expected to examine the evidence and to adjust their decision to one of "five punishments" (death, branding, cutting off the nose, cutting off the feet, or castration), one of the "five fees," or one of the "five cases of error" (exposure on the stocks or a public stone or forms of hard labor on public works). The judges are warned not to be influenced by power, private grudges, "female solicitation," bribes, or emotional appeals. When the judges are in doubt, they should refrain from convicting the accused. "When you have examined, and many things are clear, yet form a judgment from studying the appearance of the parties. If you find nothing on examination, do not listen to the case any more. In everything stand in awe of the dread majesty of Heaven" (Legge III:604). At least in theory, direct evidence would seem to have been required for conviction. The reference to "the appearance of the parties" may suggest that the character and reputation of the parties could be taken into account. I have not found use of argument from probability in ancient Chinese rhetoric, something we saw developing in the Near East and characteristic of Greek thought.

Chinese rhetoric as seen in the *Shu* generally avoids pathos except in military exhortations and in some of the more severe announcements or instructions. It is strong in ethos—the authority and character of the speaker, the tradition of the ancestors who continue to watch the living, the moral rightness of the message—but it is also not lacking in logical argument; as the Viscount of Ke said in an instruction to King Chou, "the virtue of speech is accordance with reason" (Legge III:326). Argument is chiefly inductive, based on examples, precedents, quotation of authorities, and analogies. Deductive argument in the form of enthymemes seems undeveloped. Speeches are often clearly divided into parts that perform the functions of proemium, narration, proof, and epilogue.

Records of the Grand Historian

Other works, continuing Chinese history through the classical period, also contain speeches, making it possible to observe the development of public address in different political and philosophical contexts. The *Tso Chuan* is a history of the period from 722 to 468 BCE (selections in Watson 1989). The most comprehensive and scholarly of the histories is *Records of the Grand Historian*, the work of Ssu-ma Ch'ien (also transliterated Sima Qian), who lived from about 145 to about 90 BCE (translation by Watson 1993; discussion by Watson 1962:92–103). The official known as the Grand Historian had traditionally concerned himself with astronomy and regulation of the calendar; Ssu-ma for the first time undertook to write a comprehensive, systematic history, utilizing earlier works and documents available to him in the court. His work is divided into a chronological account of dynasties and rulers down to his own times, a table of dates of principal events, discussions of the origins and development of institutions, a history of the feudal states, and a concluding section of biographies of famous or notorious individuals, accounts of foreign lands, and an autobiography of his own difficult life. He fell from favor and chose castration rather than the usual suicide to enable him to finish his great work. The function of history as Ssu-ma, like some Western historians, understood it was to teach moral lessons: to censure evil and encourage good. He thus oftens comments on events. His biographies, the earliest known in China, are largely anecdotal, identifying a variety of good and bad character types and can be compared to those of Plutarch in Greek, writing about a century later.

There are numerous speeches and documents in the *Records*, of which the most famous is probably the letter of Li Ssi, chancellor under the ruthless emperor Ch'in whose unification of China in 221 BCE has been mentioned earlier. In 213, at a social meeting in the palace various speakers eulogized the emperor in his presence, but one, probably a Confucianist, dared to suggest that flattery was compounding the ruler's errors and that if he and his rule were to survive he should imitate the example of virtuous rulers of the past. The emperor referred the matter to Li Ssi, who after some consideration replied in writing as follows (*Records*, chapter 87, in Watson 1993: *Qin* 185).

> In the past the empire was frightened and in confusion and no one was able to unite it. Therefore the feudal rulers rose up side by side, all of them declaiming on antiquity in order to disparage the present, parading empty words in order to confuse the facts. Men prided themselves on their private theories and criticized the measures adopted by their superiors.
>
> Now Your Majesty has unified all under heaven, distinguishing black from white and establishing a single source of authority. Yet these adherents of private theories band together to criticize the law and directives. Hearing that an order has been handed down, each one proceeds to discuss it in the light of his private theories. At court they disapprove in their hearts; outside they debate it in the street. They hold it a mark of fame to criticize the ruler, regard it as lofty to take a dissenting stance, and they lead the lesser officials in fabricating slander. If behaviour such as this is permitted, then in upper circles the authority of the ruler will be compromised, and in lower ones cliques will form. Therefore it should be prohibited.
>
> I request that all writings, the *Odes*, the *Documents* [i.e., the classic *Shu* discussed above], and the sayings of the hundred schools of philosophy, be discarded and done away with. Anyone who has failed to discard such books within thirty days from the time this prohibition reaches them shall be subjected to tatooing and condemned to "wall down" labour. The books that are to be exempted are those on medicine, divination, agriculture, and forestry. Anyone wishing to study these should have a law officer for his teacher.

The emperor implemented Li Ssi's proposal: books were burned and 150 scholars are said to have been buried alive. Some ancient books, including the great classics, were hidden and survived but many early works were permanently lost.

Confucius

The individual who most influenced all of Chinese thought until the twentieth century was Confucius. The standard classics of the schools were works describing his teachings or works, including the *Shi* and the *Shu*, which he was regarded as having edited. A vast body of commentary continued to be written on these Confucian classics for centuries; even philosophers who dissented from Confucian teachings often defined their thought in contrast with his or that of his followers. Confucius was a contemporary of Guatama Buddha in India and of the Greek philosophers Pythagoras and Heraclitus, though none of these thinkers had any knowledge of the others. He died in 479 BCE, ten years before Socrates was born on the other side of the world; comparison between them has been a regular feature of comparative cultural studies. Both lived in periods when traveling teachers gained some fame and sought to support themselves by speaking on political and ethical matters, and both sought to draw a line between the teachings of others and what they regarded as true wisdom. Both show some hostility toward rhetoric as practiced in their own time. Both were skilled rhetoricians who aimed to persuade those who heard them to believe what they regarded as true, beneficial, and just. Both sought to teach their followers how to live rightly. Both were rejected by contemporary society. There are also significant differences between them. Although they both engaged in dialogue with their followers, Confucius is usually represented as answering questions authoritatively, whereas Socrates often appears as the questioner and denies authoritative knowledge. Although both were personally pious, grounded virtue in the will of the gods, and put a high value on the performance of religious ritual, Confucius had little interest in metaphysics; Confucianism is a secular philosophy finding its wisdom in human traditions of an idealized past. Socrates was a mystic, believing in inspiration, and at least as presented by Plato, found truth outside human life, which was only an imitation of metaphysical reality. Confucius was a scholar who put great value on study of the written word; the Platonic Socrates was suspicious of writing and emphasized individual thinking and orality. Socrates was much given to irony; Confucius to maxims and epigrams. Socrates was much interested in epistemology and a method of dialectic that would lead to truth; Confucius was less systematic and did not develop a system of argument.

The most authoritative source of Confucius's teaching are the *Analects*, a report of what he said in different situations and his responses to the questions of his followers. The best known translations are those of Legge (reprinted 1960, I:137–354), Waley (1964), and Lau (1979). All of the remarks attributed to Confucius are short; he is never shown giving a lecture or arguing out a thesis in detail, and perhaps did not do so. His views on many subjects seem sometimes inconsistent; when taxed with this he explained that his responses differed in terms of the specific context and the understanding of the hearer. There are numerous references to speech in the *Analects*, which show some ambivalence; for example 1.3: "The Master said, 'Clever talk and a pretentious manner are seldom found in the Good'" (Waley 1964:84); 14.5: "One who has accumulated moral power will certainly also possess eloquence; but he who has eloquence does not necessarily possess moral power" (Waley 1964:180); and 17.19: "The Master said, 'I would much rather not have to talk.' Tzo-kung said, 'If our Master did not talk, what should we little ones have to hand down about him?' The Master said, 'Heaven does not speak; yet the four seasons run their course thereby, the hundred creatures, each after its kind, are born thereby. Heaven does no speaking.' " (Waley 1964:214). This contrasts sharply with biblical views of "the Word" as discussed in the previous chapter. Most of what is attributed to Confucius about rhetoric can be thought of as encapsulating qualities of good speech as found in the *Shu*.

Some important concepts in Confucian thought are the *Tao* (the "Way"), the proper course of human conduct based on the model of antiquity; *te*, often translated "virtue," a person's potentiality to act in accordance with the Way; *li*, ceremony or good manners; *yi*, the conduct fitting one's role or status; and *jen*, used as a noun to mean "noble" and as a verb to mean "be civilized" in conduct (Graham 1989:11–19). The mind/body dichotomy of Western thought was, happily, unknown to the Chinese; *jen* is not an inner state. Fingarette (1972:55) claims it was conceived as "a directed force operating in actions in public space and time, and having a person as initial point-source and a person as the terminal point on which the force impinges." It thus closely resembles "rhetoric" as a form of energy, a definition I suggested earlier in this book.

Robert Oliver (1971:136–44) sought to integrate Confucian adages about rhetoric into seven purposes of speaking and fourteen persuasive methods. He documents these from the text, but they are scattered throughout the twenty books of the *Analectics* and to list them in this way implies a systematic theory that is not at all Confucius's way of thinking. Some adages relate to the speaker, who should be wise, learned, sincere, moral, both firm of purpose and conciliatory; others to the speech, which should be restrained, clear, appropriate to the character of the speaker and the occasion, and practical. Confucius stressed the need to adapt a speech to an audience and to establish a reciprocal relationship between speaker and audience. There are elements here analagous to Plato's description of a philosophically based rhetoric in *Phaedrus*, and to Quintilian's definition of an orator as "a good man speaking well."

Chinese Philosophy

Philosophical traditions first developed about the same time in China, India, and Greece, though without any communication between thinkers in the three cultures. Perhaps this synchrony reflects a parallel stage in cultural development generally, including the use of writing and changes in traditional patterns that suggested questions not previously formulated. The Near East was something of an anomaly; there is little in Mesopotamian or Egyptian thought that is comparable to philosophy as understood elsewhere, though both those cultures had earlier made significant progress in mathematics and astronomy. The closest Near-Eastern parallel is perhaps found in Jewish theology in roughly this same period. There are significant differences between the philosophical traditions of India, Greece, and China and at least one common element. Indian thought was dominated by metaphysics; early Greek thought by explanations of the physical universe, then after Socrates by integrated explanations of metaphysics, politics, ethics, and other subjects, with the creation of disciplinary subdivisions in philosophical teaching. Chinese philosophy was always primarily political and ethical, with comparatively little interest in metaphysics. All three cultures developed logic and dialectics necessary for any philosophical project The best recent discussion of ancient Chinese philosophy is probably Graham's *Disputers of the Tao* (1989), which makes numerous points relevant to rhetoric. Graham stresses that early Chinese philosophers were little interested in the question "What is the truth?" which has dominated Western philosophy; rather, they were concerned with "Where is the Way (*Tao*)?" to order the state and conduct personal life (Graham 1989:3): "We might sum up the Chinese attitude to reason in these terms: reason is for questions of means; for your ends in life, listen to aphorism, example, parable, and poetry" (Ibid. 7). Later Chinese thinkers identified six philosophical schools that flourished between the sixth and third centuries BCE: the Confucianists, the Yang-Yin cosmologists, the Mohists, the Taoists, the School of Names, and the Legalists (Ibid. 31). In the following pages I shall say a little about each.

Mencius

The most famous follower of Confucius was Mencius (Meng K'o or Mengzi), who was born about 372 and died about 289 BCE, making him a slightly younger contemporary of Aristotle (384–322 BCE). Appreciation of Mencius's thought in the West owes much to I. A. Richards's 1932 book, *Mencius on the Mind: Experiments in Multiple Definition*. By "multiple definition" is meant the view that every logical definition is stated from a particular point of view; if something is to be understood and communicated correctly it requires description from multiple objective and subjective stances. The *Book of Mencius* (translations by Legge, reprinted 1960:II; Ware 1960; and Dobson 1963) resembles the *Analects of Confucius* in form, a report of the master's conversations, but some discourses are rather longer than those attibuted to Confucius. An important difference between Mencius and Confucius is that Mencius regarded human beings as fundamentally good, though often corrupted by seeming advantage for profit or pleasure; Confucius, on the other hand, seems to have regarded human beings as inherently neither good nor bad. Mencius lived in a period of increasing cynicism and materialism; he thought, however, that history moved in cycles, that an ideal king would soon appear who would restore society to happier conditions of the past, and that he himself was an instrument of Heaven who might play a role as an adviser to such a king (Dobson 1963:3). This millenialism can be compared to similar developments elsewhere when a society is put under strain: in ancient Israel, among American Indians in the nineteenth century, in modern Indonesia, and even to Greek utopianism such as Plato's hopes for a philosopher-king. The change Mencius looked for did not occur in his lifetime but the Han dynasty, which assumed power eighty years after his death, did sponsor a return to Confucian values and effected a partial reversal of the moral degeneration of society.

As a sample of Mencius rhetoric I quote here a passage in the translation of Dobson (1963:86–87). Kung-sun Ch'ou has asked Mencius in what respect he is superior to another philosopher, Kao Tzu. Mencius replies: "I understand 'what can be put in words.' I am adept in the cultivation of the 'greater physical vigour'(*ch'i*)" [in Legge's translation "passion-nature"]. Kung-sun Ch'ou said, "Might I ask what you mean by 'the greater physical vigour'?" Mencius said,

> It is difficult to express in words. The physical vigour [or "passion-nature"] in this sense is the greatest, the most durable. If it is nurtured by rectitude it remains unharmed and permeates the entire universe. The physical vigour in this sense is the fit recipient for Justice and the Way. Without it, man is ill-nourished. It is begotten of the sum total of just deeds. It is not to be seized and held by incidental just deeds. If an act of ours does not meet approval with the heart, then (the life force) is ill-nourished. That is why Kao Tzu has never understood Justice. He thinks it is external to man. One must render service to it; one must not regard it as an objective criterion. The mind must never let it out of its sight, but we must not try to make it grow. Let us not be like the man of Sung who, worried that his young plants were not growing, tugged at them (to help them grow). He returned home, full of fuss, saying, "What a busy day! I have been helping my plants to grow." His son hurried out to the fields to look, but the young plants had withered already. There are few men in the world today who are not "helping the plants grow." Some neglect their plants, thinking it useless to weed them. Some help their plants by giving them a tug. But this is not merely useless; it is actually harmful.

There is some similarity here to "conscience" as understood in the West and perhaps also to Aristotle's theory of how moral virtue is developed in the individual. To me, Mencius comments about "physical vigor," and his connection of it to verbal expression seems partially to overlap with my view of rhetoric as a form of energy. The passage continues as follows:

> Kung-sun Ch'ou said, "What do you mean by 'I understand what can be put into words'?"
>
> Mencius replied, "I understand what hides the other half of a half-truth. I understand the pitfalls that lie beneath extravagant statements. I understand the emptiness that lies behind evasive statements. Engendered in the mind, they cause harm to government. When they result in governmental action they cause harm to public affairs. If a Sage were to rise again he would agree with all I have said." (*Mencius* 2.1.2.11-17; for a somewhat different translation cf. Legge 1960, II:189–92)

Stephen Owen (1992:22–23) comments on the latter part of this passage as follows:

Mencius' knowledge of language is a knowledge of what the words reveal about the speaker, what they make manifest.... Words become only a surface whose shape reveals what lies within. Mencius' list of different kinds of language shows that the trained listener can make fine discriminations. Most important, what the speaker reveals in his words is involuntary—perhaps not at all what he would wish to have revealed. Error and deception are not autonomous categories here, but are subsumed under understanding the person: they are nothing more than manifestations of ignorance or the desire to deceive and as such become important pieces of evidence for us when we listen to someone speak. Recognizing the truth or accepting error, being deceived or not being deceived rest with the capacities of the listener.

For further discussion of Mencius see Watson (1962:130–32), Oliver (1971:161–81), and Graham (1989:111–32).

Yang *and* Yin

Yang and *yin* in Chinese thought were primordial entities resulting from the coalescence of chaos at the creation of the world. They are instantiated in such principles as (respectively) male and female, up and down, light and dark, life and death, yes and no, viewed as complementaries rather than as contraries; the polarization characteristic of Western philosophy is lacking. Just as some philosophical connections can be drawn between Plato's metaphysics and his rhetoric, as seen in Socrates's discussion of truth, beauty, and love in the *Phaedrus*, so there are some connections between Chinese cosmology and rhetoric. Speech is yang, silence is yin (Graham 1989:331). To achieve social order yang and yin need to come together harmoniously: "Differences of viewpoint cannot be overcome by contention.... It is advantageous to seek opportunities to present one's view to those in authority, but disadvantageous to urge ardently acceptance of one's own views" (Oliver 1971:176–77). Karl Kao (1984:326) has argued that the cosmogony of the theory of yang and yin is the source of parallelism in Chinese rhetoric, which he views as a distinctive cultural phenomenon. It may be the case that the concepts of yang and yin reinforced the continual use of parallelism in Chinese prose and poetry and influenced the discussion of style by later Chinese critics, but as I have repeatedly stressed, parallelism is a feature of composition found almost universally in traditional societies with very different cosmological views. It is not unique to China.

Mohism

Mohism originated in the teachings of Mo Tze (or Mo-tzu), who lived in the fifth century BCE, a generation after Confucius. These teachings are known from the *Book of Mo Tze*, compiled by his students and later followers (translation by Mei 1929; selections in Watson 1967:1–140). While Confucius and his followers accepted the existing stratification of society, emphasized obligations to and by rulers and family members, and sought a harmonious social order in which each person fulfilled the duty of his station in life, the Mohists believed that universal love was a principle of nature and taught the basic equality of all. The true interests of the individual and society were to be regarded as identical. A speaker should identify the needs of an audience and aim at practical results (Oliver 1971:183–93). Despite the lofty vision of Mo Tze's philosophy, he seems to have supported his doctrines by appeal to material benefits, authoritarianism, and models of conduct by ancient sages, the later of dubious authenticity (Watson 1967:11). In the fourth and third centuries the followers of Mo Tze—"the latter Mohists" as they are called—engaged in lively disputation on philosophical issues and formulated a logical system that has some resemblance to dialectic as practiced in Greek philosophical schools (Graham 1978). I shall return to this subject in the account of Chinese sophistry later in this chapter.

Taoism

The concept of the Tao, "the Way," is common to most Chinese philosophy, but the term "Taoists" is specifically applied to the followers of Lao-tzu. When he lived and when the classic work of Taoism, *Tao Te Ching*, was compiled is uncertain; dates range between about 600 and 400 BCE (translation by Lau 1982). Taoism taught passive nonaction, identification of the individual with nature, and spontaneous righteousness; it rejected verbal distinctions, categorizations, and logical argument and suggested that what seems real is often an illusion and what seems a dream may be real. Truth, however, can be found by introspection and can be expressed by simple sincerity; silence is often best. When the truth is perceived there is a possibility of communicating it by a mystical communion with others rather than by an overt attempt to persuade. Although one should not offend others and flout social conventions, one should recognize that abstract concepts, including love, honor, and charity, are artificial constructs of society. The leading Taoist philosopher of the fourth century BCE was Chuang-tzu, who considerably elaborated the rhetorical principles of the movement (Oliver 1971:246–57; Kirkwood 1995; translation of his *Sayings* by Watson 1968). Vernon Jensen (1987) has summed up the rhetorical principles of Taoism as: (1) deprecate eloquence and honor silence; (2) deprecate argumentation; (3) look inward for truths; (4) avoid willful critical thinking and instead utilize spontaneous intuition; (5) rest assertions on time-honored authority; and (6) rely on ethos: sincerity, humility, goodness, respectfulness, and trustworthiness.

Chinese Sophistry and the School of Names

The beginnings of speculation about rhetoric in the West are closely associated with the teaching of sophists, of whom the most famous are Protagoras and Gorgias. Sophistry in Greece arose in the fifth century BCE, a time of conflicting philosophical doctrines claiming knowledge of truth. The sophists were skeptical of these claims, which they undermined by verbal subtleties of argument and the use of paradox; they sought to teach practical ways of success in the world based primarily on techniques of public speaking. They were much interested in language; indeed, the sophists began the study of grammar and philology. Although Athens became the center of the sophist movement, most of the leading sophists were not Athenians but itinerant teacher-orators who supported themselves by traveling about the Greek world, giving demonstrations of their skills and offering political advice to Greek states. Something analogous to Greek sophistry had appeared in India a century or two earlier; in China it may have begun as early as the sixth century but flourished especially in the fourth and third centuries, thus overlapping the period of sophistry in classical Greece. Sophistry in some form seems to be a regular development in "sophisticated" literate societies when political, social, and moral conditions are undergoing change, conflicting philosophical schools arise, each claiming access to truth in a different way, and individual teachers appear who are independent of state bureaucracies and offer advice to rulers. All these conditions existed in China in the fourth century. What Graham (1978:15–18) has called "the metaphysical crisis of the 4th century" seems especially to have contributed to a sophistic turn in Chinese thought. This was precipitated by the teachings of Yang Chu, who argued for making judgments on the basis of the interests of the individual and introduced the concept of *hsing* into Chinese philosophy. *Hsing* is human nature, "the spontaneous tendency of the living organism throughout its life span ... we obey Heaven, not as Confucians and Mohists suppose by behaving morally, but by nurturing and harmonising the vital tendencies and spontaneous inclinations which Heaven instilled in us when we were born" (Graham 1978:16–17). This might be said to include rhetorical energy.

The School of Names opened up questions about the nature of language and exposed logical paradoxes (Oliver 1971:193–98; Graham 1989:75–94). The most famous Chinese paradox is the topic of "the White Horse." Kun Sun Lung maintained that a white horse is not a horse, for "horse" is that by which we name the shape, "white" by which we name the color. To name the color is not to name the shape. Thus a white horse is not a horse. The argument was considerably subtler than this summary statement suggests. Western readers have sometimes found Chinese rhetoric lacking in logical argument, but this is a superficial judgment. As noted earlier, the "later Mohists" in particular engaged in subtle dialectic in accordance with logical rules. Mary Garrett (1993a) has analyzed the Chinese words for argumentation and persuasion as used in this period. She identifies three that are frequently used. *Bian* often refers to dialectical disputation, usually taking the form of definition: "it is an X; it is not an X"; more loosely, it can refer to less rigorous argument employing analogies, comparison of examples, *reductio ad absurdum*, and argument by consequences. Disputers were called *bianzhe*, a word that often has a pejorative implication, as did "sophist" in Greece.

Bian was conducted as a logical contest, not intended to persuade an audience, and the winner was the person who left the opponent with no answer. *Shuo* is an explanation, and could be introduced into *bian*. A conclusion is stated, either universal or particular, and a reason given why the statement is in accordance with reality. In other words, enthymemes are stated. In argumentative writing this often takes the form of referring to some historical instance or some discussion elsewhere. *Shui*, in contrast to *bian* and *shuo*, is a speech act intended to be persuasive to a particular audience. "Labelled occurrences of *shui* incorporate appeals to emotions, to enlightened self-interest, and to idiosyncratic desires. Speakers may alter their dress and demeanor, as well as their rhetorical strategies, to ingratiate themselves with their audiences, and occasionally these rhetorical strategies slide into outright deception.... But *shui* could also include chains of reasoning about the natural and social worlds.... The term could be applied to a long-term persuasive campaign or could refer to a one-time effort" (Garrett 1993a:112).

The Greek sophists were attacked by Socrates and others as immoral in their seeming ability to make the worse seem the better cause, and Chinese sophists met similar opposition, chiefly from Confucianists. A good example of this opposition is found in the writings of Xunzi (also transliterated Hsün Tzu or Hsüntze), the leading Confucianist of the generation after Mencius (translations by Dubs 1928 and Knoblock 1988–94; selections in Watson 1967). Disillusioned no doubt by the conditions of the times, Xunzi abandoned Mencius's belief in the essential goodness of human beings and claimed that they were innately evil (book 23) but could be corrected by proper teaching. In book 18 of his work he corrects various historical and philosophical errors of the sophists; in book 21 he discusses how to remove prejudices, which are the source of all evils. One of the most interesting parts of his work is book 22, "On the Rectification (or Correct Use) of Names" (Watson 1967:139–56; Knoblock 1994, III:112–38). In *Analects* 13.3 Confucius had said "When names are not correct, what is said will not sound reasonable; when what is said does not sound reasonable, affairs will not culminate in success; when affairs do not culminate in success, rites and music will not flourish; when rites and music do not flourish, punishments will not fit the crimes; when punishments do not fit the crimes, the common people will not know where to put hand and foot" (Lau 1979:118). According to Xunzi, names (terms or words) have no intrinsic appropriateness. They arose from conventional usages which were then standarized by the early Chinese kings. To depart from these usages will confuse the relationship between names and realities. Things that are the same should have the same names. If one follows this rule, one can put a stop to such statements as "a white horse is not a horse."

> Now the sages are no more, the world is in chaos, and pernicious doctrines have arisen. Because gentlemen lack positions of authority with which to control them and lack the requisite punishments to restrain them, people

engage in dialectics (*bian*) and explanations (*shuo*).... It is when the object is not fully understood that it is "named." It is when the name still does not fully convey the meaning that it is defined. It is when the definition is not completely clear that it is explained. It is when the explanation is not fully understood that we employ dialectics....When the mind conforms to the Way, explanations conform to the mind, propositions conform to explanations, and when names are used correctly and according to definition, the real and true qualities of things are clearly conveyed. Divisions and differences should be made but not so as to introduce errors. Inferences should be made from the characteristics of the category of a thing, but not to the point of introducing fallacies. Then when we listen, it will conform to good form, and when we engage in dialectics, we will fully express all that inheres in things. (Knoblock 1994, III:132–33)

Perhaps the closest Western analogy to the "rectification of names" in Chinese was the concern of seventeenth-century philosophers, Descartes and especially John Locke, to create a precise language for philosophy and science, denying it poetical and rhetorical elements such as metaphor. Xunzi did not discuss the use of metaphor. For further discussion of Xunzi, see Oliver (1971:199–209), Cua (1985), Graham (1989:235–67), and Knoblock's introductions and notes (1988–94).

The Chinese work that most resembles Greek sophistry is *Intrigues of the Warring States*, ostensibly a history of China, complete with speeches, from 453 to 221 BCE (translation by Crump 1970). The work seems to have little historical value; Crump (1964:103) argued that it is a compilation of sophistic exercises or "persuasions"(*shui*), on quasi-historical themes resembling Greek declamations, for training men in the art of persuasion, put together from earlier materials by Chi'ien Mu sometime before 8 BCE. The speakers give advice to the kings of the warring states about how best to prevail over their opponents. The speeches show the increase in cynicism of the fourth and third centuries, some contempt for omens and other supernatural restraints, attempts to apply rudimentary theories of chance and change, and lack of concern with anything but self-interest on the part of the rulers and their advisers, against which Confucian philosophers were protesting. They also reveal the sophisticated nature of the society of the time, and are often entertaining. Later Chinese scholars condemned the ethics of the work, but praised its polished style. Speeches often begin with a paradoxical statement to arouse the readers' interest. The speaker then explains its meaning and applies it to the question at hand, using rhythmical language, antithesis, parisosis, and paranomasia, all devices of Greek sophists, with quotation from the classics, proverbs, fables, and allegories, concluding with a restatement of the original principle (Kou 1953; Watson 1962:78–80; Crump 1964:x, 88–109). The speakers' arguments make use of a number of dialectical topoi identified by Aristotle and common in Western deliberative speech: a fortiori argument, comparison, cause to effect, and especially argument from consequences (Blinn and Garrett 1993).

Legalism and Han Fei-tzu

The rhetorical tools for political advancement and the relativistic philosophy of the sophists in Greece were sometimes cynically utilized by ambitious individuals to argue for a ruthless politics of might makes right. Among the most famous examples are Callicles in Plato's *Gorgias* and Thrasymachus in the first book of the *Republic*. In India, comparable views can be found in Kautilya's *Arthashastra*, to be discussed in the next chapter. In China, power politics took the form of "Legalism," the attempt to replace traditional norms of conduct by imposing unquestioned acceptance of the law as laid down by the ruler. Social order is to be ruthlessly imposed on a public incapable of self-government rather than be inspired by ideals and actions of beneficence and gentleness. Although the beginnings of legalistic doctrines can be found as early as the seventh century, and although a totalitarian political philosophy was vigorously defended in the fourth century in the *The Book of Lord Shang* (translation by Duyvendak 1928), Legalism had its greatest successes at the time of the Ch'in conquest and unification of China in the second half of the third century. An example is the letter of Li Ssi quoted earlier.

The most famous advocate of power politics and the author of a Chinese work that most approximates a rhetorical handbook was Han Fei-tzu, probably born about 280 BCE, "the Machiavelli of ancient China" (Oliver 1971:216). Unlike most Chinese philosophers, he was of noble birth, with opportunity to influence the ruler in his native state of Han. He had studied with Xunzi, from whom he took a highly negative view of human nature but whose Confucianism he rejected in favor of Legalist pragmatic policy. He also stuttered badly and chose to expound his ideas in writing rather than speaking. These became known to the King of Ch'in, already planning to impose his rule on all of China, and Han Fei was summoned to the king's court as an adviser but was there forced to drink poison by Li Ssu, apparently out of fear that he was becoming a rival. His biography is found in the *Records of the Grand Historian*, chapter 63. There is an English translation of his writings by Liao (1939–59) and a translation of major chapters by Watson (1967: Part 3); on his political philosophy see Wang and Chang (1986).

Han Fei's work is primarily addressed to rulers and advises them how to solidify their power. Throughout there is awareness of the powers and the dangers of speech. Rulers in his view are not necessarily persons of great intelligence; they can, however, create the illusion of being a sage. The successful ruler will trust no one, neither his ministers nor members of his family. He will hide his desire and motives, for otherwise his ministers will seek to please him rather than to perform their proper functions; he will avoid any direct contact with his people and create a sense of awe and mystery around his person. He will listen to his ministers and weigh their merits by the extent to which their deeds fulfill the function of their offices and what they have promised to accomplish.

"The Way of the ruler is to make certain that ministers are called to account for the words they speak and are also called to account for the words they fail to speak" (Watson 1967:92). Successes should be rewarded, failure sternly published. The ruler will take credit for all accomplishments and cause the blame for errors to fall on others. Han Fei outlines (Watson 1967:43–48) a series of "villainies" that a ruler's ministers may be expected to use to increase their own power. One is "making use of fluent speakers":

> The ruler, because of the nature of his upbringing, has usually been cut off from ordinary conversation, and has seldom had an opportunity to listen to debates, and he is accordingly apt to be particularly susceptible to persuasive speaking. The ministers therefore search about for rhetoricians from other states or patronize the most able speakers in their own state, and employ them to plead their special cause. With clever and elegant phrases, fluent and compelling words, such men draw the ruler on with prospects of gain, terrifying him with predictions of hazard, and completely overwhelm him with empty preachments. (Watson 1967:45)

This must not be allowed to happen. Among the most dangerous potential advisers are Confucianists with their talk about the benevolence and righteousness of ancient kings. Those virtues no longer serve (Watson 1967:99). Han Fei himself often cites examples from history, but he insists that society has degenerated to the point that it can only be governed by absolute government.

> If I were to give advice from the point of view of the private individual, I would say the best thing is to practice benevolence and righteousness and cultivate the literary arts.... This is the highest goal of the private individual. But when this happens, then, from the point of view of the state, someone who has performed no meritorious service to the nation is receiving official appointment, and someone who holds no government title is enjoying honor and renown. If the government is conducted in this fashion, then the state will face certain disorder and the ruler will surely be in peril. Hence the interests of the state and the individual are mutually at odds, and both cannot prevail at the same time. (Watson 1967:106–7)
>
> In the state of an enlightened ruler there are no books written on bamboo slips; law supplies the only instruction. There are no sermons on the former kings; the officials serve as the only teachers. There are no fierce feuds of private swordsmen; cutting off the heads of the enemy is the only deed of valor. Hence, when the people of such a state make a speech, they say nothing that is in contradiction to the law; when they act, it is in some way that will bring useful results. (Watson 1967:111)

Although most of Han Fei's work is advice to rulers, he also gives advice to those who wish to influence rulers. This is found in chapter 12, "The Difficulties of Persuasion," which begins as follows (for further discussion see Oliver 1971:220–29):

> On the whole, the difficult thing about persuading others is not that one lacks the knowledge needed to state his case nor the audacity to exercise his

abilities to the full. On the whole, the difficult thing about persuasion is to know the mind of the person one is trying to persuade and to be able to fit one's words to it. (Watson 1967:73)

On first reading this sounds rather like Plato's advice in *Phaedrus*, that the speaker must know the "soul" of the listener and adapt the message to his understanding. But Plato's ideal rhetoric is grounded in truth and moral principle. Han Fei had in mind something more sophistic and manipulative, as seen in the pitfalls he outlines: if the person addressed desires a reputation for virtue and you talk about profit, you will be regarded as ill-bred; conversely, if he is interested in profit and you talk about virtue, he will think you are out of touch with reality. If in addressing a ruler you hit on his hidden motives, you will be in danger, and so on:

> The important thing in persuasion is to learn how to play up the aspects that the person you are talking to is proud of, and play down the aspects he is ashamed of. Thus, if the person has some urgent personal desire, you should show him that it is his public duty to carry it out and urge him not to delay. If he has some mean objective in mind and yet cannot restrain himself, you should do your best to point out to him whatever admirable aspects it may have and to minimize the reprehensible ones.... If you wish to urge a policy of peaceful coexistence, then be sure to expound it in terms of lofty ideals, but also hint that it is commensurate with the ruler's personal interests.... Praise other men whose deeds are like those of the person you are talking to; commend other actions which are based upon the same policies as his.... Make sure that there is nothing in your ideas as a whole that will rub him the wrong way, and then you may exercise your powers of rhetoric to the fullest. This is the way to gain the confidence and intimacy of the person you are addressing and to make sure that you are able to say all you have to say without incurring his suspicion. (Watson 1967:75–76)

Such was the road to success at the courts of the warring states in the third century BCE.

The history of rhetoric in China in the more than two millenia since Han Fei has not yet been written. Among the subjects a future historian should consider are some ways the ancient tradition of rhetoric may continue to underlie public utterances and propaganda in modern China. An effort was made beginning in 1919 to undermine the influence of Confucianism, as happened under the Ch'in, but Confucianism reasserted itself, as it did under the Han. The "Cultural Revolution" of the 1960s bears some resemblance to the bookburning and censorship of scholars of 213 BCE. Although the Communist rulers of China have eliminated the trappings of the imperial court, Chairman Mau and his successors are, it seems to me, emperors without the title and surround themselves with something like the conditions recommended by Han Fei to the Son of Heaven. Conditions within the Chinese government have some resemblance to conditions in the time of the Legalists, combined with a traditional emphasis on maintaining social order and claims of benevolence and justice for the people. Marxism in China took up many features of traditional Chinese rhetoric. The growth of Western-style capitalism in recent years may, however, over time do more than political revolutions have done to alter the assumptions and expectations on which communication is based and bring to China some features more characteristic of Western rhetoric, such as tolerance of public debate, than has been native to Chinese thought.

Chinese Literary Criticism

In Greece, the teaching of rhetoric as an art of public address, beginning in the fifth and fourth centuries BCE, was one of several factors that contributed to the development of literary criticism as seen in Aristotle's *Poetics*, Horace's *Art of Poetry*, and other treatises. In China and in India philosophers and poets also eventually advanced theories and developed systems of criticism; in neither culture, however, was purely literary or aesthetic criticism common until a time that corresponds to late antiquity or the early Middle Ages in the West. Indian criticism is concerned only with poetry and drama; something will be said about it in the next chapter. Chinese criticism discusses both poetry and prose.

Moralizing and allegorizing commentaries on the Confucian classics were already being written in the last centuries BCE; the earliest example is the anonymous "Great Preface" to the *Book of Odes* (Owen 1992:37–56; Mair 1994:121–23). Among the more important Chinese critical terms are *li-tz'u*, "parallelism"; *pi*, "metaphoric comparison" as projection of subjective emotion; *hsing*, "evocation" as an objective response to nature; *yin-yen*, "allusion" to the words of an earlier text; *yung-shih*, "historical allusion"; *chi-chu*, "borrowing" of an earlier text—what is called a cento in the West—; and *k'ua-shih*, "hyperbole" (Kao 1984). As in Greece, glossaries of synonyms were prepared for the use of writers; the first Chinese language dictionary was the work of Hsü Shen, who lived around 100 CE (Ch'ên 1961:151–52). These developments, the existence of a canonical body of literature that was regarded as an essential study for any educated person, plus the evolution of prose in the writing of essays on historical, biographical, political, and philosophical subjects opened up the possibility of literary criticism. Later, the spread of Buddhism from India to China in the early centuries of the common era brought with it some of the Indian fascination with abstractions, definitions, and categorization, which eventually found application in discussions of literature. Important factors in the growth of criticism were the popularity of the *fu*, or "rhapsody," a highly self-conscious, epideictic form of poetic prose, using parallelism and figures of speech to describe scenes and situations, often creating the voices of speaking characters, and the appearance of literary groups and literary rivalries, which increased sophistication about poetic effects.

The earliest Chinese work of purely literary criticism is the "Essay on Literature" by Ts'ao P'i (187–226 CE), the only surviving part of his collected essays; it discusses contemporary authors and the four genres of bureaucratic petitions, personal letters and essays, epigraphs, and the *fu*. In his work is found the earliest statement of *ch'i*, "vital force" (Pollard 1978), which corresponds to some extent to the theory of "vivacity" of eighteenth-century Western rhetoric and to my idea of rhetorical energy. More important are the *Wen Fu* (*wen* here meaning "literary art") of Lu Chi (261–303 CE) (translation by Hughes 1951) and the *Wen Hsin Tiao Lung* by Liu Hsieh (c. 261–303 CE) (translation by Shih 1970 under the title *The Literary Mind and the Carving of Dragons*). The former work is in verse and rather brief; the latter, in prose, is much more detailed and technical. It includes discussion of the forms of written argumentative discourse in use at the time as well as word choice, composition, figures, and other aspects of style. For discussion of Chinese literary criticism see Liu (1975), Knechtges (1976), Fisk (1986), Owen (1992), Zhao (1994), and the introductions and commentaries of Hughes (1951) and Shih (1970); most histories of Chinese literature also include some discussion of the major critics.

Conclusion

China, where writing was in use by the middle of the second millenium BCE, has a rich historiographical and rhetorical tradition, which reaches back thousands of years and contains the texts of many speeches. Some allegedly come from what was regarded as a Golden Age in the third and second millenium BCE, but there are many also from later periods. The early speeches, found in *The Book of History*, were studied as models of invention and style and were imitated by later generations. The governments of China were autocratic from the earliest known times. Deliberative speeches were, however, delivered by rulers to their courts, armies, and people, and individuals addressed speeches of advice to rulers and lesser officials. Some of these speeches are divided into a proemion, narration, proof, and epilogue in the manner of Western oratory. The authority and ethos of the speaker was the most important means of persuasion in ancient China, as elsewhere, but logical argument is employed, largely in the form of citation of examples or analogies. There is little use of pathos except in exhortations to the troops.

Rhetoric was conceptualized in ancient China and terminology was created to describe features of invention and style, but speech was not studied as a separate discipline; it was always thought of as a part of political and moral philosophy. Standards of public address as described in ancient China resemble those of traditional nonliterate societies and the canons of Ptahhotep in Egypt; they include politeness and restraint, but Chinese thinkers, beginning with Confucius, added a demand for frankness on the part of a speaker. Classical Chinese literature and oratory developed as a formal language, which continued to be employed for serious subjects for centuries.

A sophistic movement appeared in Chinese thought and flourished from the fourth to the second century BCE. It included public debate, fascination with logical paradox, and an interest in the correct use of language. Sophistry contributed to the Legalism of the third century as exemplified in the work of Han Fei Tzu, which constitutes a pragmatic and exploitive rhetorical handbook for rulers and courtiers.

Chinese states had an elaborate, hierarchical bureaucracy which, from an early time, provided for judges and courts of law. Direct evidence was required for conviction and judges were allowed to take the person of the defendant into consideration, which may have provided some opportunity for use of argument from probability in court.

The best example of epideictic rhetoric in ancient China is probably the composition, in the last few centuries BCE, of prose poems known as *fu*. In the early centuries of the common era a complex system of literary criticism, with many technical terms, was developed to describe written composition in prose and poetry.

There was no influence of Western ideas of rhetoric on ancient China, and Chinese rhetorical theory thus represents the best example of a conceptualized non-Western tradition for comparative study. Similarities, suggesting universal features, and differences, arising from a different language and different historical experiences, are evident.

References

Blinn, Sharon B., and Mary Garrett (1993): "Aristotelian Topoi as a Cross-Cultural Tool," *Philosophy and Rhetoric* 26:93–112.

Chafee, John W. (1995). *The Thorny Gates of Learning in Sung China.* Albany: State University of New York Press.

Ch'ên, Shou-yi (1961). *Chinese Literature: A Historical Introduction.* New York: Ronald Press.

Crump, James I., Jr. (1964). *Intrigues: Studies of the Chan-kuo Tze.* Ann Arbor: University of Michigan Press.

———(1970). *Chan-kuo Ts'e.* Oxford: Clarendon Press.

Cua, Antonio S. (1985). *Ethical Argumentation: A Study in Hsün Tzu's Moral Epistemology.* Honolulu: University of Hawaii Press.

Dobson, W. A. C. H. (1963). *Mencius.* Toronto: University of Toronto Press.

Dubs, Homer H., trans. (1928). *The Works of Hsüntze.* London: Probsthain.

Duyvendak, Jan J. L., trans. (1928). *The Book of Lord Shang.* London: Probsthain.

Eoyang, Eugene Chen (1993). *The Transparent Eye: Reflections on Translation, Chinese Literature, and Comparative Poetics.* Honolulu: University of Hawaii Press.

Fingarette, Herbert (1972). *Confucius: The Secular as Sacred.* New York: Harper.

Fisk, Craig (1986). "Literary Criticism," in Nienhauser, ed. (see Bibliography) (1986): 49–58.

Garrett, Mary M. (1993a). "Classical Chinese Conceptions of Argumentation and Persuasion," *Argument and Advocacy* 29:105–15.

———(1993b). "Pathos Reconsidered from the Perspective of Classical Chinese Rhetorical Theories," *Quarterly Journal of Speech* 79:19–39.

Graham, Angus C. (1978). *Later Mohist Logic, Ethics and Science*. Hong Kong: Chinese University Press, and London: School of Oriental and African Studies, London University.

———(1989). *Disputers of the Tao: Philosophical Argument in Ancient China*. La Salle, IL: Open Court.

Holzman, Donald (1978). "Confucius and Ancient Chinese Literary Criticism," in *Chinese Approaches to Literature from Confucius to Liang Ch'i-ch'ao*, pp. 21–41, ed. by Adele A. Rickett. Princeton: Princeton University Press.

Hughes, Ernest R. (1951). *The Art of Letters: Lu Chi's Wen Fu, AD 302: A Translation and Comparative Study*. Bollingen Series XXIX. New York: Pantheon Books.

Jensen, J. Vernon (1983). "Rhetorical Emphases of Taoism," *Rhetorica* 5:219–29.

Kao, Karl S. Y. (1984). "Rhetorical Devices in the Chinese Literary Tradition," *Tamking Review* 14:325–33.

Karlgren, Bernard, trans. (1950). *The Book of Odes*. Stockholm: Museum of Far Eastern Antiquities.

Kennedy, George A. (1994). *A New History of Classical Rhetoric*. Princeton: Princeton University Press.

Kirkwood, William G. (1995). "Revealing the Mind of the Sage: The Narrative Rhetoric of the *Chuang Tzu*," *Rhetoric Society Quarterly* 25:134–48.

Knechtges, David R. (1976). *The Han Rhapsody: A Study of the Fu of Yang Hsiung (53 B.C.–A.D. 18)*. Cambridge: Cambridge University Press.

Knoblock, John (1988–94). *Xunzi: A Translation and Study of the Complete Works*. 3 vols. Stanford: Stanford University Press.

Kou, Ignace Pao Koh (1953). "Deux sophistes chinois," *Bibliothèque del' Institut des Hautes Etudes Chinoises* (Paris) 8.

Lau, Dim Cheuk C., trans. (1979). *Confucius, The Analects*. New York: Penguin Books.

———(1982). *Chinese Classics: Tao Te Ching*. Hong Kong: Chinese University Press.

Legge, James, trans. (1960). *The Chinese Classics*. I: *Confucian Analects, The Great Learning, The Doctrine of the Mean*; II: *The Works of Mencius*; III: *The Shoo King, or The Book of Historical Documents*; IV: *The She King, or The Book of Poetry*. Hong Kong: Hong Kong University Press. First published 1893–95.

Liao, Wen-Kuei, trans. (1939–59). *The Complete Works of Han Fei Tzu*. 2 volumes, London: Probsthain.

Liu, James J. Y. (1975). *Chinese Theories of Literature*. Chicago: University of Chicago Press

Lu, Xing (1991). *Recovering the Past: Identification of Chinese Sense of Pien and a Comparison of Pien to Greek Senses of Rhetoric in the Fifth and Third Centuries BC*. Dissertation, University of Oregon.

Mair, Victor H., ed. (1994). *The Columbia Anthology of Traditional Chinese Literature*. New York: Columbia University Press.

Mei, Yi-Pao (1929). *The Ethical and Political Works of Motse*. London: Probsthain.

Oliver, Robert T. (1971). *Communication and Culture in India and China*. Syracuse: Syracuse University Press.

Owen, Stephen (1992). *Readings in Chinese Literary Thought*. Cambridge, MA: Harvard University Press.

Pollard, David (1978). "*Ch'i* in Chinese Literary Theory," in *Chinese Approaches to Literature from Confucius to Lian Chi'i-ch'ao*, pp. 43–66, ed. by Adele Austin Richett. Princeton: Princeton University Press.

Richards, Ivor A. (1932). *Mencius on the Mind: Experiments in Multiple Definition*. London: Kegan Paul, Trench Trubner & Co.

Shih, Vincent Yu-Chang (1970). *The Literary Mind and the Carving of Dragons by Liu Hsieh*. Taipei: Chung Hwa Book Co.

Waley, Arthur (1960). *The Book of Songs*. New York: Grove Press. First published 1937.

———— (1964). *The Analects of Confucius*. London: George Allen and Unwin. First published 1938.

Wang, Hsiao-po, and Leo S. Chang (1986). *The Philosophical Foundations of Han Fei's Political Theory*. Monographs of the Society for Asian and Comparative Philosophy, No. 7. Honolulu: University of Hawaii Press.

Ware, James R. (1960). *The Sayings of Mencius*. New York: Mentor Books.

Watson, Burton (1962). *Early Chinese Literature*. New York: Columbia University Press.

————, ed. and trans.(1967). *Basic Writings of Mo Tzu, Hsün Tzu, and Han Fei Tzu*. New York: Columbia University Press.

————, trans. (1968). *The Complete Works of Chuang-tzu*. New York: Columbia University Press.

———— (1989). *The Tso chuan: Selections From China's Oldest Narrative History*. New York: Columbia University Press.

————, trans. (1993). *Records of the Grand Historian. Han and Wu Dynasties* (2 vols.) published 1961, revised 1993; *Qin Dynasty* 1993. Hong Kong: Chinese University and Columbia University Press.

Zhao, Henry Y. (1994). "Rhetorical Invention in *Wen Xin Diao Long*," *Rhetoric Society Quarterly* 24, 3/4:1–15.

Bibliography

Ames, Roger T. (1994). *The Art of Rulership: A Study of Ancient Chinese Political Thought*. Albany: State University of New York Press.

Chan, Wing-Tsit, ed. (1963). *A Source Book in Chinese Philosophy*. Princeton: Princeton University Press.

Deeney, John J., ed. (1980). *Chinese-Western Comparative Literature: Theory and Strategy*. Hong Kong: Chinese University Press.

Dilworth, David A. (1989). *Philosophy in World Perspective: A Comparative Hermeneutic of the Major Theories*. New Haven: Yale University Press.

Hansen, Chad (1983). *Language and Logic in Ancient China*. Ann Arbor: University of Michigan Press.

Jensen, J. Vernon (1987). "Rhetoric of East Asia—A Bibliography," *Rhetoric Society Quarterly* 17:213–31.

———— (1992). "Values and Practices in Asian Argumentation," *Argumentation and Advocacy* 28:155–66.

Lang, David M., ed. (1971). *A Guide to Eastern Literatures*. London: Weidenfeld and Nicolson.

Loewe, Michael, ed. (1971). *Early Chinese Texts: A Bibliographical Guide*. Berkeley: Society for the Study of Early China.

Nienhauser, William H., Jr., ed. (1986). *The Indiana Companion to Traditional Chinese Literature*. Bloomington: Indiana University Press.

CHAPTER 8

Rhetoric in Ancient India

Archaeological excavations in the Indus valley have revealed an urban culture that flourished between 2500 and 1500 BCE. It was in contact with Mesopotamia and imitated some features of civilization there, including a form of writing. This is found on seal rings and was apparently used for commercial purposes. The remains, however, are very scanty and the language unknown. It may be an early form of the Dravidian languages still spoken in southern India.

About 1500 BCE invaders arrived in north-west India bringing a new language, a new religion, and new political institutions (Masson-Ourel et al. 1967). These were the Aryans, descendants of pastoral tribes that had once lived in the steppes of Russia and who had for reasons not well understood—perhaps changes in climate and pressure from other tribes to the east—begun migrations that brought different groups of them, speaking different dialects, into Europe, Asia Minor, and South Asia. Their original language was what modern scholars call Indo-European, the ancestor of Sanskrit, Old Persian, Greek, Latin, Old Slavic, the Germanic languages, and Celtic, and ultimately of modern Hindi and most European languages. Their religion was a worship of gods of sky and nature. Their political institutions were a chief or king, chosen with the consent of the tribe, a council of nobles, and an assembly of freemen, the warriors of the tribe. They brought with them domestication of horses and sheep and the use of implements of iron, copper, and bronze (Spear 1961:32). The Aryans established themselves as rulers in the Indus and later the Ganges valley, created kingdoms and cities with a class structure of nobles, priests (who become the Brahmins), merchants, and farmers, and assimilated some local religious traditions into their own, laying the basis of later Hinduism.

Except for the work of Robert Oliver (1971:12–83), the rhetoric of ancient India has been little studied and there are numerous impediments to a comprehensive account. India, where time often seemed to stand still, developed no strong historiographic tradition; until the invasion of Alexander the Great in the late fourth century BCE, dates and details of political history are much more scanty than in the early history of Mesopotamia, Egypt, or China. There is a vast body of ancient Indian literature; except, however, for glimpses of heroic society in the great epics, *Mahabharata* and *Ramayana*, most of this literature is religious in nature and reveals little about public address in secular contexts. Furthermore, it was for long transmitted orally. The earliest Indian alphabet, known as Brahmi, may be derived from Aramaic script, and thus ultimately from the Phoenician alphabet; it may have first come into use for commercial purposes, possibly in the eighth century BCE, but the only physical evidence is several centuries later. Some prose texts were probably written down by the sixth century; law codes dating from the fourth century or earlier refer to writing as well known (Kane 1946, III:306–7). As the discussion here will reveal, Indians put a very high value on speech, higher perhaps than that found in any other ancient culture, and in marked contrast to Mesopotamians. Even long texts were memorized and transmitted orally, and knowledge of sacred texts was guarded by priests; some may have been written down in the sixth or fifth centuries, many probably did not exist in written form until the fourth or third century, and our texts may reflect conditions of that time or have been significantly affected by the thought processes involved in writing (Goody 1987:110–22).

Despite the resistence to writing, abstract thought developed in India at an early time to a greater extent than in any other culture I have so far discussed. Why this should be so is difficult to say. It may have been facilitated by the ability of Indo-European languages to coin abstractions, which is also evident in the development of Greek philosophy. An important factor was the existence of a social class—the Brahmin priests—with the leisure for contemplation. An inclination to abstraction probably reflects some basic feature of Indian religious feeling. Certainly it is evident first in religious texts of the classical period, which are filled with definitions and subdivisions of abstract concepts. It is also evident in early Indian scholarship on law, grammar, literature, and science. Although, as in China, rhetoric in India was not differentiated from political and moral philosophy, a fully conceptualized theory of style was eventually developed by Indian thinkers and will be discussed at the end of this chapter.

Two somewhat different views of the importance, forms, and functions of speech can be traced in ancient India. One, which gave the greater value to speech and appears in a wider variety of forms, was that held by the Brahmin priests of the classical period. The other, which is in part a reaction against Brahmin dialectic, is the Buddhist tradition. Here I shall begin with the Brahmin tradition.

The Vedic Hymns

Our knowledge of the Aryans is largely derived from the Vedic hymns, and especially from the *Rigveda*, a collection of 1017 hymns to the gods (translations by Müller and Oldenberg 1891–96:vols. XXXII and XLVI and Griffith 1973). The earliest may have been composed between 1500 and 1000 BCE, but they were not written down for many centuries. Their language is an early form of Sanskrit; verses are constructed as a series of couplets, thus using parallelism, which we have encountered elsewhere in formal speech. The use of several different formal languages for religious and scholarly purposes has strongly characterized Indian discourse throughout its history (Dimock 1974:6–14). Vedic Sanskrit continued to be the language of hymns and sacrifice; classical Sanskrit, the language of the epics, was regularized (Sanskrit means "perfected") through the efforts of the great grammarian Panini (c. 400 BCE) into the formal language of Hindu religion, some Buddhist texts, and secular scholarship. It has continued in use until modern times. In the classical period Sanskrit was spoken in a variety of dialects, or Prakrits; the most important of these was Pali, which became a formal language for many Buddhist texts and continued in use long after it ceased to be spoken.

The hymns of the *Rigveda* contain references to the existence of councils and assemblies among the Aryans and a few use a simple dialogue form. Like other religious texts, they are frequently metaphorical in expression, but unlike other early or traditional poetry we have met they also often specify that something is "like" something else rather than seeming to identify two concepts. Since this is also a feature of early Greek poetry, it is tempting to think that there was something about the experience of Indo-European tribes that caused them to distinguish what was in some way "like" something else from what could be identified with something else in an undifferentiated way. Could it be that in their wanderings over vastly different landscapes, encountering different people with different ways of life and different beliefs, an experience in scale unlike that of other people I have discussed, they observed phenomena with which they could not entirely identify but which had some likeness to something they knew and found a linguistic way to express this intermediate stage of the same and the other? A contributing factor may have been the ambiguity of the Indo-European verb "to be" in all its forms. Only in Indo-European languages (and in ancient Sumerian where simile also appears) does a single verb function both as copula, which predicates some property or attribute (e.g., "This object is red"), and also means "to exist" (Dewart 1989:259–300). Thus an English phrase such as "The god is a red-burning fire" can mean that the god exists and really is a red fire and that the god has some attribute of a red fire. Indo-European and Sumerian had a greater need than other languages to specify attribute and similarity when existence and identity were not be predicated and at an early time developed the grammatical means to do so. The birth of simile would seem to be one of the stages in the development of rational and abstract thought.

The rhetoric of the Vedic hymns, like the rhetoric of hymnic poetry generally, is an effort to persuade a diety to grant favor to the community. The god is praised, his or her epithets are recited, and the prayer was accompanied by ritual sacrifice when some substance was thrown in the fire. Worshipers drank an intoxicating beverage called *soma* that facilitated their entering into the religious experience, and the god is imagined as joining in the drinking. Great importance is attributed in the hymns to speech, voice, and the word. The texts are said to originate with the gods themselves and to be a gift to humans (*Rigveda* 8.9.16): "the men come near thee for their gain, the singers with their songs of praise:/ Speech, thousandfold, comes near to thee" (7.15.9 as translated by Griffith 1973). Vak (cognate with Latin *vox* and English "voice"), goddess of speech and daughter of the sun, is "she who streams with sweetness" (5.73.8) she is the "gladdener," the "milk cow," who yields food and vigor (8.89.11). In hymn 10.125 Vak speaks, celebrating her powers in a passage that makes an interesting comparison with Gorgias's and Isocrates's celebrations of speech in Greece:

> I am the Queen, the gatherer-up of treasures, the most thoughtful, first of those who merit worship.
> The gods have established me in many places with many homes to enter and abide in.
> Through me alone all eat the food that feeds them, each man who sees, breathes, hears the word outspoken.
> They know it not, but yet they dwell beside me. Hear, one and all, the truth as I declare it.
> I, verily, myself announce and utter the word that gods and men alike shall welcome.
> I make the man I love exceedingly mighty, make him a sage, a Rishi and a Brahmin.
> I bend the bow for Rudra that his arrow may strike and slay the hater of devotion.
> I rouse and order battle for the people and I have penetrated the earth and heaven.
> On the world's summit I bring forth the Father: my home is in the waters, in the ocean.
> Thence I extend o'er all existing creatures, and touch even yonder heaven with my forehead.
> I breathe a strong breath like the wind and tempest, the while I hold together all existence.
> Beyond this wide earth and beyond the heavens I have become so mighty in my grandeur.

(GRIFFITH 1973:631–32)

Over the centuries, most of the Vedic gods and the meaning of the hymns became less and less important and the sacrifices that accompanied them became the center of attention (van Buitenen 1974:47–48). The hymns came to be understood as sounds, rather like music, that accompanied the ritual and was necessary to it but incomprehensible to any except learned priests.

Brahmin Rhetoric

Brahmins, as referred to in the *Hymn to Vak*, were the priestly class of early India; they became the intellectuals and teachers of classical times and claimed for themselves the highest rank in the notorious caste system that developed in the classical period and has characterized Indian society ever since. There is some reason to suspect that the caste system—unknown in the *Vedas*—was created or at least fostered by Brahmins in their own interests, for they were not necessarily wealthy or powerful individuals. Class, later caste, was inherited at birth, and the Brahmins especially needed to defend their prerogatives as exclusive spokesmen and interpreters of religion and knowledge against challenges created by political and economic change. The rhetorical tactic that proved most effective in this campaign was the doctrine of reincarnation: the dogma that each human self (*atman*) is reborn after one lifetime into another body. The process goes on indefinitely unless by virtue and meditation the self can escape rebirth into the timeless nirvana of untroubled being. The condition of each new life is determined by conduct in the immediate past life. If your lot is a lowly one, even an "Untouchable," the Brahmins taught that it is a just judgment for your previous life. There is no reason to protest it and seek to raise your status; what you should do is to accept your situation and act well your part, with the expectation that you will then have a better lot in your next life. This rhetoric was remarkably effective and the Hindu doctrine of caste as a result of reincarnation not only was but continues to be widely accepted by Indians living in traditional villages or in urban poverty. Somewhat irrationally, since rebirth may take place in another place and a different family, this dogma was combined with great emphasis on family hierarchy, respect for parents, and village customs, characteristic of all traditional societies.

Robert Oliver (1971:31–43) devotes an interesting chapter to "Caste as Rhetoric in Being." He discusses the rules of communication as practiced in modern times among members of a caste and between members of different castes. For example, an "Untouchable" should never use the pronoun "I" when speaking to a member of a higher caste, but should refer to himself in the third person as "your slave" and should prefix the word "old" to names of parts of his own body to indicate their worthlessness. Each caste—there are more than 3000 divisons—has its own appropriate occupation and social function, and there are traditional personal names appropriate for each cast: Brahmin names should be something auspicious, low-caste names something contemptible. The caste system is another example of the remarkable Indian obsession with categories, terminologies, and their organization into complex systems. It is also one of the most striking examples of how rhetoric has traditionally been used as a form of social control.

Indian Epic Poetry

Unlike China, India has a rich tradition of epic poetry, describing the actions of great heroes of the distant past, as does Greek epic, and using some of the same motifs, including councils and speeches on other occasions. *The Mahabharata* is an enormous work of around 200,000 lines (translation by Roy 1919–33; new translation by van Buitenen in progress 1973—with introductory essays, summaries, and notes; prose summary by Narasimhan 1965; selections in Dutt 1910 and Alphonso-Karkala 1971:85–149; brief summaries and discussions by Gowen 1968:207–37 and van Buitenen 1974:47–54). It apparently originated in legends of Aryan times sung by bards, which were combined into a narrative core describing the rivalries and wars between noble cousins and their armies. Over several centuries many new sections were added to the narrative frame by different oral poets. The epic was for long transmitted orally and perhaps first took written form sometime after 400 BCE, though additions continued to be made after that time. The most famous addition is the philosophical poem, the *Bhagavad Gita*, found in the sixth book, where it is introduced as a speech by Krishna to the hero Arjuna at a time of discouragement. Indian epic is composed in metrical units called *shlokas*, two-line unrhymed couplets, each divided into two parts of eight syllables. Since the thought is usually carried through the couplet there is not so much effect of parallelism as in the Vedas and other traditional poetry.

The *Mahabharata* deserves a detailed rhetorical analysis, which could reveal much about the forms and functions of speech in ancient India, both those reflecting older traditions and those contemporary with the work as we have it. This task, with regret, I leave to others. Ideally it should be done by someone with a good knowledge of Sanskrit. Much could probably be learned from a careful study of a translation, but the only really satisfactory English version is that by van Buitenen, of which only the earlier books have been published. Fortunately, this includes book 5, which contains many speeches, some in council, some on embassies, before the beginning of war. Although efforts for consensus and peace are made, there is also open contention, pointed argumentation, and some verbal abuse in face to face confrontation. For example, in 5.37 Vidua warns against angry and self-interested speech, but in 5.61 Bhishma breaks out against Karna, saying, "Your wits are beclouded by Time, you braggart"; in 5.131 Queen Vidura berates her son vigorously; and in 5.147 Bhishma denounces the evil Dhararashtra: "Not the son of a king and ignoble in conduct, avaricious, ill-intentioned to kin, how can you, a lout, pretend to seize this realm that others are lawfully heir to?" This sounds more like the verbal attacks of Achilles and Agamemnon on each other in the first book of the *Iliad* than the usual restraint of traditional rhetoric. The contexts are, however, comparable. In both *Mahabharata* and *Iliad*, proud, powerful, and independent nobles join or oppose each other in a great military campaign and it is not surpising that passion arises. In both cases, these nobles are the descendants of Aryan (i.e., Indo-European) chiefs and it is not unlikely that they continue some of the speech conventions of what was probably an unusually argumentative, quarrelsome society.

Van Buitenen's introduction to book five contains (III:134–38) a discussion of "the protocol of negotiations," which is a good starting point for rhetorical analysis of the book. He notes (137) the presence of "four diplomatic tactics": conciliation, subversion of allies, bribery, and punishment. He also discusses (178–84) speeches of instruction in the epic, which he divides into three types: a call to arms, a caution, and a consolation. Other rhetorical genres can be found elsewhere in the poem; for example, "lamentations" in the eleventh book. According to Oliver (1971:53) "in the *Mahabharata* the debates had largely ceased to be teaching devices and had become avowed contests, held in public assemblies principally as entertainment for the listeners." Unfortunately he cites no examples, and his statement does not seem to me to be borne out by my reading of the poem. It is clear, however, that the poem describes a society in which debate among nobles on political issues was frequent, important, sophisticated, and popular.

The second famous Indian epic, the *Ramayana* attributed to Valmiki, is shorter than the *Mahabharata*, somewhat later (c. 200 BCE?), more unified, and more approachable (translation by Dutt 1910; discussion by Gowen 1968:241–53 and van Buitenen 1974:54–80). Although a single author may have given the poem its present form, he created it out of folktales and legends that had long been a part of oral tradition. The central story is the life of Rama, son and successor of King Dasa-ratha: how in a contest with other nobles he wins the daughter of King Janak for his bride, the loss of his kingdom and wife, and his recovery of both with the aid of the monkey-king Hanman. The poem contains much moral exhortation, the characters can be viewed as examples of virtue and vice, and later interpreters allegorized it as representing the struggle of Light and Dark. Allegorization of traditional poetry is a common phenomenon in literate societies; I noted it in the case of the Chinese *Book of Odes*, and Greek epic was given allegorical interpretation by pre-Socratic, Stoic, and Neoplatonist philosophers.

At the beginning of book two of the *Ramayana* King Dasa-ratha, after a long and enlightened rule, has become old and wishes to name Rama as regent and heir apparent. He summons an assembly of chiefs and citizens to obtain their consent in accordance with Aryan tradition and addresses them in a speech from the throne. He first reminds his audience that he has toiled, like a father, for his people's welfare. Now he is old and wants to turn over rule to his son. He praises

Rama's valour and virtue and concludes by inviting those present to speak their thoughts, to suggest a better plan if they know one, or to propose a middle course. He thus shows openness to compromise and seeks consensus as generally found in deliberation in traditional societies. The people, including Brahmins and chiefs, are said to consult among themselves and with one accord answer in favor of the king's proposal, noting the king's years of toil and Rama's fitness for rule. The king, however, is not completely satisfied and says he wants to know the inner feelings of the people and to be sure they agree beyond a shadow of doubt. To this the reply is more positive in that it recounts in greater detail the admirable qualities of Rama and the homage that the people grant to him. (Dutt's 1910 translation of this passage is reprinted in Alphonso-Karkala 1971:160–63). The passage may be taken to show how deliberation on important issues should be conducted by a king, the importance of obtaining the consent of the governed, and the qualities expected of leadership.

Debate in The Upanishads

The best evidence for debates among Brahmins in the period before the fifth century BCE are the philosophical texts known as *The Upanishads*. Although they contain passages in verse, they are largely sermons and dialogues in prose and may have taken written form almost from the beginning, but additions have been made to the original corpus over many centuries. The philosophy set out in these works is a kind of pantheism or monism that unifies all nature, gods, and individuals into a single understanding of being. The discovery of *The Upanishads* in the West in the nineteenth century was greeted with great enthusiasm by philosophers as different as Schopenhauer and Emerson, and they continue to be studied and admired both by Hindus and by Westerners as an answer to the riddles of life.

Debates in *The Upanishads* illustrate efforts among Brahmins to create a more philosophical understanding of being than is found in the Vedas and also rivalries among teachers anxious to win in debate contests. Probably the best example of the latter is found in the third *adhyana*, or book, of the *Brihad-Aranyaka Upanishad* (translation by Hume 1931:107–26; discussion by Oliver 1971:49–52). King Jamaka here offers a thousand cows to the most learned Brahmin. The prize is claimed by Yajnavalkya, who admits that he wants the cows for himself and his students. Other Brahmins then ask him questions on theological issues. The questions ask for definitions, and Yajnavalkya's success seems to result largely from his ability to supply these definitions readily and authoritatively from a well-thought out system of pantheistic philosophy complete with a technical vocabulary. The interlocutors, one of whom is a woman, apparently hope to stump him with a question for which he is not prepared and they do not seek to refute his answers. Often the question invites a division of categories, which is also readily supplied. When asked, for example, how many "apprehenders" and "over-apprehenders" there are, Yajnavalkya immediately replies "eight" of each. He identifies apprehenders as breath, speech, tongue, eye, ear, mind, hands, and skin. Some of the definitions are supported by reasons and thus take enthymematic form. Of speech he says, "It is seized by name as an over-apprehender, for by speech one speaks names."

In the fourth book King Janaka questions Yajnavalkya and is instructed by him in longer speeches. The king begins by asking if Yajnavalkya has come because he desires cattle or subtle disputation. "Indeed, for both, your Majesty," is the reply. He then asks the king to tell him what he has learned from others. The king says that Jitvan Sailini has told him "Brahma, verily, is speech," but admits that he had not explained this well. Brahma is a central concept in *The Upanishads*: It might be briefly described as the ultimate principle of the world, the unity of all things, both being and non-being. Yajnavalkya elaborates the proposition that Brahma is speech by saying that the seat of Brahma is "just speech," supported in space, and to be worshiped as intelligence. He continues with an encomium of speech:

> Verily, by speech, your Majesty, a friend is recognized. By speech alone, Your Majesty, the *Rig-Veda*, the *Yajur-Veda*, the *Sama Veda*, the hymns of the Atharvans and Angirases, legends, ancient lore, sciences, mystic doctrines, verses, aphorisms, explanations, commentaries, what is offered in sacrifice and as oblation, food and drink, this world and the other, and all beings are known. The highest Brahma, your Majesty, is in true speech. Speech does not desert him who, knowing this, worships it as such. All things run into him. He, having become a god, goes even to the gods. (Hume 1931:127–28)

Sophistry in India

Although one might prefer to call Yajnavalkya a philosopher rather than a sophist, the description of the debate, with its acknowledgment of the desire to win by subtle disputation, and its celebration of speech, analogous to a famous passage in the *Encomium of Helen* by the Greek sophist Gorgias, indicate that the conditions for sophistry as found in China and Greece existed also in India. These conditions I defined in the last chapter as literacy; political, social, and moral changes; conflicting philosophical schools; and the existence of individual teachers who are not part of a state bureaucracy and offer advice to rulers. Many contending schools of Hinduism existed by the eighth and seventh centuries BCE. There were traditional themes for debate analogous to subjects discussed by early Greek philosophers and sophists: for example, "everything exists, nothing exists"; "everything is a unity, everything is a plurality" (Jayatilleke 1963:50). Sophistry, or "eel-wrangling" as its detractors called it, was an outcome of a skeptical strain in Indian thought, originating in theosophical riddles in early times and encouraged by the existence of conflicting and irreconcilable theories pertaining to religious beliefs (Jayatilleke 1963:110). Skeptical debating seems to have flourished among Brahmins by the seventh century. The closest Sanskrit term for "sophists" is *takki*, or more perjoratively *vitandanadinis*. Like the Greek sophists, *takki* are known principally from references to and criticism of them in later texts (e.g., the Buddha's *Middle Length Sayings*, translated by Horner 1954–59). Only a few Indian sophists are known by name; one was Saccaka, who debated with the Buddha. The best discussion of skepticism in India, the nature of Indian sophistry, and the Buddhist reaction against it is to be found in Jayatilleke's *Early Buddhist Theory of Knowledge* (1963:207–59, summarized in Oliver 1971:52–60). Debate in religious circles spread to the public assembly where it became a popular form of entertainment, but themes remained principally drawn from metaphysics and religion. Indian sophists did not exploit mythological and secular subjects nor paradoxes like Kun Sun Lung's "a white horse is not a horse."

Buddhism

According to Hindu belief, from time to time buddhas are born into the world. The term "buddha" means "an Enlightened One," and buddhas bring new knowledge and understanding to mankind. The Buddha *par excellence* was Siddhartha Gautama who is thought to have lived from about 563 to about 487 BCE; thus he was an approximate contemporary of Confucius in China and of Pythagoras and Heraclitus in Greece. He was a royal prince who abandonned his kingdom, wife, and child to seek knowledge and understanding of life and who broke with Hinduism to form another of the world's great religions. Compared with Hinduism, Buddhism in its original form was less interested in metaphysics, more in how to live one's life; it found truth from meditation rather than from ancient texts; although preaching was a regular feature of Buddhism beginning with the Buddha's sermons (*suttas*), oral speech was not given so strong an emphasis as it was by the Brahmins; though he regularly engaged in debate, the Buddha was hostile to sophistry as current among the Brahmins. The Buddha himself left no written texts but there is a vast body of Buddhist writings in Sanskrit, Pali, Chinese, and other languages. A work with special authority is the *Tipitaka*, which contains sermons and sayings attributed to the Buddha that were collected at a council of his followers soon after his death and amplified somewhat from oral traditions at later councils.

The "first sermon" of the Buddha (translation by Rhys-Davids 1881, reprinted in Alphonso-Kerkala 1971:230–36) was given to five ascetics with whom he had lived earlier in a vain quest for enlightenment through self-deprivation and to whom he returned after seven years of meditation had brought him the knowledge he desired. He begins by identifying two extremes that should be avoided by one seeking enlightenment: a sensual and worldly way of life on the one hand and painful, self-mortifying asceticism on the other. There is a middle path that leads to enlightenment and nirvana, "the noble eightfold path" based on right views, right aspirations, right speech, right conduct, right livelihood, right effort, right mindfulness, and right contemplation. Instead of explaining these further, the Buddha turns to the basic question of human suffering and sorrow, a problem faced by all religions, for it is on this issue that enlightenment has come to him. The origin of suffering, he says, is thirst or craving for gratification of the passions, for life, and for success. The "destruction" of suffering is attained by laying aside, getting rid of, being free from this thirst and craving. "That this was the noble truth concerning sorrow," he says, "was not among the doctrines handed down [by the Brahmins], but there arose within me the eye (to perceive it), there arose the knowledge (of its nature), there arose the understanding (of its cause), there arose the wisdom (to guide in the path of tranquillity), there arose the light (to dispel darkness from it)." Traditional doctrine, he goes on to say, recognized neither the origin nor destruction of sorrow nor the possibility that he, Tathagata ("The Perfected One"), would come to understand it: "And now this knowledge and this insight has arisen within me. Immovable is the emancipation of my heart. This is my last existence. There will now be no rebirth for me!" The five ascetics rejoice at this revelation, and all the gods give forth a great shout that "the royal chariot wheel of the truth had thus been set rolling onwards by the Blessed One."

The five ascetics had known Gautama well; they had all in a different way shared in his quest; the change that has come over him and the authority with which he speaks is the crucial factor in his persuasiveness. Many passages in the sermon are repeated verbatim and synonyms are multiplied, giving emphasis to ideas. There are no enthymemes, no supporting examples, but there is a logical structure to the sermon as a whole and the use of definition and numbered divisions suggests a systematic quality about the thought: the eightfold path, stated twice; reference to five "aggregates" (factors creating the temporal continuity of individual personality) and to "four noble truths in triple order, in this twelvefold manner." The cry of approval by the gods need not have been heard by the ascetics and is probably a rhetorical supplement by the Buddhist editors of the text to increase the authority and dramatic effect of the scene.

The "last sermon" of the Buddha (Alphonso-Kerkala 1971:236–38) is more argumentative in that the Buddha is trying to explain why, when dying, he does not want to leave specific instructions and rules to an order of Buddhist monks. "I have," he says, "preached the truth without making any distinction between exoteric and esoteric doctrine; for in respect of the truths, Ananda, the Tathagata has no such thing as the closed fist of a teacher, who keeps some things back." "Be ye a refuge to yourselves. Betake yourselves to no external refuge. Hold fast to the truth as a lamp."

Other rhetorical techniques used by the Buddha include aphorisms, found especially in the elegantly simple poetry of his sayings recorded in the *Dhamma-*

pada (translation by Carter and Palihawadana 1987), parables (Burlingham 1922), and fables, including animal fables, based on knowledge from his previous lives (Gowen 1968:312–17). Some of the latter were transmitted to the medieval West by way of Persia, the Arabs, and Spain.

Discourses attributed to the Buddha occasionally comment on speech and seem to reflect a consistent attitude toward rhetoric. Here are two examples. *The Dhammapada* is a collection of versified sayings attributed to the Buddha. Number 133 reads as follows: "To none speak harshly. Those thus addressed would retort to you. Miserable indeed is contentious talk. Retaliatory rods would touch you" (trans. by Carter and Palihawadana 1987:35). The collection of stories about the Buddha known as *The Majihima* describes a situation in which he is pressed by opponents with questions as to whether he would ever use unpleasant, disagreeable speech. He replies,

> Speech that the Tathagata knows to be untrue, false, and useless, and also unpleasant and disagreeable to others, he does not speak; that which he knows to be true, real, and useful, but also unpleasant and disagreeable to others, in that case he knows the right time to express it. Speech that he knows to be untrue, false, and useless, and also pleasant and agreeable to others, he does not speak; that which is true, real, but useless, and also pleasant and agreeable to others, that, too, he does not speak; but that which is true, real, and useful, and also pleasant and agreeable to others, in that case he knows the right time to express it. (Thomas 1975:136–37)

Here are expressed canons of speech that have some resemblance to the precepts of Ptahhotep in Egypt or those of Confucius: sincerity, restraint, frankness, but only at an opportune time, avoidance of flattery, a desire to speak pleasantly when consistent with what the speaker regards as true, real, and useful. Oliver (1971:83) sums up the rhetorical influence of the Buddha from a variety of sources in the following terms: "turn aside wrath with a gentle response; clarify and seek acceptance of your ideas by phrasing them in terms of the predilections and understanding of your listener; try to find premises so acceptable to the listener that he will himself argue for your conclusion; and keep your discourse pleasing through use of humor and homely illustrations rather than indulging in denunciation and assertive argumentation."

Contact between India and Greece

In the fall of 327 BCE Alexander the Great and his Greek army entered India through the Khyber Pass. The following year he advanced into the Indus valley, defeated the Indian king Porus in a great battle, and moved east toward the Ganges, but his troups mutinied and he reluctantly turned back toward home. Accounts of India were written in Greek by some members of Alexander's staff and by Greek visitors in subsequent years; these are the source of extant Greek writings about the country including book fifteen of the *Geography* of Strabo and the *Indica* of Arrian. Alexander had interviews with Brahmins, who are referred to in Greek sources as "sophists." Although India reverted to native rule after Alexander's retreat, a Greek dynasty ruled to the north in Bactria for 200 years. One of these Greek kings was Menander (reigned 155–130 BCE), known in Pali as Milinda. The *Milindapanha* or *Questions of Milinda* is a series of dialogues between the king and a Buddhist monk in which the latter seeks to explain his religion in terms that a Greek might understand (translation by Rhys-Davids 1890–94; selections in Alphonso-Karkala 1971:271–78).

The Arthashastra *of Kautilya*

Although dates are difficult to determine, between the sixth and the third centuries BCE Brahmin scholars began to produce systematic treatises on law and procedure, known as *dharmashastras*. The earliest were apparently concerned with sacred law (*dharma*) and the rules for sacrifices, but the subjects were extended in works called *arthashastras* (*artha* means "useful") to include rules governing the various castes, civil government and administration, crime, punishment, and judicial procedure. P. V. Kane's *History of Dharmashastras* in five volumes (1930–62), based on these writings, is a systematic account of the development and codification of Indian law and procedure from ancient to modern times. The most famous of the treatises is the versified *Code of Manu* (c. 200 BCE?), which was reintroduced by Warren Hastings, British governor of India in the eighteenth century, as the basis of native law. A fuller example of an *arthashastra* is the remarkable treatise on politics attributed to Kautilya, to which I now turn.

Kautilya's *Arthashastra* (translation by Shamasastry 1967) is a counterpart, approximately contemporary in time, to writings by Han Fei Tzu and the Chinese "Legalist" School, discussed in the last chapter. The political context was probably the Mauryan empire established toward the end of the fourth century by Chandragupta in the wake of Alexander's retreat (Spear 1961:54–55). The date was thus perhaps around 300 BCE. Kautilya advises an autocratic ruler how to acquire, maintain, and extend power; much emphasis is put on the use of spies, both foreign and domestic, and on terror, torture, and other brutal methods. The work also describes in detail the duties of a large number of officials, is a good source of information on judicial procedure in ancient India, and, again like the treatise of Han Fei-tzu, can be viewed as a handbook of political rhetoric.

Portions of Kautilya's *Arthashastra* of special rhetorical interest are those in which he lists topoi that are useful in a variety of situations and those in which he reveals the existence of a technical terminology to describe features of rhetoric. Chapter 14 of book 1, for example, deals with how to win over factions for or against an enemy's cause in a foreign state. Thirty-four different categories of people who might be disaffected are listed: those deluded by false promises, those prevented in the exercise of their rights, criminals, the oppressed, and so forth. Then suggestions are offered as to what the foreign king's spies might say to win them over. For example, to an ambitious person not receiving honor from his ruler, the spy can say, "Just as a cow reared by dog-keepers gives milk to dogs, but not to Brahmins, so this king gives milk to those who are devoid of valour, foresight, eloquence, and bravery, but not to those who are possessed of noble character; so the other king who is possessed of power to discriminate men from men may be courted" (Shamasastry 1967:25). Later, in discussing prosecution for murder Kautilya lists questions that should be asked in court; for example, the relatives of the deceased should be asked, Who called the deceased? Who was with him? Who accompanied him on his journey? And who took him to the scene of death? (Shamasastry 1967:249).

By Kautilya's time there was a well-developed system of justice in Indian courts. The king, with his advisers, was the highest court. Judges in lower courts were appointed by the king and sat in panels of three or more. Procedures were public and judges were prohibited from holding private conversations with plaintiffs or defendants. The court judged whether an allegation was true and if so then applied the penalty fixed by law. Although lawyers as such did not exist, litigants could have advisers, who were paid, or be represented by a friend. At a trial the prosecutor or plaintiff made a statement, to which the defendant responded. Elaborate rules were developed for the form these pleas should take. A defendant's answer was limited to one of four possibilities: denial of the fact; confession; admission of the fact with a plea of mitigating circumstances; or claim that a judgment had been made earlier. These categories have some resemblance to stasis theory, determination of the question at issue, as expounded by Greek and Latin writers on judicial rhetoric: fact, legality, quality, and jurisdiction. Defendants could take exculpatory oaths. Witnesses, documents, or other forms of evidence were introduced. Witnesses were examined and cross-examined. The junior members of the panel of judges then each stated an opinion that was advisory to the chief judge, who rendered the final verdict. Circumstantial evidence was admissable, and thus argument from probability must have occurred. If the direct evidence was inadequate, an ordeal by poison, water, balance, or fire could be ordered. All of these procedures are described in detail by Kane (1930–62, III:242–410).

Chapter 10 of book two of Kautilya's *Arthashastra* describes the contents and style of royal writs. It provides a list of topoi, reminiscent of some features of Near Eastern correspondence that I discussed in chapter 7, and reveals the remarkable extent to which features of rhetoric were conceptualized and named in ancient India:

> As to a writ addressed to a lord, it shall contain polite mention of his country, his possessions, his family, and his name; and as to that addressed to a common-man, it shall make a polite mention of his country and name.
>
> Having paid sufficient attention to the caste, family, social rank, age, learning, occupation, property, character, and blood-relationship of the addressee,

as well as to the place and time, the writer shall form a writ befitting the position of the person addressed.

Arrangement of subject–matter, relevancy, completeness, sweetness, dignity, and lucidity are the necessary qualities of a writ. The act of mentioning facts in the order of their importance is *arrangement*. When subsequent facts are not contradictory to facts just or previously mentioned, and so on till the completion of the letter, it is termed *relevancy*. Avoidance of redundancy or deficiency in words or letters; impressive description of subject matter by citing reasons, examples, and illustrations; and the use of appropriate and suitably strong words is *completeness*. The description in exquisite style of a good purport with a pleasing effect is *sweetness*. The use of words other than colloquial is *dignity*. The use of well-known words is *lucidity*. (Shamasastry 1967:72–73)

This passage comes close to distinguishing the "parts" of rhetoric as recognized in the West, and the stylistic qualities mentioned have some resemblance to classical rhetorical theories of the "virtues" of style: correctness, clarity, ornamentation, and propriety.

The final chapter of the *Arthashastra* (Shamasastry 1967:469–73) provides an even more extensive list of technical terms, called "paragraphical divisions." Except for the first two, they correspond in Greek rhetoric to either *topoi* or figures of speech. Although the English translation usually needs several words to convey the meaning, in the original all but one are single words. Each term is defined and an example of its use earlier in the treatise is cited. The thirty-two terms are: book, contents, suggestion of similar facts, meaning of a word, purport of reason (roughly equivalent to enthymeme), mention of a fact briefly, mention of a fact in detail, guidance, quotation, application, place of reference, simile, implication, doubt, reference to similar procedure, contrariety, ellipsis, acceptance of the opinion of another, explanation, derivation, illustration, exception, definition of terms in a special sense, citation of another's opinion to be refuted, rejoinder, conclusion, reference to something to follow, reference to something previous, command, alternative, compounding, and determinable fact. The conceptualization and naming of rhetorical techniques by Indian scholars is doubtless an extension of the analytical process that had begun in religion and philosophy. If a date around 300 BCE is valid for the *Arthashastra*, that development was taking place about the same time in India and Greece. Although they were in contact with each other at this time, there is no evidence that the development of rhetorical theory in one culture exercised any influence on that in the other.

The Edicts of Ashoka

The politics of power and intrigue that Kautilya described may well have characterized the rule of the early Mauryan kings. It was, however, at least temporarily checked under the rule of Ashoka (c. 274–234 BCE), the most famous member of the dynasty. The earliest surviving Indian inscriptions are edicts of Ashoka found on pillars and rocks in widely separated parts of the country. They witness to a remarkable conversion and an attempt to propagate a change in the values of society. Ashoka was a Buddhist; although the inscriptions indicate tolerance of all religions, he sent out Buddhist missionaries to Ceylon and even to Egypt and Greece and convened a great council of Buddhist leaders to define the faith. According to Spear (1961:57–58):

> Conscious that his empire contained a great medley of races, full of independent spirit and with the most varied beliefs, and aware that force can never maintain empires for long, he attempted to promote an imperial ethic which might bind the governing classes in a common allegiance to an impersonal law.... His method was not the sectarian encouragement of the Buddhist Church, for that would have provoked division rather than unity. Buddhist aggression would involve Brahminical reaction. So he used concepts now associated with Buddhism and tried to secure their acceptance by attaching them to the prestige of the semidivine monarch. His efforts were in line with the solar cult of Akhnaton and the emperor worship of the Romans; it was more practical than the former and more noble than the latter.

Ashoka summed up his teaching in the word *dharma*, a word with many different meanings ranging from "sacred law" to "morality" to "fate." When used by Ashoka it refers to the principles of ethics as found in universally shared insights of religion and piety. As an example of the rhetoric of Ashoka's inscriptions, here is part of Rock Edit XIII (Nikam and McKeon 1959:27–30):

> The Kalinga country was conquered by King Priyadarshi, Beloved of the Gods [i.e., Ashoka], in the eighth year of his reign. One hundred and fifty thousand persons were carried away captive, one hundred thousand were slain, and many times that number died.
>
> Immediately after the Kalingas had been conquered, King Priyadarshi became intensely devoted to the study of Dharma, to the love of Dharma, and to the inculcation of Dharma.
>
> The Beloved of the Gods, conqueror of the Kalingas, is moved to remorse now. For he has felt profound sorrow and regret because the conquest of a people previously unconquered involves slaughter, death, and deportation. But there is a more important reason for the King's remorse. The Brahmanas and Shramanas [the priestly and ascetic orders] as well as the followers of other religions and the householders—who all practiced obedience to superiors, parents, and teachers, and proper courtesy and firm devotion to friends, acquaintances, companions, relatives, slaves, and servants—all suffer from the injury, slaughter, and deportation inflicted on their loved ones. Even those who escaped calamity themselves are deeply afflicted by the misfortunes suffered by those friends, acquaintances, companions, and relatives for whom they feel an undiminished affection. Thus all men share in the misfortune, and this weighs on King Priyadarshi's mind....

King Priyadarshi now thinks that even a person who wrongs him must be forgiven for wrongs that can be forgiven....

For King Priyadarshi desires security, self-control, impartiality, and cheerfulness for all living creatures.

King Priyadarshi considers moral conquest [*dharma-vijaya*] the most important conquest....

Wherever conquest is achieved by Dharma, it produces satisfaction.... Even satisfaction, however, is of little importance.

King Priyardarshi attaches value ultimately only to consequences of action in the other world.

This edict on Dharma has been inscribed so that my sons and great-grandsons who may come after me should not think new conquests worth achieving. If they do conquer, let them take pleasure in moderation and mild punishments. Let them consider moral conquest the only true conquest.

This is good, here and hereafter. Let their pleasure be pleasure in morality [*dharma-rati*]. For this alone is good, here and hereafter.

This and similar inscriptions throughout the country publicly acknowledged the king's sin and proclaimed a new national policy. The king sought to bind his descendants to this policy by making it permanently and widely known. Their actions would be compared to his. Of course, very few of his subjects could read, but the inscriptions, in Prakrit, surely aroused public interest and those who could read them would explain the content to others so that the word would be passed on. The Mauryan dynasty lasted another hundred years, after which India was subjected to new invaders from the north and new conditions. Buddhism took permanent root in Ceylon, south-east Asia, Tibet, China, and Japan but in India faded away to a resurgent Hindu orthodoxy.

Literary Criticism in India

The conceptualization of rhetoric, to which should be added the conceptualization of grammar in the treatises of Panini and his successors, had its counterpart in the study of poetry and drama. In the early centuries of the common era Indian scholars developed a remarkably subtle system of poetic aesthetics, which stands comparison with anything known in the West. Most ancient Indian texts I have discussed were composed for religious, philosophical, or legalist reasons, not as literature to be read and enjoyed; the exception is the *Ramayana*, which is the earliest work to show the impulse of an author to create a work that could be read and enjoyed on aesthetic grounds. Centuries later, literary composition, primarily in Sanskrit, became a feature of Indian culture. Lyric poetry was fully developed by the time of Bhasa in the third century and drama by the time of Kalidasha in the fifth. Given the Indian penchant for abstract theorizing, not surprisingly this was accompanied by the development of critical systems to describe what was excellent in composition. The earliest extant works of Indian poetics, sometimes described as Indian "rhetoric," date from the sixth or seventh centuries, but continue the work of earlier thinkers (Ramanujan and Gerow 1974 provide a good overview). There were two separate traditions: *alamkara-shastra*, or "science of the figures," was the study of *kavya*, the genre of stanzaic or lyric poetry; *natya-shastra* was the study of drama. The *alamkara* critics, of whom Dandin can be taken as an example, divided poetic style into two or more types and identified "qualities" of style such as clarity, vigor, compactness, and density, as well as corresponding "defects" of style. There is some analogy here to concepts of the Greek rhetorician Hermogenes in his work *On Ideas of Style*. Indian theorists regarded simile as the basic figure, followed by hyperbole, with many subdivisions that include approximations of the Western understanding of metaphor and metonymy. This is the opposite of Aristotle's view that simile is a form of metaphor. Dramatic criticism centered on the concept of *rasa*, the "mood"—love, anger, fear, and other emotions—of a character expressed by words and gestures. For additional information on Indian poetic and dramatic criticism see Diwekar (1930), De (1960), Chaitanya (1965), Deutsch (1975), and Krishnamoorthy (1985).

Conclusion

Rhetorically, as well as geographically, India lay between China and Greece. In both India and China discussions of speech in the archaic and classical periods are found in a context of political and ethical thinking, not set off as a separate discipline, as happened in Greece. In all three countries logical argument was developed as a subtle tool, leading to a form of sophistry. There is more inclination to classification of abstract concepts and more explicit celebration of the power of speech in India, seen for example in the *Hymn to Vak* or Yajnavalkya's tribute to Brahma as speech, than in China. Both Indian and Chinese thinkers conceptualized some aspects of rhetoric and created a terminology for criticism, the Indians in greater detail than the Chinese. The best evidence is found in Kautilya's *Arthashastra*. In common with other cultures throughout the world, India developed "formal languages" for specific genres and occasions.

Indian rhetoric is connected with Greek through the common linguistic ancestry of Sanskrit and Greek, as well as by some political and cultural traditions that seem to go back to the Aryan invaders. These may include features of epic poetry in the two languages such as speeches by proud, quarrelsome nobles and possibly the use of similes, which partially replaced metaphorical expression common elsewhere. There were some direct connections between India and Greece beginning in the fourth century BCE, but there is no evidence that the rhetorical terminology used by Kautilya and others was indebted to that of Greek teachers or that Greek rhetoricians were aware of Indian teachings.

Despite the lack of texts of secular public address from ancient India, except as found in epic poetry, Indian rhetorical traditions are potentially a rich field for comparative research.

References

Alphonso-Karkala, John B., ed. (1971). *An Anthology of Indian Literature*. New York: Penguin Books.

Burlingame, Eugene W. (1922). *Buddhist Parables*. New Haven: Yale University Press.

Buitenen, Johannes A. B. van (1974). "The Indian Epic," in Dimock (1974) pp. 46–80.

———, trans. (1973—). *The Mahabharata*. Chicago, University of Chicago Press, multivolume work in progress.

Carter, John Ross, and Mahinda Pahilawadana, trans. (1987). *The Dhammapada*. New York: Oxford University Press.

Chaitanya, Krishna (1965). *Sanskrit Poetics: A Critical and Comparative Study*. Bombey: Asia Publishing House.

De, Sushil Kumar (1960). *History of Sanskrit Poetics*. Calcutta: K. L. Mukhopadhyay.

Deutsch, Eliot (1975). *Studies in Comparative Aesthetics*. Society for Asian and Comparative Philosophy, Monograph 2. Honolulu: University Press of Hawaii.

Dewart, Leslie (1989). *Evolution and Consciousness: The Role of Speech in the Origin and Development of Human Nature*. Toronto: University of Toronto Press.

Dimock, Edward C., Jr., ed. (1974). *The Literatures of India*. Chicago: University of Chicago Press.

Diwekar, H.-R. (1930). *Les fleurs de rhétorique dans l'Inde*. Paris: Maisonneuve.

Dutt, Romesh C., trans. (1910). *The Ramayan and the Mahabharata*. New York: E. P. Dutton.

Goody, Jack (1987). *The Interface between the Written and the Oral*. Cambridge: Cambridge University Press.

Gowen, Herbet H. (1968). *A History of Indian Literature from Vedic Times to the Present Day*. New York: Greenwood Press.

Griffith, Ralph, trans. (1973). *The Hymns of the Rigveda*. Rev. ed., Delhi: Motilal Banarsidass.

Horner, I. B., trans. (1954–59). *Middle Length Sayings* (of the Buddha). 3 vol. London: Pali Text Society.

Hume, Robert E., trans. (1931). *The Thirteen Principal Upanishads*. Second rev. ed. Delhi: Oxford University Press. Originally published 1877; reprinted 1992.

Jayatilleke, Kulatissa N. (1963). *Early Buddhist Theory of Knowledge*. London: George Allen and Unwin.

Kane, Pandurang V. (1930–62). *History of Dharmashastra*. 5 vols. Poona: Bhandarkar Oriental Research Institute.

Krishnamoorthy, Kerlapuna (1985). *Indian Literary Theories: A Reappraisal*. New Delhi: Meharchard Lachmandas.

Masson-Oursel, Paul, Helena de Willman-Grabowska, and Philippe Stern (1967), eds. *Ancient India and Indian Civilization*. New York: Barnes & Noble.

Müller, F. Max, and Hermann Oldenberg (1891–96), trans. "Vedic Hymns," *Sacred Books of the East*, vols. xxxii and xlvi. Oxford: Clarendon Press.

Narasimhan, Chakroevarthi V., trans. (1965). *The Mahabharata; An English Version Based on Selected Verses*. New York: Columbia University Press.

Nikam, Narayamrao A., and Richard McKeon (1959). *The Edicts of Asoka*. Chicago: University of Chicago Press.

Oliver, Robert T. (1971). *Communication and Culture in Ancient India and China*. Syracuse: Syracuse University Press.

Radhakrishnan, Sarvepalli, and Charles A. Moore (1957), eds. *A Source Book in Indian Philosophy*. Princeton: Princeton University Press.

Ramanujan, A. K., and Edwin Gerow (1974). "Indian Poetics," in Dimock, ed. (1974):115–43.

Rhys-Davids, Thomas W., trans. (1881). *Buddhist Suttas. Sacred Books of the East*, ed. F. Max Müller, vol. XI. Oxford; Clarendon Press; reprinted Delhi: Motilal Banarsidass, 1965.

———. (1890–94). *The Questions of King Milinda*. Vols. XXXV–XXXVI of *Sacred Books of the East*, ed. F. Max Müller. Oxford: Clarendon Press.

Roy, P. C., trans. (1919–30). *The Mahabharata*. 11 vols. Calcutta: D. Boise.

Shamasastry, Rudrapatna, trans. (1967). *Kautilya's Arthashastra*. Mysore: Mysore Printing House.

Spear, Percival (1961). *India*. Ann Arbor: University of Michigan Press.

Thomas, Edward J. (1975). *The Life of Buddha as Legend and History*. London: Routledge and Kegan Paul (first published 1927).

Bibliography

Lang, David M., ed. (1971). *A Guide to Eastern Literatures*. London: Weidenfeld and Nicolson.

Sources of Indian Tradition, compiled by William Theodore de Bary, Stephen N-Hay, Royal Weiler, and Andrew Yarrow. New York: Columbia University Press, 1959.

Suleri, Sara (1992). *The Rhetoric of English India*. Chicago: University of Chicago Press.

Zaehner, Robert C., ed. (1966). *Hindu Scriptures*. New York: J. M. Dent.

CHAPTER 9

Rhetoric in Greece
and Rome

Rhetoric in Greece and Rome has been more extensively studied than have the rhetorical traditions of the Near East, China, and India, since it is the origin of rhetoric as understood through western European history. I have myself sought to describe it elsewhere (Kennedy 1994, with bibliography; see also Worthington 1994). This chapter can focus on some distinctive features of classical rhetoric as compared with other traditions. Among these are the unusual contentiousness of public address in Greece and Rome, the development of judicial rhetoric beyond what is found elsewhere, and the resulting creation of a system of rhetorical education, distinct from other areas of study.

The earliest wave of Greeks, speaking an Indo-European language and practicing Indo-European religious and political customs, arrived in the peninsula in the second millenium BCE. The Minoan civilization was already flourishing on Crete and the Aegean islands. Between 1500 and 1200 BCE the Greek chieftains imitated the Minoans by making themselves into powerful kings at Mycenae, Pylos, and elsewhere on the mainland, building themselves palaces, and creating a centralized agricultural economy and bureaucracy resembling what existed in the Near East. A syllabic script called Linear B was used for record keeping. Between the thirteenth and eleventh centuries this culture was destroyed and knowledge of writing was lost. According to Greek tradition, the destroyers were the Dorians, a new wave of Greeks from the north. Destruction was, however, widespread throughout the Near East, reaching even to Egypt, and the Dorian Greeks were apparently only one wave of tribal movements throughout the region.

192 • Rhetoric In Ancient Literate Cultures

Gradually, during the ninth and eighth centuries a new culture evolved, including some Indo-European traditions, a vague memory of the Mycenaean past, and some Near Eastern practices in a distinct Greek synthesis.

The Introduction of Writing in Greece

A feature of early Greek culture was a rich tradition of oral epic, composed and performed by traveling bards chanting in verse the deeds of the gods and heroes of the past. The ultimate origin of this poetic tradition was probably songs of the Greeks' Indo-European ancestors, which found an analogous development in Indian epic. Writing was a relatively late cultural development in Greece in comparison to the societies of the Near East, never given priority over speech, and sometimes even denegrated. There were, however, close commercial and cultural contacts with the Near East (Burkert 1992), and by the eighth century BCE the Greeks had adapted the Phoenician alphabet to writing their own language, using some Phoenician consonants to represent vowels, which were not written in Semitic languages. As in the Near East and India, writing was first used to identify ownership or for commercial purposes. The earliest writing was scratched on pottery or written on wood and skins. Subsequently, papyrus was imported from Egypt and made into scrolls, which remained the most common form of book until replaced by the parchment codex in later antiquity. Some poetry, still orally composed, began to be written down for the first time by the seventh century. Original works in poetry or prose were being composed in writing in the sixth century. By that time, schools existed and written texts of poems attributed to Homer, Hesiod, and other early poets were in existence and were being memorized, recited at festivals, and studied. Although by the fifth century many Greeks could read a simple text and write their names or keep written records, books and readers of books were few until the fourth century (Finnegan 1988; Harris 1989; Thomas 1992; Robb 1994).

Early Greek Poetry

Our earliest evidence for rhetoric in Greece are the texts of the two Homeric poems, *Iliad* and *Odyssey*, perhaps the work of two different poets, and the two major poems of Hesiod, *Theogony* and *Works and Days*. There are many English translations of these works; my own preferences are versions of the *Iliad* by Lattimore (1951), of the *Odyssey* by Fitzgerald (1961), and of Hesiod's works by Athanassakis (1983). All four poems begin with an invocation of a goddess or muse and sometimes repeat the invocation in later passages: "Speak now to me, Muses holding Olympian dwellings; for you are goddesses, and you are present, and you know everything while we hear only rumor and know nothing" sings the poet at *Iliad* 2.484–86 (Solmsen 1954). Oral poets probably literally believed that their creations were "inspired" from a source outside themselves, resulting from a lack of conscious reflection about composition, which more rationally can be thought a product of original genius, imitation of traditional themes and poetic technique, an "ear" for what sounded right, and expression of cultural values and assumptions. Although there were different spoken dialects in common use and strong rivalries among the early Greek states, Greek literature from the beginning had a "pan-Hellenic" quality, appealing to a common sense of nationality and shared experience (Nagy 1989:16–17). All four works employ "formal language" that was used for poetry, oracles, and ritual but was not the spoken language of any one time or place: vocabulary and grammar is drawn from different Greek dialects; there are many traditional epithets and formulaic phrases, and the whole is cast into dactylic hexameter verse. On the other hand, early Greek poetry largely discarded parallelism, which was perhaps an earlier feature of composition and is common in traditional poetry elsewhere. The versions of Greek epic we have today are based on critical editions made by scholars at the Alexandrian Library in the third and second centuries BCE; these in turn were based on collations of manuscripts of earlier times, differing somewhat among themselves.

Metaphor in Greek Literature

In comparison to the earliest literature of China, India, and the Near East, and to poetry in traditional oral cultures elsewhere, early Greek epic seems to avoid use of metaphor, preferring instead to develop similes. What metaphors are used are chiefly either personifications of abstractions, such as the treatment of "wrath" in the opening lines of the *Iliad*, or are formulaic phrases, such as the famous expression " 'winged' words" often used of speech (i.e., speech that hits its mark like an arrow). Even early hymnic, elegiac, and lyric poetry—what are called the *Homeric Hymns*, for example, and the poems of Archilochus, Alcman, and Sappho—is comparatively nonmetaphorical, except in the sense that any poem describing a concrete experience has some universality and can be regarded as a metaphor for life in the larger sense. The ekphrasis of the making of the shield of Achilles in book eighteen of the *Iliad* is a metaphorical visualization of the contrasting worlds of war and peace and of the making of art (Becker 1995). By the fifth century, however, as seen in the works of Aeschylus, Pindar, and their successors, Greek poetry abounds in metaphor. Unlike other literary traditions, Greek thus seems to reverse the usual development: instead of movement from an early inclination for metaphorical expression to an increased literalism, we find a movement from clear, relatively literal expression toward increased exploitation of metaphorical imagery.

W. B. Stanford (1936) argued that the nonmetaphorical quality of early Greek poetry resulted from the desire of "Homer" to achieve the greatest possible clarity of expression. Although we need not attribute the use of simile in preference to metaphor to a particular individual poet, there is an underlying validity in Stanford's observation. We do not have any early Greek examples of ritual or folk poetry, such as the Vedic hymns in India or the Chinese *Book of Songs*, where metaphor would likely dominate expression. What we have instead is narrative and didactic poetry of great literary merit. The *Homeric Hymns*, for example, are highly sophisticated written works of the sixth century, not traditional, ritual praise of the gods but inventive narrative accounts of some of their doings. It seems to be a regular feature of narrative poetry, or of narrative passages in other poems, to seek clarity of expression and thus to avoid bold metaphor. Narrative poetry is intended to be understood by a general audience. In contrast, there is relatively little narrative in the Vedic hymns and much metaphor, with some short similes. In chapter 8 I tentatively suggested that the earliest development of simile might result from the experience of Indo-European peoples, ancestors of both Indians and Greeks, or be related to grammatical features of Indo-European, found also in Sumerian where simile also appears at an early time. In contrast to ritual poetry, the narrative of Indian epic—*Mahabharata* and *Ramayana*—like Greek epic, avoids bold metaphor except in epithets and formulaic phrases. The highly metaphorical quality of Greek choral lyric and of choral passages in Greek drama in the fifth century is probably related to their ritual and religious functions; the language was surely difficult for an audience to understand on first hearing, especially since choral passages were sung and accompanied by instruments, but sounds and fleeting images could create feelings of beauty, awe, or horror. As a product of conscious artistry rather than tradition, metaphorical poetry of the classical period in Greece may have been encouraged by the metaphorical thinking of philosophers of the time—Parmenides, Empedocles, and Heraclitus, for example—and facilitated by the careful composition made possible by the use of writing.

Rhetoric in the Homeric Poems

Although the *Iliad* can certainly be read as a warning of the futility of war and the dangers of pride and the *Odyssey* as a model of human resourcefulness and fidelity, and although both poems taught their audience about the gods, about great events of the past, and about the world, and together made major contributions to the formation and transmission of Greek cultural traditions, neither poem should be read as a conscious, overt attempt to persuade an audience of certain views. The poet of the *Iliad* glories in war and in pride as often as he seems to criticize them. The primary function of heroic epic for its original audience was enchantment and escape from everyday life into a fabulous and often beautiful world of the imagination (Walsh 1984).

The Homeric poems purport to describe events of the twelfth century BCE, a late phase of Mycenaean civilization at Troy, Mycenae, Pylos, and on islands of the Mediterranean, with occasional references to Egypt, but they are compositions of the eighth century and reflect some of the conditions of that time. The only reference to writing in these works is one passage in the *Iliad* (6.168–69) that speaks of "dire signs written on a folded tablet," probably reflecting some awareness of writing in the Near East. In contrast, there are several passages describing the activity of oral poets (e.g., *Odyssey* 1.325–52; 8.477–98) and many descriptions of deliberative situations in the Homeric poems. Persuasive, eloquent speech is highly valued. It was doubtless learned, as elsewhere, by imitation and practice, and was a skill expected of a leader. Phoenix is said to have taught Achilles to be "a speaker of words and a doer of deeds" (*Iliad* 9.442). Differing styles of speech and delivery are recognized and compared (*Iliad* 3.209–24). Nestor's speech flowed from his mouth "sweeter than honey" (*Iliad* 1.249), reminiscent of "honeyed words" mentioned in the biblical book of Proverbs. Formal speeches, such as Odysseus's address to Achilles in *Iliad* 9.225–306, fall into parts later standardized as proemium, narration, proof, and epilogue, and they employ techniques of logical, ethical, and pathetical persuasion (Kennedy 1994:13–14). Assemblies of the army or citizens are described in *Iliad* 2 and in *Odyssey* 2. Epideictic is represented by lamentations for the dead in *Iliad* 19.287–337 (Ochs 1993:38–41) and 24.725–75. There seems to be in the society described by the poets an awareness that speech is what Enos (1993:4–9) has called a "heuristic, eristic, and protreptic faculty." That is, a way of discovering knowledge or concealing intent and in either case of determining action, but also a form of strife and aggrandizement, and a source of wisdom and exhortation.

Rhetoric in Hesiod's **Works and Days**

Hesiod's *Works and Days* is a Greek counterpart to the "wisdom literature" composed in Egypt and the Near East, mentioned in chapter 6. The first part of the poem (up to line 764) is an exhortation to work, just living, and piety addressed to Hesiod's brother, Perses, with advice about agriculture, trading, household management, and religious duties. The poem is overtly rhetorical (Kirby 1992) in that the poet claims to have suffered from actions of his brother and from legal judgments against himself and he seeks to persuade his audience to depart from evil ways and redress wrongs, holding out the threat of the anger of Zeus at the unrighteous (267–73). Hesiod held no official position; his only "authority" is that of a poet who claims inspiration from the muses. His means of persuasion otherwise are the ethos of righteousness he projects, maxims, myths, and fables from which a moral can be drawn. Some statements are in enthymematic form. Metaphor is limited to personification of abstract or inanimate forces, and similes, unlike those in the Homeric epics, are all very short.

One of the myths in *Works and Days* is the story of Pandora (59–105). Prometheus stole fire from heaven and gave it to mankind to use. Zeus was angry; he did not take fire away from human beings, but to punish humans for using it sent "a great evil" upon them. At Zeus's order, Hephaestus made a beautiful young woman to whom Hermes gave a shameless mind and a deceitful ethos (67). Aphrodite clothed her, the divine graces and queenly Peitho, goddess of persuasion, put "golden necklaces" on her—perhaps the earliest reference to figures of speech—and Hermes contrived for her lies and crafty words (76–78). Up until this time there were no ills or sicknesses among humans; these were contained in a jar. The woman the gods have created, Pandora or "All-Gift," opened the jar, with the result that all the evils flew out to afflict humans.

The connection between sex and rhetoric is commonplace in Greek and Latin literature (Gross 1985); good examples include the *Encomium of Helen* by the sophist Gorgias and the speeches in Plato's *Symposium*. In chapter 6 I noted a similar topos in the *Gilgamesh* and in the biblical book of Proverbs, so the motif may be Near Eastern in origin; it does not seem to be common elsewhere. For Hesiod, the connection was probably emphasized by the similarity of *eros*, "sexual love," to *eris*, "strife." Kirby (1990) has explored the "triangulation" of *peitho* or "persuasion," *eros* or "passion," and *bia* or "force," as an approach to the early history of rhetoric in Greece. In Greek mythology, Peitho is often regarded as the daughter of Aphrodite, goddess of love. According to Herodotus (8.111), early in the fifth century Themistocles told the Andrians that the Athenians came to them with two great goddesses, Peitho and Anangke ("Necessity"): speech to persuade them to surrender in their best interests and the use of force to constrain them if necessary. The earliest Greek definition of rhetoric is *peithous dēmiourgos*, "the worker of Peitho," attributed by Plato (*Gorgias* 453a2) to the sophist Gorgias. "Peitho" can thus be regarded as an earlier Greek term for "rhetoric," though Greek writers commonly employ the more inclusive term *logos*, which has a wide range of meaning, including "word," "a speech," "the faculty of speech," and "reasoning." As in other cultures, the art of persuasion was originally not differentiated from other related studies into a distinct discipline. This is largely a development of the fourth century, to be discussed later in this chapter. The term "rhetoric," *rhētorikē*, seems to have originated in the circle of Socrates in the late fifth century and as used in Plato's *Gorgias* originally carried a somewhat negative association; its use in classical Greek is largely limited to writings of Plato and Aristotle, but subsequently it became widely accepted.

Judicial Rhetoric in Early Greece

The only reference to a court of law in the Homeric poems is the brief description of a trial pictured on the Shield of Achilles, made by the god Hephaestus in *Iliad* 18.497–508. The situation is not entirely clear and interpretations of the passage differ in what is at issue. A man has been killed and judges representing the community are being asked to make some decision relating to the penalty. A recent interpretation (Westbrook 1992) is that the defendant has claimed that there were mitigating circumstances: either the killing was justified in some way or was unintended. If so, he should be allowed to pay blood money, the amount to be fixed by the court. The opponent probably demanded the right to take vengeance by killing the defendant or forcing him into exile. The procedures are similar to those found in the Near East, though no written code of law existed to guide these early Greek judges as it did there.

The society Hesiod describes is one in which violence is always a threat and lies and deceit are to be found or suspected everywhere, not least in the courts of law where strife and quarrels come before bribe-taking judges (*Works and Days* 38–39). The judicial process, to which Hesiod refers several times, seems to be one in which the oath of a plaintiff, defendant, or witness was regarded as determinative (282–85). No extended speeches are likely to have been given on either side. "Oath [personified] runs with crooked judgments" and if false brings further mischief (219–24). Trial by ordeal does not seem to have been an option in case of doubt by the judges. The only vestige of trial by ordeal in Greece is perhaps the oath "by the waters of the river Styx," often taken by the gods in altercations with each other and probably of Near Eastern origin. Hesiod exhorts "kings" to be fearful of crooked judgments and the anger of the gods that will follow (248–55). On the other hand, kings, again as in Proverbs, have a special access to inspired language (Walker 1996):

> Whomever among heaven-nurtured kings the daughters of great Zeus honor and see at birth, on his tongue they pour sweet dew and gracious words flow from his tongue. All the people look to him as he settles cases with true justice. Speaking with certainty, he would swiftly and with knowledge put a stop to even a great quarrel. Kings are wise because when the people are wronged in the assembly they easily set the matter right, persuading with gentle words. (*Theogony* 80–90)

Contentiousness in Greek Rhetoric

The most distinctive feature of Greek public address in contrast to that of many other cultures is its eristic qualities. In the traditional oral and early literate societies I have described earlier, the goal of deliberative rhetoric is usually consensus and concord in accordance with conservative values, and sharp altercation is avoided if possible. Differences are usually politely or indirectly stated. In Egypt, Palestine, India, and China there are injunctions to turn away wrath with a soft answer, or even to be silent; this was not the attitude of the Greeks. In chapter 4 I noted that certain societies are unusually individualistic, combative, and sometimes argumentative, resulting probably from particular historical experience, and in all societies calm deliberation sometimes breaks down, but generally speaking, throughout the non-Western world, rhetoric has been used for purposes of agreement and conciliation, and emotionalism, except in the case of lamentation for the dead, is regarded as in poor taste. There is also often an accompanying disapproval of blatant flattery, though flattery of those in power easily develops in autocratic societies. The Greeks were contentious from the beginning, and acceptance and indulgence of open contention and rivalry has remained a characteristic of Western society except when suppressed by powerful authority of church or state.

The first book of the *Iliad*, describing the beginning of the quarrel between Achilles and Agamemnon, with fiery speeches and personal denunciations on the part of each, sets the tone of much that follows. The situation of the *Iliad*, however, is not that of normal society. Here a number of proud kings with their armed men have come together in an unusual joint operation. Within each contingent, the king's authority prevails, and contention largely arises from conflicting demands by the kings for honor from other kings. This is true also in Indian epic and presumably represents an Indo-European tradition of rivalry among chiefs. In the *Iliad*, Agamemnon is the official commander in chief, but he has difficulty imposing discipline on others who regard themselves as his equals. Contention among the kings spreads down to the common soldiers in the case of Thersites, who is a social misfit and troublemaker (*Iliad* 2.211–77). He is described as "unmeasured in speech" and as knowing many words but not how to put them together, and his attempt to turn the army against Agamemnon and return home to Greece is only silenced when Odysseus beats him.

In *Works and Days*, after a brief proem, Hesiod describes two kinds of Strife (*eris*) that are spread all over the earth (11–24). Each is personified as a divine figure. One is cruel and causes war and battle; although no one loves her, by will of the gods she is honored. The other Strife is kinder. It is she who causes men to work and to engage in rivalry with each other, which is a wholesome force in society even though "potter gets angry with potter and craftsman with craftsman and beggar becomes jealous of beggar and oral poet with oral poet" (25–26).

Strife among human beings in Greece might be thought to receive some validation from strife among the gods. In *Theogony* Hesiod describes the "generation" of the gods, which includes struggles for power among the deities and abstract forces, and in the *Iliad* the gods take opposing sides in the Trojan war, quarrel bitterly with each other, engage in lying, deceit, and other vices, and aid their favorites in the fight. Strife among gods is not uncommon in other cultures, where it often represents personification of contending forces of nature. Mesopotamian, and sometimes Egyptian, gods quarrel, and stories of the Greek gods often seem to borrow from Near Eastern sources. In traditional paganism, however, gods do not provide moral lessons for human beings. One factor that makes them gods is that they are not bound by taboos. To a lesser extent this is also true of the heroes of the past, who are often descendants of gods. What is unusual in Greece is the acceptance, even the celebration, of contention and rivalry in civic society. With the canonization of the Homeric poems as the cultural textbooks of the Greeks, the immorality of the gods in epic became a problem for ethical philosophers. As early as the sixth century Xenophanes of Colophon criticized the immorality of the Homeric gods and it was one of the reasons why Plato, in *Republic* book three, excluded poets from his ideal state. One answer to the problem was allegorical interpretation, which began with Theagenes of Rhegium in the sixth century and identified the gods as only personifications of forces of weather and nature (Pfeiffer 1968:9–11).

The pursuit of honor by aristocratic males, and later by democratic citizens, in Greece was often a "zero-sum game" in which almost any means, physical or verbal, could be justified; the more one person could be dishonored, the greater the honor to the opponent. It was an assumption of the culture that a man, and sometimes a woman, would have enemies and would attempt to defeat them. Life was regarded as a contest. After the battle of Salamis in 480 BCE the Greek commanders met at the isthmus of Corinth to award a prize of valor to the man who was judged most to deserve it in the campaign. They cast votes for first and second place. Everyone voted for himself for first place; a majority voted for Themistocles for second. Jealousy thus prevented a decision and the commanders sailed away home (Herodotus 8.123). Similar rivalry is characteristic of relations among the Greek city-states. The history of classical Greece is the history of the rivalries, plots, and wars of proud, independent city-states. Although Greeks ordinarily valued family ties and friendship, their contentiousness at times, in strong contrast to Chinese culture, even countenanced revolt of children against parents or other family members. Orestes killed his mother; in the story of the Seven against Thebes brother killed brother. Aristophanes's comedy, *Clouds*, portrays a son out-arguing and even beating his father.

Contentiousness found an important outlet in athletics, esteemed and organized by the Greeks on a scale not known elsewhere, and in oratorical contests. The earliest reference to the latter is Herodotus's account (6.129) of the competition (*eris*) among young nobles for marriage to the daughter of Cleisthenes of Sicyon early in the sixth century BCE. Personal invective and mud-slinging is also a regular feature of Greek deliberative oratory from the beginning and becomes a regular feature of judicial oratory, as seen, for example, in the verbal duels of Aeschines and Demosthenes in the fourth century. The Western world is indebted to the Greeks for the earliest models of democracy, but Greek democracies were almost always at crisis stage, riven by faction, and easily degenerated into mob rule and sometimes civil war under the influence of demagogues. Thucydides's history of the Peloponnesian war shows the process at work in Athens, Corcyra, and elsewhere. (On the development of political rhetoric in Athens, see Yunis 1996.)

Voting

The answer that the Greeks found for contention was the acceptance of the judg-ment of the majority, or in a few situations a plurality, by counting votes. One of its strangest manifestations was "ostracism" as practiced in Athens, originally intended to prevent seizure of the government by a would-be tyrant. From time to time, citizens were asked to write on a sherd of pottery the name of the per-son they would most like to expel from the city, for any reason. The person who got the most votes was exiled for ten years.

As noted in earlier chapters, trials in the Near East, India, and China in an-cient times were heard by panels of three or more judges. It is unlikely that the judges always agreed, but one of the judges seems usually to have been chair-man of the panel; he heard the opinion of the others but he himself made the final decision. When a king consulted his advisers, some informal reckoning of how many favored or opposed a course of action is likely to have taken place, even though the final decision remained with the ruler. I have not found any reference to the counting of votes in either judicial or deliberative situations in nonliterate societies or in India, China, or in the earlier periods in Mesopotamia, and in none of these countries was there ever majority rule by vote of the cit-izens as there was in Greek democracies.

Herodotus's account of Persian history in the sixth and fifth centuries does, however, mention the decision by a majority of the members of a council in some situations. It is difficult to know whether his reports can be trusted in this respect. Perhaps he imposes on the Persians his own assumptions based on Greek practice. The earliest example is his famous account (3.80–84) of a debate in 521 BCE among the seven conspirators who had overthrown the government of a usurper and who then discuss among themselves what constitution to impose on the Persians. One speaker recommends democracy, one oligarchy, and one, Dar-ius, monarchy. The four others throw their support to Darius, and thus a monar-chy under his rule is established by a vote of five to two (Herodotus 3.83.1). Herodotus admits that some of his contemporaries refuse to believe that this de-bate occurred but insists that it did (3.80.1). Most modern readers have been equally doubtful, for the whole passage reads like an example of Greek sophistry, and serious consideration of a democracy in ancient Persia seems extremely un-likely. More plausible is Herodotus's report (8.70.1) that Xerxes ordered the ad-vice of the majority of his officers to be followed in determining strategy on the eve of the battle of Salamis in 480 BCE.

Popular voting certainly originated in shouts of acclamation or show of hands in tribal assemblies, of which examples have been noted in earlier chapters and which is still practiced in some cultures. The common word for vote in classi-cal Greek is *cheirotonein*, which means "to stretch out hands." This was the pro-cedure used in the fifth and fourth centuries when the Athenian citizens gath-ered in an assembly to debate and decide on important public issues. The stages, however, in which this had developed in Greece into a counting of votes pro and con in deliberative assemblies and law courts and the use of a secret ballot in Athenian courts is undocumented. There is no hint of counting votes in the councils and assemblies of the Homeric poems and no reference to voting in Hesiod's works. In the trial scene on the Shield of Achilles, mentioned earlier, the judges are said to give judgment in turn (18.506); perhaps this implies that the decision of the majority will prevail. A mythical account of the origin of voting in the law courts is found in Aeschylus's play *Eumenides*, in which the goddess Athena as presiding judge at the trial of Orestes for murdering his mother institutes the court of the Areopagus and declares that if the votes of the judges are equal for conviction or acquittal (as they prove to be) the defendant will be acquitted (*Eumenides* 741). This may well reflect a tradition that the counting of votes in Athens originated in the Council of the Areopagus, perhaps in the seventh century when it had both deliberative and judicial functions (Larson 1949:170). The counting of votes was widely adopted in Greek states and not limited to those with democratic governments; it was, for example, also practiced in oligarchic Sparta.

Although we do not know the stages of development of voting in Greece, there are some probable reasons why it developed. It seems to imply the existence of a group of individuals with equal status and an equal claim on participation in decision making. This is a feature of Greek society emerging in the seventh and sixth centuries BCE as aristocratic government first replaced the rule of kings and subsequently as a middle class of wealthy landowners or businessmen emerged, leading the way to democracy. It is also characteristic of military organization by self-governing "hoplites" in the same period. Voting may have been the only option to civil war in some situations (Glotz 1953:65), although there remains the problem of how a sizable minority was first persuaded to accept the decision of the majority as in the best interests of all. From the Greeks the Romans borrowed voting procedures in elections, deliberation, and judicial decisions, although Roman procedures were more open to manipulation than was usually true in Greece (Stavely 1972). Voting was later a feature of councils of the Christian church and of the medieval jury system. Its use in modern times is a heritage of the classical world widely accepted in the West and in recent years adopted also in other parts of the world. When used under autocratic governments, as in Soviet Russia, voting by the public has often resulted in almost unanimous support for a single candidate and thus has differed little from the earliest custom of vote by acclamation.

The acceptance of majority decision, even a majority of one, has significant effect on rhetorical practice. If a speaker does not need to secure consensus, he need not try to conciliate the more extreme opponents, can largely ignore some of their concerns, and can concentrate on solidifying support with those already inclined to agree and winning over the doubtful. Vigorous, even personal, attack on opponents and their motives contributes to this end. Voting thus provided an answer to how to make a decision in a contentious society, but in the process polarized views and encouraged contentiousness.

Rhetoric in Herodotus's History

Herodotus's *History* of the wars between the Greeks and the Persians, written in the third quarter of the fifth century BCE (translations by Rawlinson 1947 and de Sélincourt 1954), is the earliest work to describe some actual forms and functions of speech in Greece society in the sixth and fifth centuries. At the beginning of the work, and in many later passages, Herodotus indicates that his history is a product of careful research. This involved extensive travels, collection of local traditions, interviews with witnesses or authorities, and his own reasoning about what "probably" happened. A good example of the latter is his evaluation of stories about Helen of Troy in 2.116–20. History as Herodotus conceived it was a new genre, creating a scholarly counterpart to epic in prose but dealing with recent events. He identifies two objectives in his brief preface: to prevent great and wonderful actions from being forgotten (a goal shared with oral epic) and to put on record the cause of the wars (a goal comparable to the efforts of Greek philosophers of the time to understand the causes of natural phenomena). Following the epic tradition, and comparable to what is found in the early Chinese *Book of History*, he often reports speeches by characters in his narrative. In no case had he heard the speeches and in no case was there a written version of a speech for him to consult. We have to assume that he created the speeches as a dramatic device from his knowledge of the situation, his estimate of the character and goal of the speaker, and his imagination of what might have been said. With the exception of the sermon on the nature of happiness preached by Solon to Croesus (1.30–32), the speeches are deliberative, given before a council or assembly or addressed to a ruler by an adviser.

On one occasion Herodotus criticizes the rhetoric of a speaker. Aristagoras of Miletus came to Sparta in 499 BCE to seek aid from King Cleomenes for a revolt by the Ionian Greeks against the rule of the Persians (5.49). He brought with him a map of Greece and the Near East on a bronze tablet, which he used to explain the geographical situation to the Spartans, who were quite ignorant of Asia Minor. This is, so far as I know, the earliest reference in history to the use of a visual aid by a speaker. According to Herodotus, Aristagoras spoke as follows, arguing that it would be shameful for the Spartans to neglect other Greeks, that victory over the Persians would be easy, and that the Spartans would obtain many material advantages from making an expedition to Asia Minor:

> Think it not strange, King Cleomenes, that I have been at the pains to sail hither; for the state of affairs made it fitting. Shame and grief is it indeed to none so much as to us, that the sons of the Ionians should have lost their freedom, and come to be the slaves of others; but yet it touches you like-

wise, Spartans, beyond the rest of the Greeks, inasmuch you are the leaders of all Greece. We beseech you therefore, by the common gods of the Greeks, deliver the Ionians, who are your own kinsmen, from slavery. Truly the task is not difficult; for the barbarians are an unwarlike people, and you are the best and bravest warriors in the whole world. Their mode of fighting is the following: they use bows and arrows and a short spear; they wear trousers in the field, and cover their heads with turbans. So easy are they to vanquish. Know too that the dwellers in these parts have more good things than all the rest of the world put together—gold, and silver, and brass, and embroidered garments, beasts of burden, and slaves—all which, if you only wish it, you may soon have for your own. The nations border on one another, in the order which I will now explain. (Rawlinson 1947:393)

He then pointed out the various territories and their resources on his map, where the scale made the distances seem small. Cleomenes promised to make a decision on the third day. When he then met with Aristagoras he asked how many days' journey it was from the Ionian coast to the Persian capital at Susa. Here, Herodotus says (5.50) that Aristagoras, who had been wise (*sophos*) up to this point, made a serious mistake. He should have lied; instead, he plainly said that it was a journey of three months. Before he could go on, Cleomenes interrupted and ordered him to leave Sparta by sunset: "This is no good proposal that you make to the Lacedaimonians [i.e., Spartans], to conduct them a distance of three months journey from the sea." It might be added that the Spartans, inhabitants of the area of Greece called Laconia, were famous for their "laconic" speech.

Flattery

The Greeks delighted in contentious argument; they often put a relatively low priority on telling the truth if a lie would be more effective; slanderous invective was not out of order in a court of law. Perhaps because of this, they seem to have become more tolerant of blattant flattery than most egalitarian cultures. Autocratic societies are, of course, another matter, and the existence of wealthy individuals can encourage flattery, as in the case of Hausa "roko" mentioned in chapter 4. When Socrates in Plato's *Gorgias* (463a9) is pressed to offer his own definition of rhetoric he calls it a form of flattery. What he has in mind are primarily the efforts of democratic politicians (the *rhêtores*) to gain influence by praising an audience and telling them what they want to hear rather than what is wise and just. Even the morally austere Aristotle suggests topoi for flattery in public address:

(When praising) one should always take each of the attendant terms in the best sense; for example, (one should call) an irrascible and excitable person "straightforward" and an arrogant person "high-minded" and "imposing" and (speak of) those given to excess as actually in states of virtue, for example the rash one as "courageous," the spendthrift as "liberal"; for this will

> seem true to most people and at the same time is a fallacious argument...
> (*Rhetoric* 1.9.29)

Later Greek and Roman rhetoricians offer advice about how to praise the un-worthy, and students of rhetoric exercised their wits in praise of unlikely things. The earliest example is Isocrates's reference to encomia of bumblebees and salt (*Helen* 12; cf. Plato, *Symposium* 177b); later works include Dio Chrysostom's *Encomium of Hair*, Lucian's *Encomium of the Fly*, and Synesius's *Encomium of Baldness*. Tolerance of flattery emerged in democratic Greece; it became full blown in the later encomia of Hellenistic kings and Roman emperors. It seems to have been a classical heritage to the Renaissance, where it is to be found in all kinds of compositions, and though often denigrated it remains a common feature of modern Western rhetoric. It should be added, however, that public speakers in democratic Athens sometimes found it effective to establish an ethos of moral superiority and independence by directly criticizing the values of an audience and telling them what they apparently did not want to hear. To judge from the accounts of his speeches in Thucydides's *History of the Peloponnesian War*, Pericles seems to have been able to do this with the Athenians; he had a reputation for Olympian aloofness. A century later Demosthenes, also personally aloof from others, tried the tactic with somewhat less success in his *Philippic* orations.

Thucydides's Speeches

Thucydides includes many speeches in his *History*, often arranging them into debates on two sides of a question. Thucydides had heard some of the speeches, had reports of others, and re-created what he thought the occasion demanded in terms of his interpretation of history (1.23). These speeches often sharply polarize the issue into one of expediency vs. justice. Among the most interesting examples are the debate between Cleon and Diodotus (3.37–48), in which the speakers also reflect on the strength and weakness of public debate, and the Melian dialogue (5.87–113), in which the Athenian envoys explain to the islanders that might makes right. For all its cherished democratic institutions at home, Athenian democracy easily developed into autocratic imperialism in foreign affairs, and little attempt was made to disguise this reality.

Speeches in Thucydides's work are deliberative except for the famous Funeral Oration attributed to Pericles (2.35–46). It was the custom in Athens that some distinguished individual was chosen each year to give a speech at the public ceremony in memory of those who had fallen in war. The speeches were in formal language, avoided any reference to individuals, and followed a conventional structure of topics, best seen in the example of the genre found among the works of Lysias. Their function was to bring a closure to the grief of families and friends, to unite the citizens in their patriotic duty, and to celebrate the values that had made Athens great. The speech attributed to Pericles is the classic archetype of

Western epideictic oratory, though unusually austere in tone (Loraux 1986; Ochs 1993:67–79).

Logical Arguments

Moral austerity is a form of ethos of a speaker. Slander and flattery extend ethos to the character of the subject or to the audience addressed. Ethos also is a factor in the Greek development of argument from probability beyond that found in other cultures. Argument from probability is probably already implicit in the verbals attacks of Achilles and Agamemnon on each other at the beginning of the *Iliad* or other speeches in the Homeric poems, even though what became the technical term (*eikos*) is not used there. There is an assumption that there is a connection between character and action, which makes it possible to attribute what someone has done or will do to his moral character and conversely to deduce character from actions. The earliest clear example of argument from probablity in Greek is found in the *Homeric Hymn to Hermes* (line 377), in which the infant god Hermes, brought before Zeus on the charge of stealing cattle, argues that he is in no way like (*outi ... eikotos*) a cattle thief. Hermes, the trickster-god, has no compunction about lying at any time. The classic example of argument from probability, attributed by Plato (*Phaedrus* 273a–c) to the rhetorical handbook of Tisias, suggests lying by both parties to a dispute in court:

> If a weak and brave man, having beaten up a strong and cowardly man, is brought into court, neither must tell the truth. The coward must claim that he was not beaten by a single brave man; that is, he must claim to have been attacked by two or more, whereas the other must refute this, insisting that the two of them were alone, in order to use the arguement "how could a little one like me have attacked a big one like him?"

The argument relies in both cases on what might probably be assumed about each man. Similar, though usually more reasonable, uses of argument from probability to support the innocence or guilt of an accused are a constant feature of the judicial orations of Antiphon, Lysias, Isaeus, Demosthenes, and other orators of the classical period. To modern readers, these same speeches often seem to rely excessively on circumstantial evidence, on reasoning about what probably happened, or what someone whose character can be described on the basis of other actions probably did in a given circumstance, to the neglect of direct evidence of what was actually done. One factor that apparently encouraged use of argument from probability in Greek courts was the prevalence of bribery, perjury, and the forgery of documents, on which the orators sometimes comment. To this can be added the development of Greek philosophy, where theories of physics, metaphysics, and ethics, though sometimes authoritatively proclaimed, were necessarily of a probable nature. Finally, argument from probability was a basic tool of the sophists, who were important teachers of rhetorical skills in the fifth century.

Non-Western societies, however inscrutable they sometimes seem to Westerners, value reason and engage in logical argument. Reference has frequently been made in earlier chapters to the use of enthymemes, probably going far back in human history. In literate societies, especially in China, philosophers explored systems of logical reasoning. The Greek language, even in its earliest known form, is strongly antithetical, and Greek art and mythology show a fondness for contrasting figures such as Prometheus and Epimetheus. Early Greek philosophy further developed binary thinking in terms of being and non-being, permanence and change, and other polarities (Lloyd 1966). Formal logic was first conceptualized by Aristotle, but a variety of logical techniques is evident in surviving texts of earlier philosophers, orators, and sophists, including definition and division of the question at issue, informal syllogisms, and inductive reasoning. Gorgias's *Encomium of Helen* is a good example of logical method applied in an early Greek speech. Henry Johnstone (1992) has identified concern with logical contradictions as an important aspect of Western civilization beginning with the Greeks. As the earliest example he cites a passage in Hesiod's discussion of strife (*Theogony* 782–84) in which a contradiction is met with the assumption that one statement must be a lie. It would doubtless be an exaggeration to say that speakers in other cultures do not understand logical contradiction, but it is perhaps true that Western contentiousness tends to identify and sharpen contradictions. In other cultures, and now in poststructural thought in the West, there is a greater inclination to entertain the possibility that two seemingly contradictory statements may both be true in some sense; for example, if a term is used metaphorically in one of the statements. Yang and yin in Chinese thought are complementaries, not opposites; Mencius's doctrine of multiple definitions is a Chinese example of a different form of reasoning. Western thinking, beginning with the Greeks, has tended to polarize truth and fiction, good and bad, body and soul, conservative and liberal, and other such concepts, for the sake of clarity but often unnecessarily.

Greek Sophistry

I do not feel that it is necessary here to enter into a detailed account of Greek sophistry. The subject is well known to most students of rhetoric and I have discussed it elsewhere (e.g., Kennedy 1994:17–21). As noted in previous chapters, Greek sophistry arose under conditions similar to analogous developments in China and India and shares some characteristics with them. The relativism and skepticism inherent in sophistry has, however, been a more frequently recurring feature of Western thought than elsewhere. Another feature of Western rhetoric, not unconnected with sophistry and with tolerance of lying, has been a fondness for irony (Swearingen 1991).

Greek sophists taught students how to secure success in public life by the use of speech. The teaching of public address in their schools, largely in the form of epideictic speeches by the sophist and imitation by the students, was bitterly opposed by cultural conservatives. Sophists were accused of "making the weaker seem the stronger cause" (Plato, *Apology* 18b8; cf. the dramatization of the debate between Just and Unjust Speech in Aristophanes's *Clouds* 889–1104). What is specifically being objected to here is the use of argument to support a paradox, seen for example in the speeches in favor of the nonlover in Plato's *Phaedrus*, and the fallacious use of argument from probability (Aristotle, *Rhetoric* 2.24.11). A deeper issue, however, was the conversion of rhetoric as a conservative force transmitting and enhancing traditional values, of which the funeral orations of Pericles, Lysias, and others are the best Greek examples from the classical period, into rhetoric as a tool of change, uncovering the inconsistencies and irrationality of traditional assumptions and beliefs and opening up the possibilities of objective logical argument. This process had already begun in the sixth century when philosophers, beginning with Thales of Miletus, began to create a scientific view of the world in place of the mythical mode of thought that earlier prevailed, the latter best seen in Hesiod's *Theogony*. The process is also seen in the development of democracy, with its insistence on freedom of speech and the rights of individuals. The contentiousness and personal ambition of the Greeks and the skepticism and delight in argument of the sophists—even if this sometimes took the form of trivialities and argument purely for winning—have been fundamental factors in the advance of knowledge and understanding in the West. Most social causes—the abolition of slavery or the rights of women, for example—initially seemed the "weaker cause" to the established powers of society.

Rather little of the actual speech and writings of Greek sophists has been preserved (what is known is collected in Sprague 1972). Perhaps the most interesting surviving speech is Gorgias's *Encomium of Helen* (translation by Kennedy 1991:281–88). As an example of method it illustrates division of a speech into proemium, narration, proof, and epilogue and division of the question at issue into four possibilities, as well as the use of a highly poetic "formal" style. The most famous passage in the speech is that in which Gorgias seeks to show that if Helen was seduced by the words of Paris she was morally blameless. Speech (*logos*) is here described as an irresistible divine force and compared to magic (de Romilly 1975:3–22). Neither Gorgias nor other sophists use the word "rhetoric" in extant texts; they speak instead of "speech" or "persuasion." The sophists were polymaths, interested in most everything and claiming to be able to teach anything a student might need to know. Although what came to be known as rhetoric was an important part of their instruction, it had not yet been identified as a separate discipline of study (Schiappa 1991; Cole 1991). Speech needs of Greek judicial procedure were, however, already producing handbooks of public speaking which are the antecedents of later full treatments of rhetoric (Thomas and Webb 1994).

The Greek Development of Judicial Rhetoric

Judicial rhetoric has been, at most, a minor genre outside the West. A distinctive feature of rhetoric in Greece was the development in the fifth and fourth centuries BCE of artistic judicial oratory that has been studied and imitated ever since. More importantly, it was the needs of the democratic law courts in Greece that created the discipline of rhetoric as taught and practiced in the West. This need did not exist elsewhere and as a result the conceptualization of rhetoric outside the West has been less focused, less detailed, and less distinguished from other subjects. Although judicial rhetoric developed in Syracuse and other Greek cities, Athens was the leading center for this momentous innovation.

In the Athenian democracy, criminal and civil trials were heard before large juries, made up of from 201 to 5001 citizens, impaneled by lot. The fullest description of the system and of other features of democracy is found in Aristotle's *Constitution of the Athenians*. Charges were initially heard by a magistrate who determined if a case seemed actionable and referred it to the appropriate courts. The evidence of witnesses was taken down in writing and read out by the clerk at the trial. Although the principals could question each other, there was no cross-examination of witnesses, nor was there interrogation by members of the jury. The court system was administered by public officials but there was no presiding judge to interpret the law; the jury judged law and fact. Nor was there a prosecuting attorney in criminal cases; charges had to be personally brought by an interested party. Prosecutor, or plaintiff, and defendant were ordinarily expected to speak on their own behalf, but if a person was not able to do so an advocate might be substituted. There were no professional lawyers, although as we shall see there were professional speech writers. Every trial had to be completed in one day, and there was no mechanism of appeal, though cases were sometimes reopened if there was new evidence.

The procedure in court was for each side to be allotted a given amount of time, measured by a water clock. The plaintiff spoke first, then the defendant, each giving a set speech. Sometimes there were second speeches on each side. The need to give a clear, orderly presentation of one's own case, in a limited amount of time, before a very large jury, put a great demand on a speaker's ability. He (women could not speak in court and were represented by a relative) had to demonstrate credibility, use persuasive logical arguments, and keep the jury interested. In other words, he had to have abilities in invention, arrangement, style, memory, and delivery. The law courts were often a form of entertainment, and cleverness, wit, or satire were appreciated. Athens was a litigious society, a result of Greek contentiousness, and almost any individual might be confronted with a criminal charge or a civil suit, or need to instigate prosecution. In addition, of course, democratic government required the participation of individuals in the political assembly. Some skills could be acquired by listening to speakers and imitating them, but there clearly was need for something more systematic.

This need led to the composition of simple handbooks teaching a speaker how to arrange and argue a case. The earliest was probably the work of a Sicilian named Tisias, but many others were written in the later fifth and in the fourth century. Plato gives a summary of them in *Phaedrus* (261d–67d). They were simple, practical works, which outlined the parts of an oration that would be effective in court and provided examples of topics and forms of arguments.

A second way for an individual to prepare for a court appearance was to hire someone to write a speech for him. This created the profession of the *logographos*, who furnished a client with a speech to be memorized and delivered to the best of his ability. Antiphon, Lysias, Isaeus, Demosthenes, and others wrote such speeches, of which many have been preserved as examples of eloquence. This is the earliest known circumstance in which a written text preceded a public speech, though Greek and non-Greek speakers may, of course, sometimes have prepared some notes in advance. Written speeches were, however, never read in court from a text; the illusion of extemporaneity was apparently always preserved.

The Development of a Discipline of Rhetoric

Greek thinkers of the fifth century, Heraclitus, Protagoras, and Gorgias in particular, were interested in *logos*, speech in all its varied forms and functions, but like thinkers in Egypt, China, and India they did not make a distinction between the study of politics, ethics, logic, rhetoric, or other subjects. Isocrates in the fourth century still regarded himself as a teacher of philosophy, though what he primarily taught was the composition of speeches or written works on political subjects. The identification of rhetoric as a distinct discipline, separate from other subjects, largely derives from Plato's *Gorgias* and *Phaedrus* and from Aristotle's *Rhetoric*. As it was understood by the end of the fourth century, the study of rhetoric combined teaching on several aspects of public address from a variety of sources with observation of the practice of orators of the time to create a new discipline. From the handbooks for judicial oratory came the parts of an oration (proemium, narration, proof, epilogue), the function of each (for example, the proemium should secure the good will and attention of the audience; the epilogue should recapitulate the argument and stir the emotion of the audience), and topics or arguments for each part. Sophists had compiled collections of commonplaces, arguments on opposite sides of a question, and glossaries of beautiful words. These are the beginning of the study of style. By the third quarter of the fourth century more elaborate treatises, of which Anaximenes's *Rhetoric for Alexander* is the only surviving example, combined precepts on invention, arrangement, and style into a single systematic treatise that focused primarily on judicial rhetoric but commented also on deliberative and epideictic forms. Aristotle came to regard rhetoric as a distinct subject, lectured on it, and devoted a separate treatise to it. His *Rhetoric*, which dates from about 335 BCE, recast earlier material into a more philosophical form and standardized several rhetorical concepts including ethos, logos, and pathos as basic means of persuasion and enthymeme and paradigm as the two forms of rhetorical argument. Books one and two of the *Rhetoric* deal with invention; book three has some comments on delivery followed by a systematic discussion of style, including metaphor and simile, and arrangement. Aristotle's work was not published until the first century BCE, but his theories of rhetoric were known from his students, of whom the most important was Theophrastus. One of Theophrastus's major contributions to rhetorical theory, expanding on what Aristotle had said, was the doctrine of the four "virtues" of style: grammatical correctness, clarity, ornamentation (e.g., tropes and figures), and appropriateness (Kennedy 1994:49–63).

Rhetorical schools came into existence in the fourth century, beginning with Isocrates's, where students practiced written composition on noble subjects. Oral, dialectical debates were a feature of the philosophical schools of Plato and Aristotle, and the declamation of speeches in rhetorical schools seems to have begun also in the fourth century. By the second century, rhetoric was established as the focus of secondary education in schools in Greece and the Greek-speaking Near East, and by the first century rhetorical schools were also a feature of education in the Latin-speaking West. A number of new categories were added to the system of rhetoric, among them: stasis theory (a complex system of identifying the question at issue in a speech); the distinction between tropes, figures of speech, and figures of thought, with names for many devices of style; a mnemonic system and a fully developed account of delivery. Students were taught basic rhetorical theory and intensively practiced in judicial and deliberative declamation on historical or imaginary themes. I have discussed the historical development of rhetorical theory and education in greater detail elsewhere (Kennedy 1994:81–101).

Rhetoric in Rome

Early Roman public address, before significant influence from Greece, is known from quotations of speeches by later Latin writers and speeches by historians. The Roman republic was a constitutional oligarchy of birth and wealth whose leaders shared some of the qualities seen in traditional rhetoric in many other societies: conservative values, dignity, consensus. But Rome experienced severe internal social strife, and popular leaders emerged who introduced some of the contentious elements common in Greece. Attempts were made by conservatives to stamp out the study of rhetoric in Rome, but by the time of the two brothers Gracchi in the second century BCE some of these new leaders had been trained in Greek rhetoric, and by the turn of the century wealthy Romans were regularly going to Greece to study and teachers of Latin rhetoric emerged in Rome (Kennedy 1994:102–27).

Roman writers transmitted Greek rhetorical theory and practice to the later West. The most important figure was Cicero (106–43 BCE). His youthful work *On Invention*, a compendium of the Greek theory of the time, became a basic textbook from late antiquity to the Renaissance. In his mature dialogue, *On the Orator*, he attempted a synthesis of Greek and Roman traditions and of the teachings of philosophers and rhetoricians in a vision of the orator as the dominant cultural ideal of a good society. Quintilian (c. 40–96 CE) took up this theme in *The Education of the Orator*, and Saint Augustine later adapted it to the Christian preacher in *On Christian Learning*.

Atticism and the Second Sophistic

Beginning in the first century BCE, and with greater momentum in the early centuries of the common era, teachers of grammar and rhetoric in Greece and Rome sought to redress what they perceived as a decline in linguistic standards in public address and literature; in the process they created two formal languages that had to be studied and learned and artificially preserved classical usages while the spoken languages developed in the direction of demotic Greek and Vulgar Latin. This movement is called Atticism, since in Greek it took the language and style of the Attic orators of the fourth century BCE as its norm. Like other formal languages, it thus had an archaic quality. Ciceronian Latin became the counterpart in the West. As early as the third century BCE, grammarians in Alexandria had created canons of the major Greek literary genres, constituting works to be studied in schools, and Quintilian provided a corresponding Latin canon in the tenth book of his *Education of the Orator*.

Atticism was an aspect of the movement known at the Second Sophistic, which flourished in the time of the Roman Empire, primarily in Greece, to a lesser extent in Latin. These latter-day sophists—Dio Chrysostom, Aelius Aristeides, Libanius, and many others— were often teachers of rhetoric who attained international reputations and traveled around the empire demonstrating their skills to admiring audiences in theatres, at festivals, and even before the emperors, to whom they did not hesitate to give advice. They differ from the older Greek sophists in that they were cultural conservatives, intent on preserving the heritage of Hellenism in language, literature, rhetoric, and religion (Kennedy 1994:230–56).

Conclusion

Greek society was characterized by a contentiousness that is expressed in mythology, poetry, athletics, democratic government, and public address. Personal invective was acceptable to a degree not commonly found elsewhere. Decision by majority vote was instituted as a solution, but in turn institutionalized contention. The Greek and Roman development of a theory of rhetoric, separate from political and moral philosophy, was unique, and originated with the need to learn how to give a speech before a large jury in a court of law. Beginning in the fourth century BCE rhetorical schools appeared throughout the Greek and Roman world and provided training in public address and written composition for large numbers of students. Despite some early resistence, the Romans largely took over the Greek discipline of rhetoric and transmitted it to the later West. A more detailed comparison of this Western tradition with traditions elsewhere follows in the next chapter.

References

English translations of many Greek and Latin works, if not identified in this chapter, can be found in volumes of The Loeb Classical Library, *published by Harvard University Press.*

Athanassakis, Apostolos N. (1983). *Hesiod: Theogony, Works and Days, Shield.* Baltimore: Johns Hopkins University Press.

Becker, Andrew S. (1995). *The Shield of Achilles and the Poetics of Ekphrasis.* London: Rowman and Littlefield.

Burkert, Walter (1992). *The Orientalizing Revolution: Near Eastern Influence on Greek Culture in the Early Archaic Age,* trans. by Margaret E. Pinder and Walter Burkert. Cambridge, MA: Harvard University Press.

Cole, Thomas (1991). *The Origins of Rhetoric in Ancient Greece.* Baltimore: Johns Hopkins University Press.

Enos, Richard L. (1993). *Greek Rhetoric before Aristotle.* Prospect Heights, IL: Waveland Press.

Finnegan, Ruth (1988). *Literacy and Orality; Studies in the Technology of Communication.* Oxford; Basil Blackwell.

Fitzgerald, Robert (1961). *Homer: The Odyssey.* Garden City, NY: Doubleday.

Glotz, Gustave (1953). *La cité grecque.* New edition, Paris: A. Michel.

Gross, Nicolas P. (1985). *Amatory Persuasion in Antiquity: Studies in Theory and Practice.* Newark: University of Delaware Press.

Harris, William V. (1989). *Ancient Literacy.* Cambridge, MA: Harvard University Press.

Johnstone, Henry W., Jr. (1992). "Strife and Contradiction in Hesiod," in *Intimate Conflict: Contradiction in Literary and Philosophical Discourse,* pp. 35–38, ed. by Brian G. Caraher. Albany: State University of New York Press.

Kennedy, George A. (1991). *Aristotle on Rhetoric: A Theory of Civic Discourse.* New York: Oxford University Press.

———(1994). *A New History of Classical Rhetoric.* Princeton: Princeton University Press.

Kirby, John T. (1992). "The 'Great Triangle' in Early Greek Rhetoric and Poetics," *Rhetorica* 8:213–28.

———(1992). "Rhetoric and Poetics in Hesiod," *Ramus: Critical Studies in Greek and Roman Literature* 21:34–60.

Larson, J. A. O. (1949). "The Origins and Significance of the Counting of Votes," *Classical Philology* 44:164–81.

Lattimore, Richmond, trans. (1951). *The Iliad of Homer*. Chicago: University of Chicago Press.

Lloyd, Geoffrey E. R. (1966). *Polarity and Analogy: Two Types of Argumentation in Early Greek Thought*. Cambridge: Cambridge University Press.

Loraux, Nicole (1986). *The Invention of Athens: The Funeral Oration in the Classical City*, translated by A. Sheridan. Cambridge: Harvard University Press.

Maidment, K. J. (1941). *Minor Attic Orators, Vol. 1: Antiphon and Andocides*. Loeb Classical Library. Cambridge, MA: Harvard University Press.

Nagy, Gregory (1989). "Early Greek Views of Poets and Poetry," in *The Cambridge History of Literary Criticism, I: Classical Criticism*, pp. 1–77, ed. by George A. Kennedy. Cambridge: Cambridge University Press.

Ochs, Donovan J. (1993). *Consolatory Rhetoric: Grief, Symbol, and Ritual in the Greco-Roman Era*. Columbia: University of South Carolina Press.

Pfeiffer, Rudolf (1968). *History of Classical Scholarship from the Beginnings to the End of the Hellenistic Age*. Oxford: Clarendon Press.

Rawlinson, George (1947). *Herodotus, The Persian Wars*. New York: Modern Library. Originally published 1858 and frequently reprinted.

Robb, Kevin (1994). *Literacy and Paideia in Ancient Greece*. Oxford: Oxford University Press.

Romilly, Jacqueline de (1975). *Magic and Rhetoric in Ancient Greece*. Cambridge: Harvard University Press.

Schiappa, Edward (1991). *Protagoras and Logos: A Study in Greek Philosophy and Rhetoric*. Columbia: University of South Carolina Press.

Sélincourt, Aubrey de, trans. (1954). *Herodotus: The Histories*. New York: Penguin Books.

Solmsen, Friedrich (1954). "The Gift of Speech in Homer and Hesiod," *Transactions of the American Philological Association* 85:1–15.

Sprague, Rosamond K., ed (1972). *The Older Sophists*. Columbia: University of South Carolina Press.

Stanford, William B. (1936). *Greek Metaphor: Studies in Theory and Practice*. Oxford: Basil Blackwood.

Staveley, E. S. (1972). *Greek and Roman Voting and Elections*. London: Thames and Hudson, and Ithaca: Cornell University Press.

Swearingen, C. Jan (1991). *Rhetoric and Irony: Western Literacy and Western Lies*. New York: Oxford University Press.

Thomas, Carol G., and Edward Kent Webb (1994). "From Orality to Rhetoric: An Intellectual Transformation," in *Persuasion: Greek Rhetoric in Action*, ed. Ian Worthington, pp. 3–25. London: Routledge.

Thomas, Rosalin (1992). *Literacy and Orality in Ancient Greece*. Cambridge: Cambridge University Press.

Walker, Jeffrey (1996). "Before the Beginnings of 'Poetry' and 'Rhetoric': Hesiod on Eloquence," *Rhetorica* 14:243–64.

Walsh, George B. (1984). *The Varieties of Enchantment: Early Greek Views of the Nature and Function of Poetry*. Chapel Hill: University of North Carolina Press.

Westbrook, Ramond (1992). "The Trial Scene in the *Iliad*," *Harvard Studies in Classical Philology* 94:53–76.

Worthington, Ian, ed. (1994). *Persuasion: Greek Rhetoric in Action*. London: Routledge.

Yunis, Harvey (1996). *Taming Democracy: Models of Political Rhetoric in Classical Athens*. Ithaca: Cornell University Press.

Bibliography

Enos, Theresa, ed. (1996). *Encyclopedia of Rhetoric and Composition*. New York: Garland Publishing.
Lausberg, Heinrich (1973). *Handbuch der literarischen Rhetoric*, 2nd ed. Munich: Max Hueber Verlag.
Martin, Josef (1974). *Antike Rhetorik; Technik und Methode*. Munich: C. H. Beck.
Ueding, Gert, ed. (1992–). *Historisches Wörterbuch der Rhetorik*. Tübingen: Max Niemeyer Verlag.

Conclusion

Rhetoric is apparently a form of energy that drives and is imparted to communication. Some awareness of this can be found in Chinese thought—in Mencius's theory of "physical vigor" and in "vital force" in later Chinese criticism, in Aristotle's concept of *energeia*, the "actualization" of a text (*Rhetoric* 3.11), and in "vivacity" as understood by eighteenth-century British rhetoricians. When an individual encounters a situation that threatens or seems to offer an opportunity for advancing self-interest, an emotional reaction takes place; it may be fear, anger, hunger, lust, indignation, pity, curiosity, love, or some other emotion. This emotion, often unconsciously, prompts response that expends energy in utterance or physical action directed toward fulfilling the need. Rhetorical energy in its simplest form is conveyed by volume, pitch, or repetition; more complex forms of rhetorical energy include logical reasons, pathetic narratives, metaphor and other tropes, or lively figures of speech such as apostrophe, rhetorical question, or simile. All communication carries some rhetorical energy; it may be slight, some phrase of conventional etiquette, but there is no zero-degree rhetoric. If there were no rhetorical energy no utterance would take place nor would any communication be perceived by an audience. If the speaker is tired, the rhetorical energy is reduced and less is accomplished.

The rhetorical energy of an utterance can spark a reaction in the audience, for the utterance can either threaten or seem to offer an opportunity to advance the self-interest of the audience as individuals or a group. This reaction may take the form of expressed objection or agreement and may lead to judgment and action. Rhetorical energy is also inherent in utterances when no human audience is present. The utterance may be directed to a god, an animal, or natural force, such as the weather, it may be directed to the speaker who seeks to urge himself or herself to some action or belief, or it may be only a form of release of pent up energy of desire, frustration, or other emotional reaction.

It seems probable that the origin of rhetoric in nature is the instinct for self-preservation and the preservation of the genetic line, the family, and the social group of which the individual is a member. Nature has favored the use of communication by utterance or body language over the use of force; although sometimes costly in energy, it is less dangerous to the individual than physical conflict. Among social animals, communication is primarily concerned with establishing a territory, securing a food supply, finding a mate, deterring enemies, maintaining a social hierarchy, and strengthening relationships among members of the species or group. Much of human communication can be reduced to these same essential functions. First in biological evolution, then in human cultural evolution the communicative instinct has been generalized to a desire to secure not only the necessities of life, but also what is perceived as the qualities of a good life. The basic function of rhetorical communication is defensive and conservative; but to secure or preserve the quality of life for one individual or one group may seem to require offensive actions and efforts at change. Traditional human societies have been strongly resistant to change, which is usually perceived as change for the worse. The major function of rhetoric throughout most of human history in most of the world has been to preserve things as they are or to try to recover an idealized happier past. In times of stress, the latter sometimes takes the form of millenialism, prophecy of the return of a Golden Age or the coming of a messiah. Occasionally, influential individuals have undertaken rhetorical programs for change; examples cited in earlier chapters include Akhenaton in fourteenth-century BCE Egypt, Moses as described in the Old Testament, Solon in sixth-century Greece, Ashoka in India, and the Legalists in China. Popular belief in the possibility of progress and thus openness to change for the better is largely limited to classical Greek and modern Western societies and even there often resisted.

As a phenomenon of nature, rhetoric is prior logically and historically to human speech. Human speech is a development from animal communication, specifically from that of primates. As described in chapter 1, many features of human rhetoric can be found in animal communication. The development into human language was facilitated by physiological evolution of the brain and the vocal apparatus. In the earliest stages of human speech, gestures played an important role in associating specific sounds with specific meanings. Social groups are by nature hierarchical, and the sounds made by high-status individuals probably had an important role in determining what came to mean what. Speech surely developed primarily in everyday domestic and hunting contexts. Song also has antecedents in animal communication; as it developed side by side with everyday language it enriched vocabulary and furnished aesthetic, acoustical features. All human societies have more than one level of discourse, used in different situations. These probably derive from the basic distinction of speech and song.

"Formal language," required in ceremonial or official contexts, often has poetic features and often seems archaic. Archaism certifies the authenticity of the message by suggesting its conformity with beliefs of the past. Use of formal language has to be learned and is not available to everyone; it thus exercises social power of a conservative sort.

Traditional societies all over the world have admired effective and eloquent orators. Most languages have a word for "orator," and orators everywhere have recognized functions in deliberation. Ability at speaking is partly a natural endowment, but enhanced by listening to older speakers to learn traditional techniques and topics, by imitating good speakers, and by opportunities to practice, in private or in public. Acquisition of an ability to use formal language is analogous to acquisition of an ability to recite oral poetry or perform rituals. A good speaker must know the conventional speech forms of the society, must have self-confidence, and should observe and adjust to the reaction of an audience.

Most early literate societies shared the traditional admiration of oral societies for an orator. The conspicuous exception is absence of any expression of admiration for oral eloquence in texts from ancient Mesopotamia. There, the scribes, probably in the interest of their own power and influence, were silent about the power of oral discourse and subordinated speech to writing. In ancient China, India, Palestine, Egypt, and Greece, the other early literate societies, eloquence was admired, written examples were preserved and imitated, and precepts describing it were formulated.

Western rhetorical practice differs from other traditions in being more tolerant of contention, personal invective, and flattery. Elsewhere, there have been greater pressures for consensus, politeness, and restraint. The vote of the majority of a group, not a feature of politics elsewhere, was introduced in Greece as a way to reach a decision in the face of conflict. Although it performs that function, it also sharpens disagreement.

In the introductory chapter of this book I said that one objective of my studies was to try to test the Western conception of rhetoric against rhetorical practices in other parts of the world. To what extent are the categories and terminology of rhetoric as taught in the West satisfactory descriptions of rhetoric as a universal phenomenon? Not surprisingly, perhaps, the short answer is: Some of them are and some of them are not. I have no desire to impose Western notions of rhetoric on an understanding of other cultures. Indeed, my objective is rather the opposite: to modify Western notions by comparison with other traditions in the interests of coming to an understanding of rhetoric as a more general phenomenon of human life.

Our word "rhetoric" derives from the Greek *rhêtorikê*, meaning the technique or art of a public speaker. This word first came into use among followers of Socrates at the beginning of the fourth century BCE and by the end of that century had been accepted as the title of a systematic discipline, taught to young men to provide them a facility in speaking in public. Beginning in the fifth century BCE the structure of a judicial speech and useful topics had been set out in Greek handbooks. By the first century BCE this Greek theory of public address had been taken over by the Romans and largely achieved the form it was to take through the history of Western civilization. So far as I can discover, the word "rhetoric" does not exactly correspond to any term in non-Western languages. In nonliterate cultures, in addition to a word for an orator, there are often terms for different occasions for public address, for formal, indirect, or informal speech, and sometimes for other features of rhetoric but not for rhetoric as an abstract entity. These words constitute a structure of thought within the culture but do not reflect a desire to conceptualize or analyze it. Exclusively oral societies usually think in specific terms and feel little need to erect systems of abstract thought. Their religion too is primarily mythological, not philosophical. Abstract, theoretical thought and precepts about rhetoric, as about philosophy, politics, and nature, are developments of literate societies, and there, in ancient China, India, Palestine, Egypt, and Greece, we find some approximations to the concept and teaching of rhetoric. Before *rhêtorikê* was coined there was among the Greeks awareness of the power of speech, of eloquence and artistry, and of certain conventional techniques of public address. *Peithô*, or Persuasion, was a goddess in early Greece, just as *Vak*, or Speech, was a goddess in early India. Eloquent speech in early Greece was compared to honey, as it was in ancient Israel. The speeches in their early epic poetry were studied by Greeks and helped to provide models of content, structure, and style, just as archaic written speeches were studied and imitated in China. The closest Chinese word to "rhetoric" is probably *pièn*, which means "persuasive argument."

A significant difference between rhetoric as it came to be conceptualized in Greece and what is found elsewhere is that in Greece, and thus in the Western tradition generally, rhetoric was identified as a distinct, academic discipline that could be taught, studied, and practiced separately from political and moral philosophy. The secondary level of public education in Hellenistic Greece and in Rome was devoted entirely to study of rhetoric, something not found elsewhere. Though it necessarily draws on topics from politics and ethics, as a discipline Western rhetoric is a tool for oral and written composition with no political or ethical doctrine, and its techniques can be applied to either side of any case. This can be socially justified by the assumption that truth will prevail if there is free discussion of the issues, but this justification was rarely explicitly enunciated; in Aristotle's *Rhetoric* it is only mentioned once, and briefly (1.1.12). The goal of rhetorical training was how to persuade and how to win. Plato's attack on rhetoric in *Gorgias* contributed to the separation of rhetoric as practiced in his time from philosophy, but in *Phaedrus* he outlined the possibility of a reintegration, and Cicero in *On the Orator* restated this in a more practical form. Rhetorical practice in the West has continued to be tolerant of deception, equivocation, and lies. That has been a constant basis of criticism of it, but also a source of practical strength. In ancient Egypt, China, and India there were technical writings that discuss techniques of persuasion, but always as a part of political or ethical thought. At times the political and ethical thought of which rhetoric was a part was a philosophy of power politics and autocratic rule, seen, for example, in the writings of Han Fei Tzu in China or Kautilya in India. Here deception is justified as in the interests of the greater good of an orderly society.

The primary reason why rhetoric was disciplinized in Greece was the development of constitutional democracy there, which required the participation of ordinary citizens in the decision-making process to a degree not existing in other literate cultures. Male citizens were expected to speak in the political assembly and were required to speak on their own behalf in prosecution and defense in the courts of law. Juries in democratic courts were large, ranging in Athens from 201 to 5001. Each speaker had a limited amount of time, measured by a water clock, to present a case. A speech needed to be well organized, well argued, and well delivered if it was to succeed. Circumstantial evidence was admissible and required some imaginative development. In non-Western societies, in contrast, there has been less need for rhetorical skill before a court of law: Direct evidence has usually been expected, litigants were permitted to speak but were often interrogated by the judges and were not expected, or not allowed, to deliver an oration. The systematic teaching of rhetoric in Greece thus originated in the need to instruct a person in how to give a speech in a court of law. Some of these skills could also be utilized in speeches in political assemblies. Greek and Roman rhetorical treatises from the fourth century BCE to the end of antiquity continued to be predominantly concerned with judicial rhetoric, a genre that was never highly developed in other societies.

Consistent with its disciplinary independence, the Western rhetorical tradition has often separated thought from expression, content from style, implying that any given thought can be expressed in a variety of different ways, though advice that style be appropriate to subject is often added. The separation of style from thought has, of course, also sometimes been protested, but again, it has in practice prevailed. Non-Western literate cultures have been slower to make this distinction. It is perhaps an assumption in the Egyptian story of the Eloquent Peasant and begins to appear in discussions of literary style in China and India in the postclassical period.

Greek and Roman writers on rhetoric taught that there was a series of steps in the composition of a speech, which by the Hellenistic period became the "parts" or as they are sometimes now called "canons" of rhetoric: invention, or the planning of the thought and arguments; arrangement of the contents into a systematic structure; and casting of the contents into an appropriate style of words and sentences, artistically adorned; then the memorization of the speech, and finally its delivery with good control of the voice and effective gestures. These five steps originated as a pedagogical device for novices. Mature orators everywhere often plan speeches in advance, and in literate societies they may make notes or even write out a speech before delivery, but the process is much more organic. The closest non-Western analogy to the parts of rhetoric that I have found is the statement of the Indian political theorist Kautilya, quoted in chapter 8, that the necessary qualities of a writ are arrangement, relevancy (which includes invention), completeness, sweetness, dignity, and lucidity, but Kautilya and other non-Western writers on rhetoric view composition as organic, not a series of separate steps. Artificial as the "parts" of rhetoric are, they do have a certain universal validity in that the thought, the arrangement, the style, and a speaker's ability to remember what he planned to say and to say it effectively are features of good oratory. The existence of elements of invention, arrangement, style, memory, and delivery in animal communication suggest that they are all natural parts of rhetoric.

The chief occasions for public address in classical Greece were in the law courts, in political assemblies, and on ceremonial occasions at public festivals. Aristotle divided rhetoric into the three species of judicial, deliberative, and epideictic. The logical basis for his distinction was the function of the audience. An audience is either called on to make some decision or take some action or it is not. If asked to make a decision about the justice or legality of an action in the past, the species is judicial. If asked to make a decision about the advantage of some future action the species is deliberative. If no decision is required other than whether or not a good speech has been given, the species is epideictic. Although as noted above, classical rhetoricians devoted most attention to judicial rhetoric, these three species became fundamental categories in Western rhetorical theory and have remained so. How well do they describe rhetoric outside of Greece?

I have already said that the development of artistic judicial rhetoric is unique to the Greeks. Judicial rhetoric exists elsewhere, but is not a fully developed form and, with the exception of the Eloquent Peasant in Egypt, there seem to be no examples of judicial speeches that were admired, studied, or imitated by future generations, as there were in Greece and Rome. In many societies, crimes have been avenged with community acceptance and without a trial and personal disputes negotiated privately by "go-betweens." In the latter case, considerable rhetorical skills are required, but a non-Western thinker constructing a system of rhetoric would probably not have given any attention to judicial oratory.

Deliberative rhetoric, in contrast, is a universal genre and can be said to be recognized as such. Nonliterate egalitarian societies and those with more or less autocratic chiefs or kings both regularly engage in formal deliberation, and formal deliberation has been a feature of all literate societies, although under autocracies often limited to a small group of officials of state. Deliberative rhetoric also occurs outside political assemblies when an individual gives advice to others. Often this requires allegorical or other forms of indirect language, as in the case of Managalese *ha'a*.

The function of deliberation in traditional societies is the achievement of consensus: not the acceptance of the view of a majority but explicit or tacit unanimity. The pressure for consensus is so great that if the process breaks down, as it sometimes does, open fighting may occur, dissenters may move away, or may be forcibly silenced. Lack of unanimity is a threat not only to leaders but to the maintenance of society. Non-Western societies that have accepted Western democracy often continue to try to impose uniformity of public opinion in a way disquieting to Westerners; Singapore is a good example. The appearance of uniformity remains an important value in China and many Third World countries. Comparative study of rhetoric helps understanding of why this inclination is natural.

Deliberation in traditional societies achieves apparent unanimity by politeness, restraint, and the use of formal language. A speaker may offer a suggestion and indicate willingness to withdraw it or compromise. Individuals are referred to by position or by honorable epithets. Criticism is made indirectly or by telling a story without summarizing its application. Emotion is controlled. Opponents allow each other to "save face." Silence is taken to mean agreement. As I noted in chapter 4, the use of formal language can make a speech unanswerable in terms acceptable to the culture.

Even before the advent of democracy, Greek civic rhetoric differed sharply from traditional deliberation as I have described it. Greek orators were characteristically quarrelsome and emotional, inclined to bitter personal attacks on each other, highly resentful of such attacks on themselves but tolerant of verbal fights by others. Alone among ancient civilizations the Greeks also developed competitive athletics. The other ancient society in which open contention is common is that described in the ancient Indian epic, *Mahabharata*. Since the ancient Greeks and the Aryan invaders of India derived their language and some of their cultural institutions from the same ultimate source, the Indo-Europeans, this may be a heritage from contentious tribesmen who once roamed the steppes of Russia. Contention among pagan gods is a feature of Near Eastern, Greek, and some other religions, where it probably originated in the anthropomorphizing of contending forces of nature. Outside of Greece, however, imitation of the gods in this respect did not achieve general acceptance. It is everywhere a feature of mythology that divine or semidivine figures can do what human beings cannot do, including breaking taboos, and pagan gods are not regarded as appropriate models for human imitation. Greek writers, beginning with the poet of the *Iliad*, show an unusual inclination to explore the private life of the gods, making it more entertaining, more like the lives of the audience, and under the influence of rational philosophy by the end of the Hellenistic period, as seen, for example, in the poetry of Ovid, all but emptying the gods of religious significance. The self-destruction of Greco-Roman paganism provided an opening for the spread of Christianity.

As an answer to sharp political differences the Greeks invented decision-making by majority vote. The antecedent of voting was the show of hands or cries of acclamation practiced in a number of cultures, but only the Greeks counted votes and accepted a majority of one. How they came to do so is not well documented. It was probably the only alternative to civil war in some cases.

Acceptance of contentious debate and majority rule by the counting of votes is a western tradition, still very much alive, though one that has often been suppressed by autocratic rulers. In the form of freedom of speech, it has been an important and constructive Western value. Open contention in debate is a major source of vigor in Western rhetoric. Majority rule has had effects on Western rhetoric as well. A speaker who only needs a majority of one can ignore the concerns of parts of the audience, concentrate on rallying supporters, and bringing in the undecided. Majority rule results from the tolerance of contention and at the same time sharpens it.

The third species of rhetoric in Western teaching is epideictic. Aristotle's description of it is specific to his own culture and it needs revision in any General Theory of Rhetoric. He regarded it as a speech of praise or blame that was concerned with what was honorable or dishonorable. Funeral orations were the prime example of speeches of praise; most invectives were delivered in either a judicial or deliberative context, though there are later Greek invectives against Christians or pagans. Some rhetoricians lumped all artistic discourse that was not specifically judicial or deliberative, including poetry, into epideictic. It should be remembered that poetry in classical times was publicly performed or read aloud in private; thus it was a form of speech. The problem of the classification of epideictic oratory was eventually met by Greek rhetoricians—Menander Rhetor's discussion is the fullest—by identifying a large number of genres: funeral orations, speeches of greeting to an arriving or departing official or friend, speeches on anniversaries, speeches at religious festivals, and the like. What such speeches chiefly have in common is that they are connected with some ceremony.

There is a large body of oral and written discourse in non-Western cultures that is not easily classifiable as judicial or deliberative. This includes performances of traditional myths, legends, and songs as well as speeches. One solution would be to dispense with the concept of epideictic and content oneself with identifying speech genres practiced in each culture. Those genres that are not judicial or deliberative do, however, seem to have something in common. They are often connected with some festival or ceremony, including funerals. In common with Greek epideictic genres they are almost universally concerned with transmitting and enhancing traditional values. They often utilize the more extreme forms of formal language that would not be employed on other occasions. Examples that I have discussed in earlier chapters include Australian mythological songs and dances, the chants of Cuna chiefs, Aztec *huehuetlatolli*, and others. The term *huehuetlatolli*, "speeches of the elders," approximates epideictic in that it includes a large number of different genres sharing a cultural message and a formal style.

Are there species of public address that cannot be easily classified as judicial, deliberative, or epideictic? The most ambiguous case is that of magic. Much magic is practiced in secret by individuals, but in many traditional cultures magical rites are publicly performed in connection with the agricultural seasons, trading expeditions, hunting, or warfare. Sorcerers recite spells and perform ritual actions intended to compel spirits, natural forces, or objects to act in a certain way. This is certainly not judicial rhetoric. If the spell can be thought of as "persuading" the object to act in a certain way, it could be regarded as deliberative. The sorcerer speaks with authority but makes no use of artistic ethos and there is no element of logical reasoning on the part of of the object, which is thought to have no choice if the magic is properly performed. The real effect of the magic is psychological and addressed to the human witnesses, whose belief in the value of the cultural tradition and whose expectations of good results are strengthened by the ritual. From that point of view, the public address of magic could be regarded as epideictic.

Aristotle and later rhetoricians made a distinction between artistic and nonartistic means of persuasion. Nonartistic means are such things as the testimony of witnesses, written documents, and oaths that have been taken by litigants; they are "used" but not "invented." It might be argued that if an oath of purgation was determinative of an issue, as it could be in the Near East and in Greece, it had a kind of magical power since it put a constraint on the deity invoked. Could magic be best classified as "nonartistic"? Magical formulas are "used" and not "invented" by the speaker. I do not see any authoritative answer to the classification of magic under the three species of rhetoric. Perhaps it is best to regard magic as a separate species, not provided for in Greco-Roman rhetoric. Public magic was not practiced in Greece or Rome. Magic went underground, where it was practiced in private by individuals, largely of the lower classes, to secure a lover or harm an enemy. Both Judaism and Christianity opposed magic, but Christian priests have practiced exorcism.

The artistic means of persuasion in classical rhetoric are ethos, pathos, and logos. Aristotle viewed ethos as the demonstration in a speech that the speaker was to be trusted. Later writers on rhetoric, beginning with Cicero, recognized, however, that there were other forms of ethos that regularly came into a speech. For example, a speaker might appeal to the moral character of the audience, and in judicial rhetoric the ethos of the opponent and of witnesses was often an issue. Thus even in classical rhetoric the concept of ethos was broadened. Ethos also has a nonartistic form, something that is brought to the occasion and not invented, maybe not even mentioned in a speech. That is the authority of the speaker, known to the audience from his position or previous actions. Both nonartistic authority and artistic ethos are primary means of persuasion throughout the world, often adequate in themselves to secure persuasion without rational argument. Many examples have been cited in previous chapters.

Pathos in its original, Aristotelian conception was the emotion of the hearers aroused by a speech that moved them to accept what the speaker said. The rhetorical energy of a speaker is transmitted through the emotion of a text to an audience. Delivery may be a major factor. In composing or analyzing a text pathos has to be judged from what is contained in the text, not from how a speaker delivers it or how an audience receives it. Emotion is generally avoided in traditional non-Western deliberation. Its most common appearance is in epideictic performances, including funeral lamentations, which may have a cathartic function. In his dialogue *On the Orator* (2.182–98) Cicero recast the Aristotelian theory of the means of persuasion to make ethos and pathos degrees of emotion: Ethos is an expression of moral character and thus of the gentler emotions associated with moral character such as friendliness or pity; pathos is the expression of strong emotions such as anger or outrage, but there are many intermediate degrees. Probably Cicero was right, that the sharp distinction of ethos and pathos in rhetorical theory is artificial. Emotional expression is really a part of the ethos of the speaker or writer. What arouses strong emotion is often culturally specific: A statement that is amusing or conventional in one culture may be outrageous or insulting in another. It seems to be the case that open expression of pathos, including personal attack, has been relatively more characteristic of Western than of non-Western rhetoric, as has been contention and flattery.

The persuasive effect of character and emotion is often seconded by logical reasons. I have repeatedly noticed the existence of enthymemes in discourse in traditional societies. The simplest and earliest form of the enthymeme seems to be what I have called "enthymeme by juxtaposition," that is two statements, one of which gives a reason for the other, but without any logical connective such as "because, for, since, etc." Primitive human beings had some understanding of cause and result, as do most animals, but perhaps no linguistic means of articulating it. As I have sought to show earlier, primitive human beings and members of some nonliterate cultures today also do not naturally express universal propositions from which particulars are then deduced. The universal propositions are assumptions and part of the assumed wisdom of the culture; as such, they do not need to be stated. Proverbs sometimes take the form of universal propositions—"You can lead a horse to water but not make him drink"—and proverbs are used as a basis of argument in many cultures, but not in all, especially those with little technological development. I noted the absence of proverbs among the Austrialian aboriginals and North American Indians. A complex chain of logical argument is not a feature of persuasion in nonliterate societies. Ability to use it is apparently a development of literate societies where arguments can be worked out in writing and can be read and reread by others with the leisure to follow the argument. The best examples of complex argument outside Greece are found among the later Mohists and other Chinese philosophers.

Enthymematic argument, or its fuller form in syllogistic reasoning, is deductive of a conclusion from a major premise, whether expressed or not. The other form of argument recognized by Greco-Roman rhetoricians is inductive, from one or more examples, though again the universal proposition that logically connects the terms of the argument need not be expressed and the reasoning is from particular to particular: "X successfully defeated the enemy by use of a certain strategy; we can do so too." A paradigm, or argument from example, can be restated as an enthymeme in which the example becomes the minor premise: "We can defeat the enemy by use of this strategy because X did earlier." Aristotle says (*Rhetoric* 3.17.5) that the use of paradigms is especially appropriate in deliberative rhetoric, since knowledge of the future is based on experience of the past. Discussion in earlier chapters suggests that argument from example is probably the most common form of reasoning widely used all over the world. Examples are drawn from mythology, from analogies with nature, and from events of the past known to an audience.

The classification of logos as the use of either enthymemes or paradigms seems a valid one on the basis of comparative evidence. I have not found any logical argument that does not fit these classifications. Another universal feature is the use of topoi. These are of two sorts. Dialectical topics are forms of argument applicable to many subjects and include argument from the greater to the lesser, from cause to result or the opposite, and argument that something is possible or important, or the opposite. The topic of cause and result is certainly a universal feature of rhetoric. Some of the more self-conscious dialectical topoi such as definition and division seem to be developments of literate societies and can be found in China, India, and the Near East as well as in Greece.

The other kind of topoi are those specific to a particular subject. Deliberation, for example, can deal with what is advantageous and with such issues as war and peace, finances or resources, national defense, imports and exports, and framing new laws. Traditional societies debate these subjects in their own contexts except for the framing of laws. A proposal to change some law, which would be an unwritten custom of the society, is rarely if ever debated in traditional societies. They do, however, sometimes debate a few other issues, such as whether some religious rite should be performed. Another specific topic that is widely found is the duty of a good ruler. But some topics are specific to a culture. These include such things as qualities conventionally perceived in another tribe—perhaps they are regarded as lazy or given to drunkenness—and topics drawn from the religion, mythology, agriculture, or activities of the group. A list of the common topics of any given society could doubtless be drawn up. Among non-Western writers, Kautilya in India gives the fullest list of topics.

This is a convenient place to recapitulate what has been said in earlier chapters about sophistry on a comparative basis. Sophistry emerged in Greece in the fifth century BCE and was characterized by celebration of the power of speech, philosophical relativism or skepticism, questioning traditional beliefs of the society; fascination with an apparent ability to demonstrate a paradox or prove two sides of an issue; and an interest in the nature of language and linguistic experimentation. Greek sophists made much use of epideictic oratory and claimed to have lofty ideals, but when applied to deliberative oratory by their students, sophistry sometimes exploited a policy of expediency.

Something analogous to Greek sophistry appears in India by the sixth century BCE and flourished in China in the fourth and third centuries. Indian sophistry first appears in the debates of Brahmins on metaphysical or religious issues. Chinese sophistry has its first major development in the logical debates of Mohist philosophers. Sophistry is unknown in traditional, nonliterate cultures. It seems to be a recurring phenomenon in literate and "sophisticated" societies (those with wealth, leisure, and refinement of artistic taste) where there are competing and irreconcilable philosophical schools and where traveling teachers seek to impress audiences with their verbal skills and to gain influence with rulers or leaders of the society. These conditions do not seem to have existed in the Near East, where there was at most a potential for sophistry in scribal schools that occasionally practiced exercises in praise or blame. A sophist aims to win, and sophistry is thus by definition contentious. Sophistic debates in China and India permitted individuals to exercise their skills against others, but only certain individuals and only on certain subjects. Political issues were not discussed by Chinese and Indian sophists but in both countries sophistic techniques were later adapted to the support of autocracy.

Sophistry had a second important period in Greece in the time of the Roman empire. In the West it has been regularly repressed by political autocracy, philosophical idealism, and religious orthodoxy, but some aspects of it appear in medieval dialectic—for example, in debates between nominalists and realists—features of it reemerged in the Renaissance, and avant-garde twentieth-century thinkers often resemble sophists. Sophistry flourishes in the Western tradition of tolerance of controversy, individual ambition, and freedom of speech. There seems to be less of a sophistic tradition in Chinese and Indian thought, though the subject has not been thoroughly studied.

The second "part" of classical rhetoric is arrangement. In the teaching of rhetoricians, invention was often subordinated to arrangement in that the topics and arguments of each of the conventional parts of a judicial speech were discussed in the order in which these should normally occur: proemium, narration, proof, and epilogue, sometimes with other parts inserted, such as proposition and division of the question, preparation for the proof, refutation, or digression. Non-Western discussions of rhetoric do not offer precepts about the structure of a speech as a whole, but Kautilya in India discussed the arrangement of a writ.

An organized structure of the whole is, however, often a feature of actual non-Western speeches when we have complete texts. A good example is the presence of a proemium, narration, proof, and epilogue in the speech of King Pwan-kang discussed in chapter 7. Official letters in the Near East also had a standard rhetorical structure. I see no objection to the use of Western terminology to describe parts of a non-Western discourse when these are clearly present. In animal communication, a sense of structure can be heard in the songs of some birds, an opening note calls attention to the speaker and the body of the song consists of a succession of variations on themes. Often the song ends abruptly, but occasionally there is a concluding flourish. Classical rhetoricians recommended recapitulation and pathos in the epilogue, but some classical epilogues are very simple. A famous example is the end of Lysias's speech *Against Eratosthenes*: "I shall end my accusation. You have heared, you have seen, you have suffered, you have the case; judge." Demonstrative speeches often have only a simple epilogue calling for action. Elaborate ones are chiefly features of long judicial speeches. In Greek poetry, the Homeric epics have elaborate and pathetical epilogues, Greek tragedy has simple conclusions. An elaborate epilogue, however, is more characteristic of the West than of other cultures. It probably results from studying rhetoric and has come to satisfy Western needs for closure.

Samoan *fono* and other formal speeches in non-Western societies adhere to an established order of topics, though here the Western terminology is less applicable. Speeches in nonliterate societies sometimes have extended narrations, primarily to establish the ethos of the speaker. In chapter 5 I noted some speeches of American Indians which consist largely of narratives of the deeds of the speaker, followed by his proposal for action. Some sense of beginning, middle, and end seems the most natural structure of discourse and can be found in many speeches in traditional societies, but the end need not recapitulate the message and is likely to be calm, rather than an attempt to arouse the emotion of the audience. Plato's advice (*Phaedrus* 264c), "It is necessary for every speech to cohere like a living thing having its own body so that nothing is lacking in head or foot, but to have a middle and extremities suitable to each other, sketched as a whole," is advice that would be understood in most cultures.

Style, meaning the choice of words and their combination and arrangement into an artistic text, is the third part of classical rhetoric. Comparative study reveals that human societies all over the world recognize a variety of different styles of speech in their native languages, styles that are regarded as appropriate for certain occasions or subjects. Probably the oldest distinction is between the styles of speech and song, followed by a development of styles of formal speech, which often borrow vocabulary or compositional devices from song: for example, rhythm, alliteration, and assonance. The more formal and serious the occasion, the more formal the language should be; the most extreme elevated language is that of religious ritual, which may be incomprehensible to all except those initiated into it. Formal political deliberation usually requires the use of some degree of formal language.

The earliest and most common distinction among styles in classical rhetoric is that of a grand, middle, and plain style. The first description of these is found in the *Rhetoric for Herennius* (4.11–16), written in the early first century BCE, but this goes back to earlier sources. Aristotle had made some distinction between oral and written style and deliberative, judicial, and epideictic style in *Rhetoric* 3.12. The theory of the three kinds of style, however, does not well describe rhetoric as viewed cross-culturally. For one thing, all three classical styles can be used on the same formal occasions. Another distinction made by classical rhetoricians is between Atticism, the use of the language of fourth-century Greece or a Latin approximation, and Asianism, the use of a flamboyant, sententious, or highly rhythmical style as cultivated by rhetoricians in Asia Minor in the Hellenistic period. This does not well describe the general phenomenon either. No Greek rhetorician ever acknowledges that Koine Greek as developed in the Hellenistic period was appropriate for some kinds of speech or writing (though it was widely used, the most famous example being the New Testament).

Beginning with Dionysius of Halicarnassus in the late first century BCE and continuing with Hermogenes and others in the time of the Roman Empire, attempts were made to create a more subtle description of the different kinds of style used by the orators, historians, and philosophers of classical Greece whose works had been canonized in the schools. Hermogenes identified seven basic "ideas" or "types" of style: clarity, grandeur, beauty, rapidity, character, sincerity, and force, and described the choice of words, figures of speech, construction of sentences, and rhythm productive of each. His work *On Types of Style* (translation by Cecil W. Wooten, University of North Carolina Press, 1987) remained authoritative throughout the Byzantine period. It was not taken up by rhetoricians writing in Latin until the Renaissance, when it exercised some influence in the West. Hermogenes's approach has some similarity to concepts in postclassical Chinese and Indian literary criticism and some potentiality for stylistic analysis of any discourse.

A general theory of style, however, should begin with the concept of "formal language" as defined by Judith Irvine and discussed in chapter 4. The concept applies to the history of style in the West where efforts were made to create a style superior to colloquial language for formal occasions in Greece beginning in the fifth century BCE and in Rome beginning in the first century BCE. The Atticism of the Roman Empire is a formal language, and continued in use even when it was largely uncomprehensible to those not specially trained in it. Latin remained a formal language in the West after the vulgate languages replaced it in everyday use and was revived and restored to classical standards in the Renaissance. Beginning with Dante's efforts on behalf of Italian, formal levels of the vulgate languages were created in the West.

The human inclination to develop formal languages is one of many indications of the basically conservative function of rhetoric in human history. Formal languages are often archaic or revivals of what is regarded as the pure form of the language used in the past. They thus contribute to the preservation of other past values. The requirement to use them for serious discourse helps ensure preservation of the status quo on the behalf of those in power and limits the ability of marginal groups, untutored in elitist language, from effecting change.

The classical distinction between tropes, figures of speech, and figures of thought is not found outside the West. Chinese and Indian writers on language and literature name and define a number of individual tropes and figures but do not classify them under these three headings. Some Chinese and Indian observations about kinds of metaphor or other devices of style, discussed in the later parts of chapters 7 and 8, are very subtle and might have some application in analysis of poetry in other languages. Greek and Roman rhetoricians produced long lists of tropes and figures, named and illustrated in handbooks, but these works tend to be pedantic and ordinarily view the devices solely as ornaments, artificially added to the thought. I see no objection to the cross-cultural use of the more common names of tropes and figures in describing features of non-Western language.

The earliest, most natural, and most universal tropes are metaphor, synec-doche, and metonymy. Metaphor is usually regarded as the most important by modern theorists. Its great rhetorical importance is that, unlike other tropes, it can carry emotional value and is thus an important manifestation of rhetorical energy. It seems possible to say something about the history of metaphor on the basis of comparative study. The most common early form of metaphor was per-sonification, including anthropomorphization of animals and natural objects; this surely reflects the animistic world view of ancient and some modern societies in which spirits are everywhere in interaction with human life. A variety of metaphorical predications can merge into a shifting image without the mind be-ing troubled by rational feelings of contradiction. The earliest stages of spoken language probably lacked words to articulate a comparison as a simile rather than a metaphor. The differentiation of simile from metaphor seems to have occurred at an early time in Vedic Sanskrit and Greek, both Indo-European languages, and may have had its origin in either some historical experience of the Indo-Europeans or some feature of their language. Similes also appear at an early time in Sumerian, which is not regarded as an Indo-European language but which shares the double connotation of forms of "to be," meaning that something ex-ists or that something carries some quality. Possibly this feature of language en-couraged the differentiation of metaphor from simile.

Synecdoche is the use of the genus for the species or the species for the genus or of whole for part or part for whole. This even occurs in animal communi-cation, as described in chapter 1. In human communication it was and is the simplest way of denoting objects, actions, and qualities when linguistic resources do not provide specific terms. A particular culture then may find a practical need for greater differentiation. The most famous example are the twenty words for different kinds of snow in Eskimo.

Intelligent nonhuman animals easily come to understand or even use meton-omy, in which an object or term carries meaning on the basis of contiguity rather than similarity. Metonymy does not seem to have been as common in early lan-guage use as metaphor or synecdoche, but like synecdoche it may have been in-voked when no specific term was available. Metonymy is difficult to distinguish from synecdoche in the case of whole for part or part for whole.

Figures of speech such as anaphora, alliteration, or assonance probably came to speech from song. They impart emphasis, thus carry some rhetorical energy, and like verse and prose rhythm facilitate memorization of formulas and topoi. Among figures of thought, the most common everywhere seems to be rhetorical question. It, and apostrophe (turning from the nominal audience to address someone or something), carries a high degree of rhetorical energy originating in the emotion of the speaker and evocative of the emotion of the audience.

I have found my excursus through the cultures of the world enlightening. Many of the things I discovered were, of course, well known to others in special fields, but they deserve to be better known to students of rhetoric. Among things that have specially impressed me are the discovery of the rhetorical features of animal communication, the many forms of formal language used all over the world, including varieties of indirect speech, the large corpus of distinguished oratory preserved in Chinese historical works, the emergence of forms of sophistry in India and China, and the remarkable epideictic oratory of the Aztec *huehuetlatolli*. Classical rhetorical theory turns out to have some universal features, some features unique to Greek and Roman culture—especially its focus on judicial oratory—and a number of central concepts, including epideictic and ethos, that require some redefinition if they are to describe rhetoric in general. Finally, I have been much impressed by the generally conservative function of rhetoric all over the world, which seems to help confirm my suggestion that rhetoric has its origin in the instinct for self-preservation and is a form of energy transmitted through signs to persuade an audience to act in securing or preserving the best interests of the speaker. As I stressed in the Prologue, this book is not intended as an authoritative statement of comparative or general rhetoric. Revisions and additions are surely needed, but I hope I have provided a starting place for future study.

Index